intimate entanglements in the
ethnography of performance

Eastman/Rochester Studies in Ethnomusicology

Ellen Koskoff, Series Editor
Eastman School of Music
(ISSN: 2161–0290)

Burma's Pop Music Industry:
Creators, Distributors, Censors
Heather MacLachlan

Yorùbá Music in the Twentieth Century:
Identity, Agency and Performance Practice
Bode Omojola

Javanese Gamelan and the West
Sumarsam

Gender in Chinese Music
Edited by Rachel Harris, Rowan Pease, and Shzr Ee Tan

Performing Gender, Place, and Emotion in Music:
Global Perspectives
Edited by Fiona Magowan and Louise Wrazen

Music, Indigeneity, Digital Media
Edited by Thomas R. Hilder, Henry Stobart, and Shzr Ee Tan

Listen with the Ear of the Heart:
Music and Monastery Life at Weston Priory
Maria S. Guarino

Tuning the Kingdom:
Kawuugulu Musical Performance, Politics, and Storytelling in Buganda
Damascus Kafumbe

New York Klezmer in the Twentieth Century:
The Music of Naftule Brandwein and Dave Tarras
Joel E. Rubin

Songs for Cabo Verde:
Norberto Tavares's Musical Visions for a New Republic
Susan Hurley-Glowa

The Kecak and Cultural Tourism on Bali
Kendra Stepputat

Walking with Asafo in Ghana: An Ethnographic Account of
Kormantse Bentsir Warrior Music
Ama Oforiwaa Aduonum

intimate entanglements in the ethnography of performance

race, gender, vulnerability

Edited by
Sidra Lawrence
and
Michelle Kisliuk

UNIVERSITY OF ROCHESTER PRESS

Copyright © 2023 The Editors and Contributors

All rights reserved. Except as permitted under current legislation, no part of this work may be photocopied, stored in a retrieval system, published, performed in public, adapted, broadcast, transmitted, recorded, or reproduced in any form or by any means, without the prior permission of the copyright owner.

First published 2023
Reprinted in paperback 2025

University of Rochester Press
668 Mt. Hope Avenue, Rochester, NY 14620, USA
www.urpress.com
and Boydell & Brewer Limited
PO Box 9, Woodbridge, Suffolk IP12 3DF, UK
www.boydellandbrewer.com

ISBN: 978-1-64825-063-7 (hardback)
ISBN: 978-1-64825-067-5 (paperback)
ISSN: 2161-0290 ; vol. 13

Chapter 4 was previously published as "Performing Desire: Race, Sex, and the Ethnographic Encounter," *Ethnomusicology* 61 no. 3 (Fall 2017): 468–85. It is reprinted here with permission.

Chapter 9 is from *Congo's Dancers* by Lesley Nicole Braun. Reprinted by permission of the University of Wisconsin Press. © 2022 by the Board of Regents of the University of Wisconsin System. All rights reserved.

Library of Congress Cataloging-in-Publication Data
Names: Lawrence, Sidra, editor. | Kisliuk, Michelle Robin, editor.
Title: Intimate entanglements in the ethnography of performance : race, gender, vulnerability / edited by Sidra Lawrence and Michelle Kisliuk.
Other titles: Eastman/Rochester studies in ethnomusicology ; 13.
Description: Rochester : University of Rochester Press, 2023. | Series: Eastman/Rochester studies in ethnomusicology, 2161-0290 ; 13 | Includes bibliographical references and index.
Identifiers: LCCN 2022053600 (print) | LCCN 2022053601 (ebook) | ISBN 9781648250637 (hardback) | ISBN 9781800109520 (pdf) | ISBN 9781800109537 (epub)
Subjects: LCSH: Ethnomusicology. | Music--Performance—Social aspects. | Intimacy (Psychology) | Africans—Music—History and criticism. | African Americans—Music—History and criticism. | Music—United States—History and criticism. | Music—Africa—History and criticism. | Music and race.
Classification: LCC ML3798 .I65 2023 (print) | LCC ML3798 (ebook) | DDC 780.89—dc23/eng/20221230
LC record available at https://lccn.loc.gov/2022053600
LC ebook record available at https://lccn.loc.gov/2022053601

A catalogue record for this title is available from the British Library.

This publication is printed on acid-free paper.

Printed in the United States of America.

Michelle:
In loving memory of Roy Kisliuk who taught me compassion
and Ingrid Kisliuk who showed me how to persevere.
If only we could have held their hands.

Sidra:
To my grandmother Rose,
a model of all that is worth pursuing in life.

Contents

Foreword: Let It Get into You   ix
Deborah Kapchan

Acknowledgments   xiii

introduction: on intimate entanglements   1
Sidra Lawrence

1   Yusef's Breath: Jazz Love, Cross-Racial Identification, and Paying Dues   23
Tracy McMullen

2   Three Reflections, with Epilogue   47
Steven Cornelius

3   Modulating Flawed Bodies: Intimate Acoustemologies, Chronic Pain, and Ethnographic Pianism   57
Mark Lomanno

4   Performing Desire: Race, Sex, and the Ethnographic Encounter   86
Sidra Lawrence

5   Thick Descriptions   107
Catherine M. Appert

6   Entering the Lives of Others: Entangled Intimacies, Trauma, and Performance   114
Ama Oforiwaa Aduonum

7   Ethnomusicological Empathy: Excavating a Black Graduate Student's Heartland   150
Danielle Davis

8 Ethnomusicological Becoming: Deep Listening as Erotics in the Field 159
   Carol Muller

9 Mirror Dancing in Congo: Reflections on Fieldwork as Blanche Neige 175
   Lesley N. Braun

10 ethnography and its double(s) // theorizing the personal with Jews in Ghana 194
   Michelle Kisliuk

   Notes on Contributors 243
   Index 247

Foreword

Let It Get into You

Deborah Kapchan

When I left New York City for Morocco in 1982, my flute teacher gave me his most recent cassette as a parting gift. He took out the cardboard insert, imprinted with a picture of him playing his golden Muramatsu on one side and a list of compositions on the other, and wrote "Let it Get into You" across the cover. It was good advice for a fledgling performer, off to explore North Africa for the first time.

My teacher's playing had already gotten into me, of course. He combined the pure blue-glass tones of a classical musician with the fluent looseness of someone not bound by genre. He played Bach as well as he played Brazilian samba, and his own compositions were haunting and hip. He was also an accomplished and exhibited visual artist, his paintings full of bold color and the abstract patterns of Kente cloth. They lined the walls of his studio, where I went for my lessons, a loft in the Village, not far from the one where Barry Harris gave his weekly classes on jazz improvisation. I attended those too, thanks to my teacher's introduction.

But my teacher, male, African American and twenty years older than me, also captivated me in other ways. It happened one day when I was practicing my pentatonic scales for him.

"Who *are* you?" he asked, breaking the spell of my playing and casting another. Not long after, we climbed the stairs to his loftbed to find out.

There was no coercion. He was attractive and I was a lusty young woman in awe of his talent. There was a seduction, however. Had I chosen this? My agency in this situation is hard to pin down. Bodies are connected, and desires move through them in ways not always subject to conscious decision.

Like the intertwining of sound and environment, so yearning reshapes flesh in its image.[1]

When my teacher had taught me everything he could about the flute, he suggested I study with *his* teacher, a professor at Brooklyn College. The following year I had a scholarship there to do my second BA, this time not in literature, but in flute performance.

Who was instrumentalizing whom? I had sought him out, after all, in a club on Bleecker Street. After listening to him play a set with percussionist Nana Vasconcelos, I approached him and asked if he gave lessons. I wanted what he had—to have a free instrument, to let the music flow through me unimpeded.[2] I hadn't thought of him as a potential lover, at least until the fateful day that he changed the key of our duet.

We all have stories like this or know people who do—tales of affection that never become public. Aesthetic proximities of all kinds are alluring and dangerous.[3] Perhaps this is why there are so many taboos about "going native," or losing one's objectivity; as if to be a scholar means to close down empathy and remain impermeable (something philosopher Martha Nussbaum demonstrates is impossible, since all rational decisions are inflected with emotion).[4]

As the authors in this volume demonstrate, intimacy is where we are most vulnerable, easily wounded, soft and enmeshed, most animal but also most malleable and sublime. Music, like love, takes us places we could never go otherwise, into what Kisliuk calls the "deep eyes" of difference.[5] And sometimes it beaches us there, broken on a reef, gasping for air.

Yet power, as Lawrence notes, is often "multi-directional."[6] In McMullen's piece in this volume, she quotes a Black woman vocalist in the novel *Another Country* by James Baldwin. The character is talking to a wealthy white woman. "What you people don't know," she says, "is that life is a bitch, baby.

---

1 Philosopher Maurice Merleau-Ponty defines "flesh" (*la chair*) as an element of being like water, air, earth, and fire. For him, it is a porous, reversible, and renewable substance. "The human body is flesh, but it intertwines with the flesh of the world like a pulsing rhythm or a condensation of vibrations. Flesh is the continuity that links the perceiver's body with the world. Flesh is an isthmus, a kind of fascia or connective tissue. It traverses at the same time that it forms. It is, we might say, always *trans*forming." Kapchan 2021, following Merleau-Ponty 1969.
2 Lomanno this volume.
3 Kapchan 2021.
4 Nussbaum 2001.
5 Kisliuk this volume.
6 Lawrence this volume.

It's the biggest hype going. You don't have any experience in paying your dues and it's going to be rough on you, baby, when the deal goes down. There's lots of back dues to be collected, and I know damn well you haven't got a penny saved."[7]

My teacher was Black. I was white. He was male. I was female. He was in his forties and I was in my twenties. Let it get into you.

We pay our dues in love, and we pay them in our profession. We pay them when our children and students temper us and show us our failings. We pay them in the challenges and traumas of life.

I'm not sure social theory protects us from the aftershocks of that. In fact, it doesn't protect or exempt us from anything at all. While feminism has given me the tools to excavate my own internalized hegemony, and critical race theory has allowed me to see my complicity with racisms inherited from family and society, they have not prevented me from making the mistakes caused by the thick amorphous stuff of my humanity. It sticks to my sinews and bones like desire. More than theory, my intimate mistakes have been my teachers and my intimate teachers have taught me more than most.

You have to pay your dues, and it's a bitch, but there's no way around it. You have to let it get into you, because that's the only way to know it, to understand and earn it, and maybe to recompose it and give it back changed. Who *are* you? he asked me. That may be a pretty clichéd come-on line, but it is also one of the most vital questions of our existence. Who are we, together and separately, in all the complexity of our human being?

I went to Morocco. I married. I had a baby. I let it get into me, as my teacher suggested. There are some who would think this has nothing to do with ethnography, but I disagree. My intimacy with Morocco and Moroccans challenged all my beliefs and assumptions, it put me through changes that were total and irrevocable, placing me at the nexus of culture and transformation. This was not just personal.[8] While the encounter with difference is painful and fraught, it is also the most important thing we can do—lingering in the space of discomfort until something shifts;[9] until, as the authors in this volume note, the intractable dissolves and we modulate together in unexpected directions.[10] For either we learn the lessons of empathy, or we

---

7 Baldwin 1993/1962, 350, quoted in McMullen this volume.
8 This is also an integral step in forging a unique configuration of "collective becoming" (Kisliuk this volume).
9 Kapchan 2017.
10 Necessitating what Lomanno (this volume) calls "a modulation of somatic modes" of being.

are exiled from every hope in the human condition. I realized this with my senses—which is the only way to learn it—and now I teach it to my students: the exigency of ethnography.

Let it get into you. I am grateful to my teacher for giving me that advice. He knew something I didn't know then. He was a devoted and high-functioning artist, and he gave me that example. I have no regrets. But the conundrums don't go away: white privilege, the exotification of the Black body, the fetishization of youth, the power of age. We are caught in the webs of our cultural stories, and it is up to each one of us to write, teach, and perform our way out, and through.

We know about kinship, patriarchy, religion as a cultural system, language acquisition, and the performance of gender. We know about ragas and maqam, about sonatas and symphonies. We know about carbon dating, cosmology, shamanistic chanting, and spirit possession. The information is in a keystroke and in a glance at the web.

What is left to do when the "exotic" is near and yet we are still so far from ourselves and each other?

After decades in the Academy—that institution based on the mind/body fallacy—I am convinced that there's no *other* way forward except through embodied experience and *its subsequent story*.

Read on. The stories are here. Let them get into you.

References

Baldwin, James. 1962/1993. *Another Country*. London: Penguin Books.
Kapchan, Deborah. 2017. "The Splash of Icarus: Theorizing Sound Writing/Writing Sound Theory." In *Theorizing Sound Writing*, edited by Deborah Kapchan, 1–24. Middletown, CT: Wesleyan University Press.
———. 2021. "The Aesthetics of Proximity and the Ethics of Empathy." In *Oxford Handbook of Phenomenology in Ethnomusicology*, edited by Harris M. Berger, Friedlind Riedel, and David VanderHamm. https://www.oxfordhandbooks.com/view/10.1093/oxfordhb/9780190693879.001.0001/oxfordhb-9780190693879-e-15?rskey=A20q9g&result=1.
Merleau-Ponty, Maurice. 1969. *The Visible and the Invisible*. Translated by Alphonso Lingus. Evanston, IL: Northwestern University Press.
Nussbaum, Martha C. 2001. *Upheavals of Thought: The Intelligence of Emotions*. Cambridge, UK: Cambridge University Press.

Acknowledgments

We thank Julia Cook, production editor at the University of Rochester Press and acquisitions editor for the Eastman/Rochester Studies in Ethnomusicology series, who shepherded the volume with patience and skill from its nascent beginnings through to publication, and Ellen Koskoff, series editor, for her wise council and steady backing of this project. What began as a panel idea long before the COVID-19 pandemic survived through to publication after many twists and turns and growth spurts, which is a testament to their solid support.

Sidra:

My first acknowledgments go to the authors presented in this volume. I am grateful for their scholarship, their willingness to be vulnerable, open, and honest in their writing, and their patience. I am privileged to have been able to engage in conversations with each of them about their ideas contained here. I thank them, too, for allowing us to publish their extremely fine work with this volume.

This volume developed from papers presented at the Society for Ethnomusicology Annual Meeting in 2013. Though the direction of the volume as a whole has expanded over time, I would like to thank the original panelists, Ama Aduonum, Catherine Appert, Nicol Hammond, Carol Muller, Patty Tang, and Michelle Kisliuk, for being willing to present difficult work and for challenging our discipline to address uncomfortable truths. Much of the theoretical groundwork of this book emerged out of conversations we had during that initial panel, as well as post-presentation conversations, collaborations, and coalitions.

It was at that meeting when Michelle and I began strategizing about how to approach building a volume that would open space for engaged, embodied, ethnographic writing that would also provide critique of our disciplinary methods, theories, and institutions that prevent or regulate such work. We connected deeply on the importance of vulnerability, porousness, and poetics of ethnographic writing, and on what we felt was at stake for our discipline if we failed to pursue more just and empathetic encounters. These initial conversations, were, for me, an important aspect of finding an intellectual home. When I was a graduate student, Michelle, along with Katherine Hagedorn, Carol Babiracki, and Eileen Hayes, were the models for conducting work that critically addressed ethnography as a process in which the researcher, their identity, and their experiences are fully present. Their attention to the embodied, performative, and expressive aspects of research, and their commitment to writing expansively, created space in ethnomusicology for others to pursue such work. I am thankful to them for their visions, their courage, and every battle they fought so that others could move those conversations forward. Having the opportunity to work with Michelle and to find a shared vision through which to build this collection has been spiritually and intellectually nourishing.

I would like to acknowledge and thank Sonia Seeman, whose graduate seminars at the University of Texas at Austin were the spaces where I was first exposed to issues of critical ethnographic work, and in which I was nurtured into finding a voice and the courage to use it. She gave me the tools and support to work through these ideas intellectually. She was also very personally supportive of my work in these areas.

Any project is the product of a community of support and care; I have been enriched and sustained by the many people who have, in various ways, created space for me to develop ideas and get critical and crucial feedback, and who made it possible to persevere. For my friends from graduate school, who remain my central support system in all intellectual matters, and whom I trust unquestioningly for their assessments and advice: Kathryn Metz, Michael O'Brien, Mark Lomanno, Ryan McCormack, and Dan Sharp, thank you for listening, for strategizing, and for helping me recover after setbacks with the warmest intellectual community anyone could hope for. I am especially grateful to Justin Patch for reading numerous drafts, for talking through each and every facet of the project at all stages, and for cheering me on even in the darkest of times; he's the truest of friends. For my friend, Katherine Meizel, who is the finest and most supportive colleague imaginable. Reading drafts, offering advice on matters from publication to theory, and listening to me work through ideas on walks with Dusty—it's been nearly a decade of her ceaseless support; I am appreciative and honored to have her in my life. I would like to thank Gavin Steingo and Travis Jackson for reading early drafts of my essay and offering such excellent and keen perspectives. Thank you to Suzanne Cusick for teaching my essay, and the graduate students at New York University for inviting me to present this work, for challenging me to sharpen my frameworks, and being such rigorous thinkers. To Pete Sigal and Zeb Tortorici, who gave me a platform to write, to present, and to share community with like-minded thinkers, I thank you for your bold visions. Conversations with Yun Emily Wang have been particularly delightful, motivating, and simultaneously enriching and hilarious. This volume was made immeasurably better by the important insights from the anonymous peer reviewers, and from Omi Osun Jones, a mentor who makes me feel seen, appreciated, and challenged to always strive to be better.

To Nick, thank you for being my best friend, my rock, and my joy. I thank my mother for her wry insight on all topics and for teaching me the values of compassion and empathy.

I would like to thank the Society for Ethnomusicology for allowing me to reprint my essay here.

And finally, for Kiko, my fluffy and loyal editorial assistant.

Michelle:

I met Sidra in 2013 at the first SEM meeting after the death of my dear friend Katherine Hagedorn. I was not sure I would ever find joy at those meetings again. But Sidra made clear to me during our memorial gathering for Katherine that, though she had never had the chance to meet her, Katherine's strong spirit and important work had helped pioneer a new generation of writers in the field—especially women writers—who would not compromise in our dedication to the centrality of human relationships in our research and would turn to poetics for understanding musical, spiritual, and politically embedded lives. Sidra, along with many of the contributors to this volume and many more friends, colleagues, teachers, and students, revives my conviction that rigorous work that is laden with our idiosyncrasies and foibles makes us who we are, and that this work is in the service of life. I am grateful to Sidra for her tenacity in bringing forward a brave vision for a kind of research and writing that does not yet fully exist.

A few days before my mother died in 2020, I was talking to her over Zoom—she in her COVID bed just after my father had died. I could not tell how much of what I was saying she could understand. She could no longer speak and would slip in and out of consciousness. As I tried to keep a thread of conversation going across that terrible electronic divide, I realized I had never told my mother what an inspiration she was to me. When I was a child, I felt that her decision to pursue a doctorate in French literature meant that I was not as important to her as were her studies. I didn't understand. I felt abandoned. But in reality, her choice to fulfil her intellectual and interpretive dreams was crucial for me. As a woman and mother in the 1960s and 1970s it took a lot to do that. Because of her perseverance, I could follow in her path as if it were the most normal thing to do. But I had never told her so. When I said it, her eyes widened unmistakably. She understood. My most fundamental thanks go to my mother.

introduction

on intimate entanglements

Sidra Lawrence

When two hands touch, there is a sensuality of the flesh, an exchange of warmth, a feeling of pressure, of presence, a proximity of otherness that brings the other nearly as close as oneself. Perhaps closer. And if the two hands belong to one person, might this not enliven an uncanny sense of the otherness of the self, a literal holding oneself at a distance in the sensation of contact, the greeting of the stranger within? So much happens in a touch: an infinity of others—other beings, other spaces, other times—are aroused.

When two hands touch, how close are they? What is the measure of closeness? Which disciplinary knowledge formations, political parties, religious and cultural traditions, infectious disease authorities, immigration officials, and policy makers do not have a stake in, if not a measured answer to, this question?

–Karan Barad, "On Touching"

I like to think of this volume as a form of radical intimacy—the kind of intimacy that happens when we allow ourselves to be open, to be touched, to be vulnerable in our expressions.[1] Willing to reveal and to explore dimensions of our desire to know, of our seeking, of our being that are rarely sounded. Some forms of intimacy revive us, they reaffirm our visions, our truths, our shared humanity. Not all intimacies are pleasing; there are forced and coercive intimacies that assume a closeness to which we or others have not consented. The chapters in this volume lay bare this range of vulnerabilities, and

---

1   We follow the feminist convention of subverting masculinist writing norms and practices by not capitalizing the words of our volume title.

they do so with tremendous courage and a willingness to expose themselves and the raw and sometimes unpleasant realities of human engagement.

intimate entanglements originally emerged out of a Society for Ethnomusicology conference panel (2013) exploring erotic subjectivity in ethnographic research. Those papers addressed the myriad ways that erotics and intimacies shape our experiences as field researchers, as scholars, and within and beyond our institutions. We argued that these dimensions of our epistemologies are crucial to the knowledge we produce and are also regulated by gatekeeping mechanisms institutionally and disciplinarily. The chapters in this volume expand on those original concerns, widening the scope and also deepening the theoretical interrogation of the multifaceted relationships between erotics, intimacy, and trauma as produced through sound, movement, and embodied experience. We call attention to the particular power dynamics of ethnography that have allowed for some to move seemingly unmarked through the field, while generating the lenses through which all subsequent knowledge claims are refracted; we then clarify the modes of knowledge production that have been obscured by such hegemonic ethnographic epistemologies. Central to our goals is to think about ourselves as scholars, activists, and musicians alongside and within the work we produce, as well as the tensions that emerge in trying to *write* these truths. In a moment when ethnomusicology is seeking more just and ethical modes of research and teaching, we suggest that efforts to do decolonial work in our discipline must maintain higher levels of accountability and vulnerability when it comes to matters of ethnographic engagements, methodologically, theoretically, and pedagogically.

During that initial conference panel, and then expanded in this volume, the voices come not coincidentally from researchers, mostly women, whose work is located within and from Africa and the African diasporas. Authors in this volume work from the premise that the coding around racialized, gendered, and sexualized bodies profoundly shapes our human engagements, systems of learning, and environmental experiences. Intersectional feminist critique forms the basis for understanding how overlapping systems of oppression coalesce to generate trauma (cultural, spiritual, physical, intellectual, and emotional) and produce systems of violence.[2] We build from this framework, engaging with critical theoretical orientations that presume the

---

2   A small sampling of such work includes Moraga and Anzaldúa 2015; Combahee River Collective 1979; Collins 2000; Collins 2004; hooks 2000; Lorde 1984a; Smith 1977; Hull, Bell-Scott, and Smith 1982.

centrality of the body both in articulating epistemologies of trauma and in generating transformational possibilities.[3] We commit ourselves to thinking through the painful and damaging iterations of trauma, as well as to the processes of healing and emancipation that emerge from wounded states, and to the human intimacies both momentary and lifelong that produce new shared realities. Through performance, sounding, and embodied experience we explore the sensory knowledge that is frequently left unattended to in ethnographic work. *intimate entanglements* proposes the possibility of aesthetic and discursive transformations through new conceptions of intimacy as emergent, performative, and sonically enabled.

Working toward expansive and intersecting understandings of the erotic, intimacy, and trauma, this volume explores numerous manifestations of these concepts in performance, ethnography, and in institutional and disciplinary settings.[4] The chapters explore the contours of what is painful, traumatic, or violent (both interpersonally and systemically), but also find and foreground healing practices, intimacies, and joyful, sensual connections. These multiplicities are not dichotomous, but reveal the tensions implicit in human engagements that occur within systems of power imbalance. Bringing together discourses on trauma, intimacy, and erotics allows us to think more deeply about how the seeming polarities of pleasure and violence are bound up in shared discourses of power; we recognize those tensions and articulate around a wealth of embodied experiences along this continuum. Theorizing the interstices of these categories provides increased space for authors to discuss race, gender, sexuality, and ability as categories that intersect with citizenship, proficiency, safety, healing, ethics, and spirituality. Authors explore the acoustemology of intimacy, woman-centered eroticism generated through musical performance, desire and longing in ethnographic knowledge production, and listening as intimacy. On the other end of the spectrum, authors engage with and question the fetishization of race in jazz; conceptions of vulgarity and profanity in movement and dance-ethnography; and address pain, trauma, and violation, whether physical, spiritual and/or

---

3   Authors work across a range of theoretical paradigms, including queer theory, dance and movement scholarship, performance theory and practice, Black, Chicana, and African feminisms, postcolonial feminism, and disability and pain studies.

4   This theoretical frame follows from works by interdisciplinary scholars who have provided models for such expansive interpretations of erotics, including Lorde 1984b; Gill 2018; Gill 2012; Gill 2010; Alexander 2005; Waterman 2008; McCartney 2016; Anzaldúa 2002; Allen 2012; Allen 2011.

political. Ultimately, we seek to develop new conversations about performed sensory and sonic modalities through which we navigate and manage these entanglements as engaged, embodied, scholars.

Ethnomusicology, Colonialism, and Ethnographic Knowledge

In the current moment, the practice of ethnomusicology is grappling both with the historical tensions that were formulated during colonialism and the ways in which those systems and ideologies continue to shape our ethnographic engagements, knowledge production, and quotidian practices. The unresolved tensions between ethnographic acquisition, consumption and circulation, and colonialist desire are contributing to a fraught discipline that has not yet adequately grappled with its own racist past, present, and futures. Systems of domination have bound exotic fantasy, racialized images, and authority in such ways that ethnographic consumption and circulation often unwittingly reiterate these hierarchies.[5] In her open letter to ethnomusicology and music education, Danielle Brown writes,

> Getting it means understanding that an organization, whose predominantly white members by and large research people of color, *is and can be nothing other than a colonialist and imperialist enterprise.* Period. It is a hard pill to swallow but swallow we must. No matter how hard we try to convince ourselves otherwise, until ethnomusicology as a field is dismantled or significantly restructured, so that epistemic violence against BIPOC is not normalized, Black lives do not matter. And that's real talk.[6]

As Brown points out, to continue to conceal how power reinforces itself destines us to return to the same place over again. In this volume, we see racialization as a meaningful marker of ethnographic knowledge production. Authors address the afterlives of slavery and colonialism in performance, the racial imagination of Otherness that drives a yearning to know and acquire, the legacies of colonialism carried through bodies, genres, and

---

5   Art historian Kelly Dennis goes so far as to suggest that imperial regimes structured the racial imagination to the extent that "pure ethnography" does not exist "independent of erotic motivation and colonial determination." Dennis 1994, 23.
6   Brown 2020.

sound production, and the histories that connect whiteness to both violence and privilege. By bringing race to the analytical foreground, this volume takes seriously the need to critique how ethnographic desire is implicated in violent entanglements and to seek responses that are ethical, reflective, and grounded in specific geographic, cultural, and political frameworks. In doing so, we unmask the type of disciplinary power imbalances that Brown articulates and offer reimagined analytical and interpretive ethnographic possibilities.

All knowledge production is filtered through experiential frames, whether or not we acknowledge it, and what the authors here are doing is demonstrating very clearly how the methods, theories, and institutional frameworks that undergird ethnomusicology have been inadequate to provide space to speak truths about intimacies, violence, and erotics.[7] Additionally, we draw clear attention to the challenges of speaking these truths and how the discipline continues to gatekeep what conversations can happen and who can participate. Rather than joining in with those disciplinary histories and practices that conceal power and that would sidestep these concerns, we face them, we expose them, and we open space for honest dialogue. We choose vulnerability, radical empathy, and openness as modes through which we re-cooperate the discipline by interrogating the categories from which we emerge and proceed. The future of ethnomusicology should not be to retreat from ethnographic engagement, but rather to seek an empathetic future, one that is accountable for who we are as researchers, where we do our work, our institutional policies and responses, and the creative and political engagements we honor and lift up.

In the North American academy, there remains rigorous gatekeeping around writing, and concepts of difference and otherness continue to shape basic assumptions about ethnographic work. The marriage of these two issues contributes to the pushback against having the type of conversations present in this volume. The notion of intractable power differentials between researcher and research subjects has, over the past decades, been addressed at length by postmodern anthropologists, feminist anthropologists, and ethnomusicologists.[8] Within these bodies of literature, those who have discussed sensory approaches, intersubjectivity, and intimacies have challenged

---

7   See Appert 2017, in which she discusses the implications for neglecting the experiential and gendered aspects of ethnography.

8   See for example, Abu-Lughod 1990; Stacey 1988; Hahn 2007; Minh-ha 1989.

the presumption of inherent difference, research ethics, and representational politics. We believe that by exposing these concerns and tackling them with thoughtful, engaged, and ethical research models, such as those shared by the authors in this volume, we do the work of generating meaningful disciplinary change.

The authors in this volume work predominantly in Africa and the African diasporas; and the majority of the scholars represented in the volume are white.[9] Rather than sidestepping the realities of our demographics, we wish to foreground them, pointing to the precise disciplinary structures that create such imbalance. One of the challenges for discussing topics contained in the volume is the vulnerability inherent in having such conversations. This vulnerability is not evenly felt and actually does result in making it more difficult for people in certain subject positions to readily risk speaking into volumes such as this.[10] One of our hopes is that by centralizing these issues, we continue to create spaces for more people to be able to address their lived experiences, and for the discipline of ethnomusicology to be more willing to grapple with its own racialized histories and practices. We are attempting to open such a conversation but do not claim to have eradicated imbalance. Many of the contributing authors (including white authors) specifically and directly confront these histories, and we hope to encourage ongoing discussion and disciplinary change. Open conversation about the ways in which the racial imagination has shaped ethnographic desire and process is required in order to have fuller dialogue about intricacies of ethnographic work as racialized. Feminist scholars and scholars of color are both particularly well situated to understand the specific ways we are vulnerable to sanction when we challenge the patriarchal/colonialist/white supremacist norms in work exemplified within this volume, and this professional vulnerability helps explain why relatively few scholars of color are represented here.

---

9   See Kisliuk (this volume) for further discussion on the complexity of racialized coding as both a historical and geographic construct.

10 See Hayes 2010, in which she not only addresses subjectivity in ethnography via multiple and overlapping categories of identity but also points the reader to challenges faced by Black scholars doing ethnographic research that foregrounds their identity. Likewise, Ama Oforiwaa Aduonum, this volume, explores the complications of insider/outsider identity; she teases out the many ways that ideas about belonging are filtered through historical and geopolitical layers of perception and expectation, all of which bear down upon the researcher.

In order to begin a theorization of intimate entanglements in ethnographic work conducted in particular in Africa and the diasporas, it is useful to think through the ways in which the construction of racialized sexuality is linked to colonialism, and by extension to colonialist visions of Otherness. In the context of ethnography, the political consequences of erotics are produced via the same mechanisms that have historically constructed and produced racialized forms of violence, including the ethnopornographic gaze, which trades in circulations of the racial imagination.[11] As other scholars have shown, regimes of colonialism, imperialism, and racialization created systems of eroticized racial othering that continue to have afterlives that impinge upon ethnographic desire.[12] It is the silence around such histories that cloaks their insidious consequences in ethnographic writing. The presumed white male ethnographic subject as a stand-in for universal-knowledge-producer is reinforced if research and writing fail to account for our particular positions within these histories—histories that have enabled theories, methods, and narrative modes emerging from patriarchal, racist, and colonialist systems. As contemporary scholars, we cannot distance ourselves from the relationships between violence and sexuality in colonialist discourse, racialized labor systems, and ethnographic projects.[13] Anthropologist Neil L. Whitehead wrote,

> Certainly, the gender categories and sexual modalities fostered in colonial contexts are still with us and, ontologically speaking, the postcolonial will never actually arise since it is a temporal and not a historical construct. So, if there is no final escape from the legacies of colonialism, only a reworking of colonial legacy—in itself a highly contingent and variant set of circumstances when viewed cross culturally—then the roles of the sexual and the violent in cross-cultural relationships are ever present and always connected with each other—a concern about today no less than about yesterday.[14]

Seeking alternative and reimagined modes of ethnographic connection and representation requires both conscious efforts to interrogate the systems we work within and the willingness to openly engage with how these histories

---

11 Sigal, Tortorici, and Whitehead 2020.
12 Stoler 1995; Stoler 2002; McClintock 1995; McClintock, Mufti, and Shohat 1997; Collins 2000; Collins 2004; Sigal, Tortorici, and Whitehead 2020.
13 McClintock 1995; Patton 2018; hooks 1992; Ipsen 2020; Berry and Harris 2018; Jones-Rogers 2019.
14 Sigal, Tortorici, and Whitehead 2020, 245.

shape knowledge production. Part of the disciplinary anxiety around work that attends to intimate entanglements in Africa and the diasporas may be about the risk of unintended reinforcement of stereotypes around Blackness as paired with hypersexuality. But while such concerns regarding stereotypes must be addressed, anxiety that censors the realm of intimacy and erotics and the disclosure of pain and trauma ironically results in the erasure of the necessary nuanced conversations about ethnographic experiences that enable the fuller interpretive work that in fact mediates power imbalance both in the field and in our institutions. Erotics is a critical theoretical position that, rather than reinforcing stereotypes, actually facilitates a deepened interrogation of the webs of racialized, sexualized power constructs through which we all move. Studies of erotic subjectivity call attention to particular ways in which these webs impinge on lives and relationships; they also provide models of mutuality, dismantle legacies of Othering, and deepen the representations of myriad forms of human connections. Anthropologist Don Kulick notes that "silence about erotic subjectivity of fieldworkers also works to keep concealed the deeply racist and colonialist conditions that make possible our continuing unidirectional discourse about the sexuality of the people we study."[15] He refers here to anthropological accounts of sexuality such as those by Malinowski, who famously produced a unidirectional racialized fantasy-cum-diary that illuminates the danger of the presumed white male omnipotent ethnographic subject.[16] The ways in which erotics is being mobilized overall in this volume and in the work of our authors who specifically address erotics (see Braun, Lawrence, Lomanno, Muller this volume) is antithetical to such fetishization and works to combat the damage of those discourses. The frame of erotics as it is used by these authors is via intersubjective connection, love, and intimacies; these visions of erotics are liberatory and move us toward models of ethnographic engagements that we believe are more just, ethical, and decolonizing.

---

15 Kulick and Willson 1995, 4.
16 See Malinowski 1967. Malinowski's diary was published posthumously; his fieldwork journals contained information not in his published work, including racial fantasy, lustful, and misogynistic thoughts. The publication of the diary created a critical stir in anthropology and was important in generating self-reflective critique about the objectivist stance in anthropology.

Erotics, Intimacy, and Vulnerable Ethnography

> I write to record what others erase when I speak, to rewrite the stories others have miswritten about me, about you. To become more intimate with myself and you. To discover myself, to preserve myself, to make myself, to achieve self-autonomy. To dispel the myths that I am a mad prophet or a poor suffering soul. To convince myself that I am worthy and that what I have to say is not a pile of shit. To show that I *can* and that I *will* write, never mind their admonitions to the contrary. And I will write about the unmentionables, never mind the outraged gasp of the censor and the audience. Finally, I write because I'm scared of writing but I'm more scared of not writing.
>
> —Gloria Anzaldúa, "Speaking in Tongues"

By disrupting the masculinist model of unidirectional representation, erotic subjectivity as a field of inquiry has focused on intersubjective processes and power negotiation. As Pete Sigal and Zeb Tortorici point out, "the lack of consent on the part of those observed is what signifies such materials as parts of a project of domination and control."[17] In traditional ethnographic texts, the voyeuristic gaze of the invisible ethnographer, coupled with representational modes that obscure the intimacies of knowledge production, conceal intersubjective and processual ethnography. In the introduction to *Women Writing Culture,* anthropologist Ruth Behar exposes the gendered assumptions implicit in ethnographic modalities that fail to account for the observer as a fully human part of the process. She says that the breasts of the "native," of the "other" are "exposed" in our writing, and yet the breasts of the anthropologists remain "concealed, privileged, different." Behar continues, "yet it is at her own peril that she deludes herself into thinking that her breasts do not matter, are invisible."[18] By exposing the intersubjective nature of engagement through such an intimate metaphor, Behar, and the authors' work in that volume, not only disrupt the gendered imbalance of ethnographic innovation but also call attention to many forms of intimacy as crucial to ethnography. In my contribution to this volume, I explore the hermeneutics of vulnerability as an ethnographic posture that dislocates colonizing methodologies and writing styles. Such vulnerability is a decolonizing gesture that draws attention to power dynamics rather than conceals them; intentional

---

17 Sigal, Tortorici, and Whitehead 2020, 19.
18 Behar 1995, 1.

and vigilant ethnographic openness will "broaden not just what we know but what we consider to be knowledge. These are not just personal stories, these are truths that open up possibilities to ways of knowing and experiencing shared encounters."[19] The chapters in this volume do the labor of exposing vulnerabilities as interpretive possibilities. They each reach toward greater understanding of knowledge as something which *becomes* and are working toward allowing unresolved tensions to live in their writing.[20]

Such vulnerable ethnographic postures intersect with erotic subjectivity as modes through which we can access and explore their broader context. Thinking of erotics as a field of action, rather than as a set of behaviors, helps us situate the interpretive framework of erotics within systems of power. Erotics is a culturally situated epistemological position through which we are able to interpret and understand human connectivity, desire, and mutuality. In the introduction to *Taboo*, anthropologist Don Kulick expanded upon the performative labor that erotic subjectivity does:

> Erotic subjectivity does things. It performs, or, rather, can be made to perform, work. And one of the many types of work it can perform is to draw attention to the condition of its own production. That is, for many anthropologists, desire experienced in the field seems often to provoke questions that otherwise easily remain unmasked, or that only get asked in a rarified manner once back at home seated comfortably behind one's computer. The questions are basic, quite uncomfortable ones. They are questions about the validity and meaning of the self-other dichotomy, and about the hierarchies on which anthropological work often seems to depend. They are questions about exploitation, racism, and boundaries. They are questions, in other words, about issues that lie at the heart of anthropological knowledge.[21]

---

19 Lawrence 2017, 483.
20 There has been much work on the masculinist, objectivist assumptions generated in ethnographic writing that normalize (even as they make invisible) male researchers. While it is not the project of this book to outline the history and practices of feminist ethnography, we do situate ourselves within a genealogy of studies that theorize gender and sexuality as crucial components to ethnographic methods, theory, and practice. These studies show that truth is incomplete and emergent, and they intentionally reveal the process of ethnography as integral to the claims being made. See, for example, Abu-Lughod 1990; Stacey 1988; Minh-ha 1989; Behar 1995; Hayes 2010; Hagedorn 2001, 2002; Kisliuk 2001.
21 Kulick 1995, 5.

Kulick suggests that by "unmasking" ethnographic questions about erotics as a field of inquiry and exposing and critically interrogating the answers we come closer to dismantling the often-solidified self-other dichotomies that plague ethnographic research.[22] By doing so we reveal multidirectional power flows, negotiations of intimacy and proximity, and the exchange between knowing subjects. The "exchange" in question does not have to be sexual to be erotic, though it certainly can be. Through this interpretive framing, erotics provides a means to think through myriad forms of human connectivity.

Examinations of erotics that move away from sexual identity, behavior, or spaces enable us to think about how desire, pleasure, joy, collaboration, and other forms of creative agency are realized through this framework.[23] Sound scholar Ellen Waterman wrote, "A 'feminist erotics of creative improvisation' is one contribution to the larger project of critical studies in improvisation, an emerging field that seeks to understand the potential of certain forms of music to decentre, even transform, entrenched social hierarchies and power structures."[24] Waterman draws from philosophical texts to argue that pleasure is realized in nonsexual forms of creative capacity and such erotics are key in reimagining power imbalance. Audre Lorde similarly claimed, "when I speak of the erotic, then, I speak of it as an assertion of the lifeforce of women; of that creative energy empowered, the knowledge and use of which we are now reclaiming in our language, our history, our dancing, our loving, our work, our lives."[25] By broadening the scope of desire and the language we use to describe it, scholars have queered erotics; focusing on same-sex intimacies, rejecting a heteronormative framework for relationship- and community-building, and calling attention to nonsexual modes of erotic expression have demonstrated the liberatory potentiality of erotics (see also Muller, Aduonum, this volume).[26] Scholars, too, have viewed erotic agency as a mode of engaged citizenship, a form of shared sensuous experience that

---

22 Gloria Wekker makes a similar assertion in *The Politics of Passion: Women's Sexual Culture in the Afro-Surinamese Diaspora* (2006). See also Babiracki 2008.
23 See for example Gill 2010; Gill 2012; Gill 2018; Anzaldúa 2002; Allen 2011; Allen 2012; Alexander 2005; McCartney 2016.
24 Waterman 2008, 1.
25 Lorde 1984b, 55.
26 Lorde 1984b; Marcus 2007; Newton 1993; Barz and Cheng 2020.

builds creative and social bonds, political orientations, expressive possibilities, and embodied freedom.[27]

Authors in this volume offer reflective ethnographic details to generate theories of erotics and intimacy as they emerge from within situated contexts, effectively expanding erotics to include shared emotional and spiritual bonds, shared pleasure, sensual aspects of knowing, and the political dimensions of desire. The essays they craft are attendant to the colonialist, racialized histories that enable and shape ethnographic visions and endeavors, even as they provide alternate possibilities of connection and closeness. They also gesture toward the ways in which critical positionality generates intimacy.

Trauma, Pain, and Transformation

Artist and performance studies scholar Omi Osun Jones connects radical transformation with spiritual, creative, embodied work. She calls on women to "write the truths their bodies have been terrorized into keeping silent" as "radical acts of self-making and social transformation."[28] By doing so, we embark upon empathetic, collective, and sensory experiences of liberation. We proceed from the view that by attending to those aspects of ethnographic knowledge that have historically remained silent we contribute to such social transformation. Examining multiple iterations of trauma, the authors in this volume think through pain, surveillance, injustice, and rupture as modes through which we create more empathetic encounters. By creating space to breathe into areas of discursive discomfort, we also ask our readers to consider these experiences not as isolated personal experiences but as indicative of the ways our methodological, theoretical, and disciplinary frameworks render inaudible these aspects of knowing and being. What silences do we need to listen to? What pain have we turned away from? And how might more attentive listening create a more empathetic and just future?

Several authors position trauma within the experience and process of ethnographic research. The investigation of violence and trauma in ethnographic work has been largely separated from accounts of erotics and intimacy.[29] The

---

27 Lawrence 2021; Sheller 2012; Alexander 2005; Gill 2018.
28 Jones, Moore, and Bridgforth 2010, 10.
29 Notable exceptions include Eva Moreno's chapter in *Taboo* (1995) in which she discusses being raped by her research assistant. In Gloria Wekker's *Politics of Passion* (2006), she discusses how an intimate relationship in the field

literature on trauma in ethnography has attended to methodology, ethics, the danger and safety of researchers, the challenges and consequences of disclosing trauma, and the disciplinary implications of harm and violence in the field.[30] Some of the chapters here explore a range of related issues, notably the failure of methods training to prepare students adequately for violent encounters, sexual assault and harassment, and negotiating gendered expectations in the field. They also discuss the institutional implications and difficulties of meaningfully engaging these experiences analytically. Ethnographic work is unevenly marked according to categories such as gender, sex, race, ability, and citizenship status, for example. Approaches to the study of ethnography and violence have attended to the ways in which identity categories, marked bodies, and sociocultural parameters affect who is subjected to violence, under which circumstances, and the legal, social, and political consequences of such violence.

This volume enters into this discourse by providing space to think about the interpersonal aspects of trauma in ethnographic work, as well as the disciplinary and institutional implications for such conversations. Authors analyze their subject positions within these frameworks to provide localized, grounded, interpretive models and exploring the sensorial manifestations of racism, both as it impinges upon and orders racial subjectivity, knowledge, and imagination. Authors offer visions of transformation and healing through empathy, coalition building, and attentive listening.

---

opened space for her to be maligned by the woman with whom she was intimate. I discuss safety, surveillance, and physical violence in "Under White Men's Eyes" (2020). Julie Beauregard's master's thesis, "Ethnomusicologist Sexed and Sexualized: Theorizing a Woman in the Field" (2019), explored both trauma and erotics in depth; its contribution is unique among the ethnomusicological literature for drawing out a relationship between these two spheres of experience.

30 Hagedorn 2001; Hagedorn 2002; Kenyon and Hawker 1999; Sharp and Kremer 2006; Huang 2016; Kloß 2016; Cai 2019; Ghassem-Fachandi 2009; Hanson and Richards 2019; Yates 2013; Heinze 2020; Clark and Grant 2015; Berry, Argüelles, Cordis, Ihmoud, and Estrada 2017; Pollard 2009; Clancy 2013; Moreno 1995.

The Chapters

Tracy McMullen invites spirituality into questions of intimacy. Exploring racial fetishization in jazz, she asks questions about what it means to learn traditions cast as Other, while she considers her own experiences with jazz and Buddhism as ways of "dreaming the world." In seeking answers, she offers the frameworks of devotion as a practice based on love, humility, and paying dues. In speaking of desire, she writes, "This means having the humility to seek out knowledge not in order to gain 'power over' but to learn from someone or something that you recognize knows more than you do, and to honor that knowledge and carry it forward." By bringing Buddhism to the front of her love for jazz, McMullen offers a spiritual reflection on musical performance as a mode of healing, of heightened connection to others, and as an opportunity to honor a love of and a desire for knowledge.

In his chapter, Steven Cornelius, too, reveals spiritual intimacies that emerge through a series of memories woven into evocative portrayals of the tensions between our desires, our minds, our bodies, and the divine. Writing across time, he takes the reader along a sensory journey of listening and knowing, to be "a silent and nameless witness to timeless infinity." The desire to know but not possess or be possessed emerges as a tension in this chapter. The subsequent memories reveal ever deepening layers of spiritual, emotional, and physical trauma and healing, even as they wind back to wrestling with the deity Ogún, for power, for self-determination. "Now, more than ever," he writes, "I find it imperative to learn to listen with ever greater care, so that the life I live (and the stories I write) will be more whole. I am trying to listen inwardly, into silence."

Mark Lomanno's chapter queries the state of the performing body as it is conflated with proficiency in jazz, using details from a performance ethnography in the Canary Islands to reimagine ethnography as an intimate acoustemological experience. Lomanno challenges ethnographic norms that are informed by ableist assumptions about access, mobility, perception, and interaction. Focusing on the "flawed body" via the subject-in-pain, they explore the embodiment of trauma-centered improvisation that posits an ethnographic posture that accounts for disability. Lomanno compels us to seek vulnerability as a source of intimate connection to others and ourselves in our writing, our musical performance, and our ethnographic encounters.

My reprinted essay, "Performing Desire: Race, Sex, and the Ethnographic Encounter," challenges disciplinary presumptions about dichotomous power differentials in ethnographic research. I illustrate how a focus on quotidian ethnographic experiences is instructive in theorizing power as multidirectional and negotiable. By incorporating intersubjectivity as a narrative mode, ethnographers represent multiple perspectives on cultural engagements, human connectivity, and the interpretive frameworks through which we derive meaning. I argue that this narrative strategy can move us away from overly simplistic, ahistorical social categories and toward the nonlinear, complex, and sometimes contradictory realities of human engagement.

In a creatively redacted "fieldnotes" essay, Catherine M. Appert visually draws our attention to that about which fieldworkers often cannot write. She demonstrates how ethnographic trauma and the fear that prohibits full accounts of gendered forms of violence remain difficult or impossible to include in research accounts. Her chapter, "Thick Descriptions" taunts the Geertzian framework that has compelled ethnographic research for half a century by revealing precisely how violent our norms and processes are. She asks, "What might it mean to invert that thickness, throwing the unseen into relief?" Informed by feminist scholarship that insists on listening to silence and inaudibility, Appert sharply critiques our institutions, methods, and the gatekeeping around academic publications and knowledge production. Her innovative visual play heightens our awareness of the layers of silence in such experiences; she asks us "to dwell in the unvoiced."

Ama Oforiwaa Aduonum's chapter confronts the complex terrain of a Ghanaian woman, who now lives and works in the United States, as she variously connects and disconnects with others via shared trauma, historical memory, and racial performativity in locations spanning Senegal, Ghana, and the United States. Aduonum discusses the ways in which her body became the repository for notions of race in a sliding doors portrait that points to the fissures of ideologies of race in the United States and Africa. Pointing to the dissociative trauma of racism and entangled intimacies with women of African descent, Aduonum provides examples of performance as a mode of protest, recovery, and healing.

Danielle Davis brings us to the embodied performativity of pedagogy by examining the traumatic consequences of anti-Blackness in academic spaces. Through details drawn from graduate coursework, conference spaces, and interactions with professors, Davis charts the visceral, emotional, and intellectual trauma of failed connections and harmful performances. This essay reveals the layers of interiority that are wounded by anti-Black systemic violence and the complicity of academic institutions in upholding, defending, and excusing such violence. Davis imagines an empathetic future, providing insights into building multiracial coalitions grounded in accountability, solidarity, listening, and an embodied interconnectedness.

Carol Muller illustrates the erotics of fieldwork in a highly evocative portrait of intimacies generated by listening, working alongside people, and building community. She reflects upon the racial and class divides that characterized her fieldwork in South Africa and then demonstrates, via the music of Shembe women, the ways that listening becomes an erotic, spiritual bridge that carries us into a remade world of connectivity, longing, and safety. In developing a theory for the erotics of fieldwork, she specifically challenges ethnographers to deepen our listening practices, to create balanced dialogue, and to reflect on how relationships and embodied ethnographic practices can be modes through which we challenge inequality.

Exploring localized constructs of the erotic through movement and dance-ethnography, Lesley N. Braun reflects upon her experiences in Kinshasa as a dancer in urban "musique moderne," frontloading the embodied experience of movement in a genre considered improper for Congolese women. Braun brings readers into the sensuality of experience, within which she explores themes of vulgarity, profanity, pleasure, and the erotics of exposure in Congolese dance worlds, and in so doing questions both insider and outsider assumptions about those categories. This essay offers a vulnerable portrait of dance as an intimate knowledge system through which moral critique, surveillance, and women-centered pleasure are performed.

Michelle Kisliuk's chapter elucidates many of the volume's thematic materials. Rich in ethnographic detail from her research with Jewish people in Ghana, she theorizes the ways in which critical positioning enacts "empathetic intercultural bonds for healing across smoldering colonial/anti-colonial and other divides." Kisliuk demonstrates via her narrative the labor that such positioning offers as means to think more carefully and in nuanced, context-situated ways about layers of identity and belonging. If the volume poses a question, this essay offers some answers: in a moment when disciplinary conversations are questioning the ethics of ethnographic research and turning away from the possibilities of fully human connections across categories of difference, this essay demonstrates the ways that ethnography can instead build intersubjective, empathetic futures and reminds us of the political, social, and spiritual necessity to create meaningful human bonds.

Tension—To Stretch, or to Extend

The willingness of the volume authors to be vulnerable in profound ways, to expose their interior emotional, spiritual, and intellectual longings and pain, is humbling to me. I find a creative embodiment of intimacy in the chapters of this volume. The porous openness of the writing creates space for the reader to enter, to find themselves reflected back. As Omi Osun Jones states,

> This truth telling is dangerous business. It leaves one vulnerable—but our vulnerability is our strength. It leaves one exposed, but exposure allows the wind to whip through all those dank and musty spaces of terror and blow away isolation and fear. Truth telling leaves us free—and that is, after all the point.[31]

Jones wrote that liberation is possible. It is possible when we are vulnerable, when we honor truth, even when that truth is not convenient, pretty, or easy. In a personal communication with Jones, she wrote, "Now breathe into those spaces that show you how you got up each day, how you found the 'radical interconnectedness' you tell us is so important." As I sought to find the language to communicate the importance of spiritual connection as a healing practice, her advice to "breathe into the spaces" of my writing opened me to find the places where I was still afraid to go and to seek solace in the solidarities about which I was writing. I found freedom in her gentle nudge to speak my truth.

And yet I write this knowing that not everyone is able to write their truths, speak their truths in such ways. There are still a number of silences in this volume, and a volume that calls attention to unsounded histories, experiences, and perspectives needs to be accountable for what remains absent. Disciplinary, institutional, and social forms of violence, regulation, and governmentality continue to bear down unevenly upon individuals, making it difficult to speak back. As Jones articulates,

> This truth telling is especially dangerous for a Black queer woman, for me. My very safety is at stake when I speak the truth, the truth of my life, and the truth of the world as I know it. My truths challenge the very foundation of the systems around me, systems that variously support and denigrate me, systems that applaud and slap me.

---

31   Jones 2010.

So, as I walk, I look for mirrors, for allies who are also committed to everyone's freedom, allies willing to risk their own safety in order to insure [sic] mine.[32]

Any time we claim to create space with our writing, we must also be accountable for ways of speaking and writing that are outside of our immediate peripheries, are written in languages that are not widely circulated, or are spoken rather than written. Circulations of knowledge within the academy remain woefully narrow, and we must remain attentive and honest about our complicity in silencing, marginalizing, and speaking over other voices. I'll conclude with a remark that I believe is in the spirit of this book: just as we carry forward the work of those who created space for us, we must extend further, stretch further, listen more fully to that which remains unsounded so that there is more space into which we can all breathe.

References

Abu-Lughod, Lila. 1990. "Can There Be a Feminist Ethnography?" *Women and Performance: A Journal of Feminist Theory* 5 (1): 7–27.

Alexander, M. Jacqui. 2005. *Pedagogies of Crossing: Meditations on Feminism, Sexual Politics, Memory, and the Sacred*. Durham, NC: Duke University Press.

Allen, Jafari. 2011. *¡Venceremos? The Erotics of Black Self-Making in Cuba*. Durham, NC: Duke University Press.

———. 2012. "One Way or Another: Erotic Subjectivity in Cuba." *American Ethnologist* 39 (2): 325–38.

Anzaldúa, Gloria E. 2002. "now let us shift … the path of conocimiento … inner work, public acts." In *this bridge we call home*, edited by Gloria E. Anzaldúa and AnaLouise Keating, 540–78. New York: Routledge.

Appert, Catherine M. 2017. "Engendering Musical Ethnography." *Ethnomusicology* 61 (3): 446–67.

Babiracki, Carol M. 2008. "What's the Difference? Reflections on Gender and Research in Village India." In *Shadows in the Field: New Perspectives for Fieldwork in Ethnomusicology*, edited by Gregory F. Barz and Timothy J. Cooley, 167–82. 2nd ed. New York: Oxford University Press.

Barz, Gregory, and William Cheng, eds. 2020. *Queering the Field: Sounding Out Ethnomusicology*. New York: Oxford University Press.

Beauregard, Julie. 2019. "Ethnomusicologist Sexed and Sexualized: Theorizing a Woman in the Field." M.A. Thesis, University of Rochester.

---

32 Jones 2010.

Behar, Ruth. 1995. "Introduction: Out of Exile." In *Women Writing Culture*, edited by Ruth Behar and Deborah A. Gordon, 1–29. Berkeley: University of California Press.

Berry, Daina Ramey, and Leslie M. Harris, eds. 2018. *Sexuality and Slavery: Reclaiming Intimate Histories in the Americas*. Athens: University of Georgia Press.

Berry, Maya J., Claudia Chávez Argüelles, Shayna Cordis, Sarah Ihmoud, and Elizabeth Velásquez Estrada. 2017. "Towards a Fugitive Anthropology: Gender, Race, and Violence in the Field." *Cultural Anthropology* 32 (4): 537–65.

Brown, Danielle. 2020. "An Open Letter on Racism in Music Studies, Especially Ethnomusicology and Music Education." June 12.

Cai, Yifan. 2019. "Confronting Sexual Harassment in the Field." *Made in China Journal* 4 (3). https://madeinchinajournal.com/2019/10/25/confronting-sexual-harassment-in-the-field/.

Clancy, Kate. 2013. "'I Had No Power to Say "That's Not Okay"': Reports of Harassment and Abuse in the Field." *Context and Variation, Scientific American Blog Network*, April 13, 2013. https://blogs.scientificamerican.com/context-and-variation/safe13-field-site-chilly-climate-and-abuse/.

Clark, Imogen, and Andrea Grant, eds. 2015. "Sexual Harassment in the Field." Special issue of *Journal of the Anthropological Society of Oxford Online* 7 (1). https://www.anthro.ox.ac.uk/jasoonline-2011#collapse392631.

Collins, Patricia Hill. 2000. *Black Feminist Thought: Knowledge, Consciousness, and the Politics of Empowerment*. New York: Routledge.

———. 2004. *Black Sexual Politics: African Americans, Gender, and the New Racism*. New York: Routledge.

Combahee River Collective. 1979. "The Combahee River Collective Statement." In *Capitalist Patriarchy and the Case for Socialist Feminism*, edited by Zillah R. Eisenstein, 362–72. New York: Monthly Review Press.

Dennis, Kelly. 1994. "Ethno-Pornography: Veiling the Dark Continent." *History of Photography* 18 (1): 22–28.

Ghassem-Fachandi, Parvis, ed. 2009. *Violence: Ethnographic Encounters*. London: Routledge.

Gill, Lyndon K. 2010. "Transfiguring Trinidad and Tobago: Queer Cultural Production, Erotic Subjectivity and the Praxis of Black Queer Anthropology." PhD diss., Harvard University.

———. 2012. "Chatting Back an Epidemic: Caribbean Gay Men, HIV/AIDS, and the Uses of Erotic Subjectivity." *GLQ: A Journal of Lesbian and Gay Studies* 18 (2–3): 277–95.

———. 2018. *Erotic Islands: Art and Activism in the Queer Caribbean*. Durham, NC: Duke University Press.

Hagedorn, Katherine. 2001. *Divine Utterances: The Performance of Afro-Cuban Santería*. Washington, DC: Smithsonian Institution Press.

———. 2002. "Sacred Secrets: Lessons with Francisco." In *Mementos, Artifacts, and Hallucinations: From the Ethnographer's Tent*, edited by Ron Emoff and David Henderson, 31–44. New York: Routledge.

Hahn, Tomie. 2007. *Sensational Knowledge: Embodying Culture through Japanese Dance*. Middletown, CT: Wesleyan University Press.

Hanson, Rebecca, and Patricia Richards. 2019. *Harassed: Gender, Bodies, and Ethnographic Research*. Oakland: University of California Press.

Hayes, Eileen M. 2010. *Songs in Black and Lavender: Race, Sexual Politics, and Women's Music*. Urbana: University of Illinois Press.

Heinze, Jerika Loren. 2020. "Gauging the Toll: Auto-Reflexivity, Sexual Violence, and Fieldwork." Member Voices, *Fieldsights*, September 1, 2020. https://culanth.org/fieldsights/gauging-the-toll-auto-reflexivity-sexual-violence-and-fieldwork.

hooks, bell. 1992. *Black Looks: Race and Representation*. London: Turnaround Press.

———. 2000. *Feminist Theory: From Margin to Center*. 2nd ed. Cambridge, MA: South End Press.

Huang, Mingwei. 2016. "Vulnerable Observers: Notes on Fieldwork and Rape." *Chronicle of Higher Education*, October 12, 2016. https://www.chronicle.com/article/vulnerable-observers-notes-on-fieldwork-and-rape/.

Hull, Akasha Gloria T., Patricia Bell-Scott, and Barbara Smith, eds. 1982. *All the Women Are White, All the Blacks Are Men, but Some of Us Are Brave: Black Women's Studies*. Old Westbury, NY: Feminist Press.

Ipsen, Pernille. 2020. "Sexualizing the Other: From Ethnopornography to Interracial Pornography in European Travel Writing about West African Women." In Sigal et al., *Ethnopornography*, 205–24.

Jones, Omi Osun Joni L. 2010. "The Role of Allies in 2010." Keynote Address, presented at the Women's and Gender Studies Graduate Student Conference and Abriendo Brecha Activist Conference University of Texas at Austin, February 19, 2010. https://liberalarts.utexas.edu/cwgs/news/wgs-student-conference-keynote-dr-omi-osun-joni-l-jones.

Jones, Omi Osun Joni L., Lisa L. Moore, and Sharon Bridgforth, eds. 2010. *Experiments in a Jazz Aesthetic: Art, Activism, Academia, and the Austin Project*. Austin: University of Texas Press.

Jones-Rogers, Stephanie E. 2019. *They Were Her Property: White Women as Slave Owners in the American South*. New Haven, CT: Yale University Press.

Kenyon, Elizabeth, and Sheila Hawker. 1999. "'Once Would Be Enough': Some Reflections on the Issue of Safety for Lone Researchers." *International Journal of Social Research Methodology* 2 (4): 313–27.

Kisliuk, Michelle. 2001. *Seize the Dance! BaAka Musical Life and the Ethnography of Performance*. Oxford: Oxford University Press.

Kloß, Sinah Theres. 2016. "Sexual(ized) Harassment and Ethnographic Fieldwork: A Silenced Aspect of Social Research." *Ethnography* 18 (3): 396–414.

Kulick, Don, and Margaret Willson, eds. 1995. *Taboo: Sex, Identity and Erotic Subjectivity in Anthropological Fieldwork*. New York: Routledge.

Lawrence, Sidra. 2017. "Performing Desire: Race, Sex, and the Ethnographic Encounter." *Ethnomusicology* 61 (3): 468–85.

———. 2020. "Under White Men's Eyes: Racialized Eroticism, Ethnographic Encounters, and the Maintenance of the Colonial Order." In Sigal et al., *Ethnopornography*, 118–35.

———. 2021. "Sonic Intimacies: Performative Erotics and African Feminisms." *Senses and Society* 16 (2): 177–92.

Lorde, Audre. 1984a. *Sister Outsider*. Freedom, CA: Crossing Press.

———. 1984b. "Uses of the Erotic: The Erotic as Power." In *Sister Outsider*, 53–59. Freedom, CA: The Crossing Press.

Malinowski, Bronislaw. 1967. *A Diary in the Strict Sense of the Term*. New York: Harcourt, Brace, and World.

Marcus, Sharon. 2007. *Between Women: Friendship, Desire, and Marriage in Victorian England*. Princeton: Princeton University Press.

McCartney, Andra. 2016. "How Am I to Listen to You?: Soundwalking, Intimacy, and Improvised Listening." In *Negotiated Moments: Improvisation, Sound, and Subjectivity*, edited by Gillian Siddall and Ellen Waterman, 37–54. Durham, NC: Duke University Press.

McClintock, Anne. 1995 *Imperial Leather: Race, Gender, and Sexuality in the Colonial Contest*. New York: Routledge.

McClintock, Anne, Aamir Mufti, and Ella Shohat, eds. 1997. *Dangerous Liaisons: Gender, Nation, and Postcolonial Perspectives*. Minneapolis: University of Minnesota Press.

Minh-ha, Trinh T. 1989. *Woman, Native, Other: Writing Postcoloniality and Feminism*. Bloomington: Indiana University Press.

Moraga, Cherríe L., and Gloria E. Anzaldúa, eds. 2015. *This Bridge Called My Back: Writings by Radical Women of Color*. 4th ed. Albany: State University of New York Press.

Moreno, Eva. 1995. "Rape in the Field: Reflections from a Survivor." In Kulick and Willson, *Taboo*, 166–89.

Newton, Esther. 1993. "My Best Informant's Dress: The Erotic Equation in Fieldwork." *Cultural Anthropology* 8 (1):3–23.

Patton, Stacey. 2018. "Why #MeToo Needs to Talk about Predatory White Women." *Dame Magazine*, October 23, 2018. https://www.damemagazine.com/2018/10/23/why-metoo-needs-to-talk-about-predatory-white-women/.

Pollard, Amy. 2009. "Field of Screams: Difficulty and Ethnographic Fieldwork." *Anthropology Matters* 11 (2). https://www.anthropologymatters.com/index.php/anth_matters/article/view/10/10.

Saavedra, Martha. 2013. "Quick Bibliography on Personal Safety, Sexual Harassment and Sexual Violence Considerations for Field Work Researchers." Center for African Studies, UC Berkeley, August 29, 2013.

Sharp, Gwen, and Emily Kremer. 2006. "The Safety Dance: Confronting Harassment, Intimidation, and Violence in the Field." *Sociological Methodology* 36:317–27.

Sheller, Mimi. 2012. *Citizenship from Below: Erotic Agency and Caribbean Freedom.* Durham, NC: Duke University Press.

Sigal, Pete, Zeb Tortorici, and Neil L. Whitehead, eds. 2020. *Ethnopornography: Sexuality, Colonialism and Archival Knowledge.* Durham, NC: Duke University Press.

Smith, Barbara. 1977. "Toward a Black Feminist Criticism." *Conditions: Two* 1 (2): 25–44.

Stacey, Judith. 1988. "Can There Be a Feminist Ethnography." *Women's Studies International Forum* 11 (1): 21–27.

Stoler, Ann Laura. 1995. *Race and the Education of Desire: Foucault's "History of Sexuality" and the Colonial Order of Things.* Durham, NC: Duke University Press.

———. 2002. *Carnal Knowledge and Imperial Power: Race and the Intimate in Colonial Rule.* Berkeley: University of California Press.

Waterman, Ellen. 2008. "Naked Intimacy: Eroticism, Improvisation, and Gender." *Critical Studies in Improvisation / Études critiques en improvisation* 4 (2): 1–20.

Wekker, Gloria. 2006. *The Politics of Passion: Women's Sexual Culture in the Afro-Surinamese Diaspora.* New York: Columbia University Press.

Yates, Diana. 2013. "Team Reports on Abuse of Students Doing Anthropological Fieldwork." April 15, 2013. https://news.illinois.edu/view/6367/204840.

Chapter One

Yusef's Breath

Jazz Love, Cross-Racial Identification, and Paying Dues

Tracy McMullen

> Freedom and innocence are antithetical. You can't have both.
> —James Baldwin

I used to think I was a fast learner. Indeed, I could understand concepts quickly, but only because I was so able to ignore the particulars. I was a bullet train toward my destination, the landscape out the windows blurred into invisibility. It was many years into practicing Buddhism, years after one of my Buddhist teachers described herself as a slow learner and I felt smugly relieved to not have that problem, that I realized I, too, was slow. Glossing quickly over the surface, I held more complex engagement at a distance, essentially afraid to lose myself within something—because how could I judge then? How could I know I was smart, that is, smarter than others, if I could not locate myself for comparison?

Along with Buddhism, my road to more realistically assessing my capacities included my efforts to learn jazz. I had loved the saxophone since the age I began playing in my Fairbanks, Alaska, junior high school "jazz" band, even as my primary exposure was "String of Pearls" by way of the Glenn Miller Orchestra, Phil Woods's alto saxophone solo on Billy Joel's *Just the Way You Are*, and the 1970s instrumental pop group Spyro Gyra, which I dutifully transcribed with earnest and rotund eighth notes for my first gigs in a prom band. I'm sad to say that it was only after I graduated from college that I encountered what I think I can call fairly unproblematically "real" jazz. I had given up the saxophone my senior year of high school and still recall the moment outside the band room when I had the thought: this is not what grown women do. But I would tear up when I'd hear a saxophone on a pop song in college. If I had kept it up, I hope I would have discovered jazz in college. But it was only after graduating that I encountered a bevy of young, white, male, experimental-minded recent college grads in San Francisco who listened to Coltrane, Miles, Ornette, Dolphy, and Ayler and dragged refuse into their rented flats to bang on in improvisatory and drug-fueled splendor day and night. Joining this cohort, I bought an old Martin tenor from a shop South of Market and started practicing, beginning with "free jazz," as it were, and working my way back.

Five years later, living in Oakland and attending jam sessions led by the accomplished pianist Ed Kelly at the Bird Cage bar and tavern, I became so frustrated with my self-conscious mind, which seemed to separate me on one side and the music on the other, that I opened my phone book and searched for Buddhism (I had recently read a book that led me to believe Buddhism could help). I asked the Buddhist Center if they had any programs where I could learn an instrument as part of a spiritual practice. I was ready to even give up the saxophone and play a Buddhist ritual instrument because I wanted to (really) play music and I felt like I couldn't—my pestering ego would not shut up and let me play. They said they had no such programs, but they could help me connect with my saxophone. And one thing I have in common with the great jazz pianist, Herbie Hancock: I turned to Buddhism initially to help me play better. And then Buddhism, but also jazz, became much bigger than my personal ability to make music.[1]

Therefore, almost thirty years ago, jazz and Buddhism started to turn my mind from what I see now as an impoverished and impoverishing way of relating to the world to a deeper, more nourishing relationship with experience. In jazz, I found a commitment to excellence and beauty that whispered to me in pop music even before I directly encountered John Coltrane or Dexter Gordon. Buddhism helped me connect with my instrument in a way that furthered me on the path my exemplars had traveled. Jazz and Buddhism continue to help me connect with my experience, heal my neuroses, and reveal how life has a purpose. These are qualities my "home tradition" as a

---

[1] For Herbie Hancock's description of how Buddhism affected his life and musicianship, see Hancock and Reiss 2007.

white, middle-class girl did not teach me. The lessons I personally learned in that tradition (growing up in my family and community) led to alienation, neuroses, and purposelessness, something the Western philosophers would further articulate for me but not effectively counter. It is my home tradition—the European post-Enlightenment tradition—that is increasingly recognized as a ubiquitous, yet failed tradition—one that cannot sustain a livable world. A rising tide of voices affirms that our global way of life is something that needs to be "dreamed again."[2] This means having the humility to seek out knowledge not in order to gain "power over" but to learn from someone or something that you recognize knows more than you do, and to honor that knowledge and carry it forward. It means having the confidence to know you can be in and act in the world honestly and through that honesty discern right from wrong.

In this chapter, I trace through my engagement with jazz as a white woman encountering an African American tradition. My individual experience of dreaming the world again comes primarily from my engagements with Buddhism and jazz, and I use my personal journey to shed light on a central problem within such an undertaking: the potential for white exoticization and appropriation of otherness. I begin this essay with an examination of racial identifications in the process of embodying the jazz tradition, including my identification with Black male saxophonists and what I argue is resistance on the part of many white men to bringing the sound of Black men into their bodies. This leads to an interrogation of white women's location within the narrative of Blackness as the embodiment of hip. If white men have a history of appropriating Blackness in order to perform "hipness," where does the white woman fall in this story? Finally, I make an argument for how a white American can learn from traditions and from people who have been constructed as "other" to and for her. This entails understanding why she is seeking knowledge. It entails paying dues as a white, female American, which is not distinct from any other definition of paying dues in jazz, I argue, but everyone's dues are not precisely the same.

I have sought the lessons I could learn from jazz—lessons about commitment, devotion, focus, generosity, and love. This learning takes place amid the racial neuroses of the United States and forces me to confront my ignorance and my complicity in white supremacy. John Murphy describes the relationship of jazz artists to those who came before as not the Bloomsian anxiety of influence but a "joy," a way to "celebrate their debt to their

---

2   Lopez 2019.

precursors" (9) by incorporating their precursors' work and efforts into their own. What does this mean for white American musicians and their specific debt to their Black American precursors? Can it be a practice of joy for all and not an ignorance that just takes what it wants because it is too afraid to look more closely at the full picture? What is the debt I have to a tradition that whispered, spoke, and called to me in a language that was not taught to me by my family?

Racial Identifications in Jazz

What are you going to put in your body?

When Yusef Lateef plays, you hear him breathe. His body resonates his breath in preparation for his horn to sound. His breath reminds you of his body, that he is there. That there is effort, commitment, energy. It is not just a saxophone. It is a man playing the saxophone. It is a person. His breath sounds his commitment. He is putting his body on the line. For what? For something very important. You can hear it in his breath.

When I first starting practicing jazz seriously in my early twenties, I began by playing with records. I imagined myself as John Coltrane and Sonny Rollins as I played along with "Tenor Madness." I did the same with the recordings of Yusef Lateef, Gene Ammons, Wayne Shorter, Dexter Gordon, Joe Henderson, George Coleman, Pharoah Sanders, and Frank Foster. I would try to fully embody these saxophone players while playing their solos. I would try to *be* them in that moment, imagine that I *am* them. I read interviews and books, watched documentaries and concert videos, but it was the sound on records that was laying the path that I wanted to follow. Nicholas Payton recently articulated this near-universal desire of serious jazz aspirants, saying of his early years studying the trumpet, "I wanted to know what [Clifford Brown] had for breakfast. I wanted to be him" (quoted in Hill 2020). Whatever it was that was happening in their body to produce that music, I tried to have that happen in mine. This type of love and recognition can happen in a white girl from Fairbanks, Alaska, initiating her on a journey about which she will initially know nothing. It can foster an admiration that drives her to want to understand the musicians and the music. What happens to Payton on that road? What happens to me? Wanting to know, care, be moved, heal, find meaning, give?

The tenor saxophonists I tried to sound like were all Black men (I added Gato Barbieri and Jim Pepper to the repertoire later). This should not be surprising, given that it was jazz and the tenor saxophone that spoke to me. I heard beauty and a message in the tone and the music, especially in John Coltrane, that made me want to listen to whomever he listened to and so on. *And* we live in a racist country (the "and" here replacing "but" or "however"). For me to engage with Coltrane in this way was for me to have to acknowledge I had a race, something the structure of race itself is designed to hide.[3] A white person who wants to become a jazz musician should face discomfort along racial lines because this is a price of the long history of racism in our country. Dealing directly with the history of jazz (wanting to know what Clifford Brown had for breakfast) means engaging with racism in the United States, which means looking at oneself in racial terms. White people generally have no tolerance for paying such a price, expecting to be treated as an "individual" and judged by their merit, not by race! Jazz education in universities and high schools has developed in such a way as to "go around" this price by creating white-dominated jazz populations. Paying the real price of the ticket onto the jazz train currently involves independent study for a white student.

To investigate this price, I begin with an examination of my musical preferences. The rich, complex timbre of the saxophonists I mention above, the swing of the ensembles, the way the edges are not smoothed down into a perfect blend—these were (and continue to be) aesthetic approaches that I often prefer, and they stem from an African American tradition of music. People have different tastes and I maintain that there is some mystery around this. Although we all grow up in certain traditions, most of us don't stay only within the aesthetic tradition of our upbringing. Our modern world exposes us all to genres of music that cross space and time. I believe that personal taste has an element of obscurity that cannot be explained by social forces; that there is an enigmatic and idiosyncratic call of certain styles to individuals that crosses racial and cultural boundaries and that cannot be fully explained by a constructivist logic about raced, gendered, or sexual allegiances. Equally, we cannot escape the culture that we are born into. Thus, whatever the mysterious call we have toward "our thing," it will, at minimum, be imbued with the cultural hierarchies and definitions that channel these impulses. Thus,

---

3 Whereas white people tend to think of themselves as "without race," recent popular books like Irving 2014, DiAngelo 2018, and Kendi 2020 have helped bring a deeper understanding of race and white supremacy to a mainstream population. For a recent in-depth analysis of the origins of race, see Mbembe 2017.

my taste both can't be adequately explained and has been affected by racism and sexism in the United States. We can examine constructions of race and aesthetic traditions and understand that our taste takes place within and, to greater or lesser extent, through these structures.

Therefore, these aesthetic choices cannot be separated from alliances I've also made within and in response to a racist and sexist culture. First, I was introduced to jazz by my young, white boyfriend who preferred the African American stylistic tradition; at the time, neither of us had interrogated the "problem with white hipness."[4] Many scholars have helpfully delineated the problem of white exotification of Blackness and this will continue to be necessary.[5] I will add to this discussion particularly in terms of white women within that discourse. What I also want to add, however, is something that I have not yet seen addressed: my alliance with a tenor saxophone sound that was abetted by my interpretations of certain white men and their espoused values from which I wanted to distance myself. On the one hand, I don't want to overdetermine this, because I do not see a world where I would prefer the sound of Michael Brecker, say, to that of Yusef Lateef. Nonetheless, I also felt my alliance with a Black aesthetic tradition deepen in the face of sexist white men with whom I did not identify and, indeed, from whom I wanted to dissociate myself. These were men and values I encountered in the Bay Area as I began to learn jazz and that I encountered in an even more unalloyed form at the University of North Texas at the turn of the millennium. I met these men and their evaluations as soon as I started practicing and playing gigs. They had snide, regularly proffered comments to me and to other young women, generally along the lines of how we weren't original and only copied licks. My white male roommate in our four-person Mission District flat belittled my practicing with Coltrane albums in a way that was almost hysterical, angrily and breathlessly volunteering that artists don't spend their time "copying others." Another man proffered to me how a local female saxophonist who was clearly one of the best jazz musicians around (and went on to play with the Diva Orchestra in New York City) was a "good copier." This view that white women only copy and are inauthentic has been detailed especially in popular music scholarship.[6]

I will always recall a basketball coach describing the diet soda, Tab, in the 1970s: "if cancer had a taste …" Well, if these men had a sound in my mind,

---

4   Monson 1995.
5   Lott 1995, Monson 1995, Brooks 2010.
6   Coates 2003, McGee 2009.

it was the tenor saxophone sound of Michael Brecker. In the late 1980s when I bought my Martin tenor, Brecker was "the man" in white male jazz circles. I did not identify either with Brecker's sound or with the sea of saxophonists who modeled themselves on him. I found them too abstract in their emphasis on symmetrical patterns, too show-off-y, too, in my opinion, "measure my dick"-y. They sounded shallow and self-centered.[7] I didn't hear any grain.[8] Nor did I hear a message like I heard in Coltrane or Lateef or Dolphy. I associated this sound with competitive and sexist white men of all ages who laid claim to jazz in a way that made it about what you could measure: how fast, how precise, how "in-tune," how timbrally "even," how logical. It was a positivist approach to art, a type of jazz combine where "the best" was what can be objectively verified: speed, clear articulation, the completion of a logical symmetrical pattern laid over harmonic changes.[9]

At North Texas I found the source of this definition of jazz skill. As the oldest postsecondary jazz program in the country, UNT has remained a paragon of jazz as defined by the intellectual and aesthetic sensibilities of the white men who founded college jazz programs. At present, because the school is so large, it is possible to find musicians who enjoy a variety of musical styles and approaches, but the norm (primarily enforced through the auditions for the famous "lab bands") remains a type of positivist approach to evaluating "good jazz." This "competition jazz" style now begins for students in junior and high schools where the instructors were trained in these college programs. Jazz competitions developed many decades ago and many organizations led by African Americans have also created such competitions, including Jazz at Lincoln Center's Essentially Ellington competition for high school big bands and the longtime Thelonious Monk (now Herbie Hancock)

---

7   I met Michael Brecker years later at UNT and he struck me as a deep, thoughtful, and caring person. What his sound represented to me is not tantamount to who he was as a person. In this chapter I am attempting to articulate how certain sounds accrued their meanings for me, which has to do with that person's individual sound combined with how it is read and taken up in culture.

8   Barthes 1975.

9   Football and other professional sports leagues hold a national "combine" every year to measure the abilities of young athletes seeking a position in a national league. These combines have been critiqued for their reductionist emphasis on what can be measured and inability to grasp the more elusive and holistic qualities of top athletes. Tom Brady, for example, was not impressive when he performed in the NFL combine as a young athlete.

Institute's jazz competition.[10] A jazz student summarized the general sensibility in high school jazz programs: "In my high school jazz experience people who played very fast, long, intricate, bebop style solos were the people who got the most attention and praise from instructors ... It was always a technical beast that won the medal."[11] This student went on to describe how what I'm calling "competition jazz" as a style encourages students to play a certain way and how saxophonists like Wayne Shorter and Joe Henderson are considered worthy of less consideration than "[early/middle period] John Coltrane, Sonny Rollins, or Michael Brecker," whose melodic lines and approaches can be more easily formalized. This viewpoint undergirds the proffered opinions of many young white men, including those who shared with me during my time at UNT that Eric Dolphy was not a good jazz musician because "he just plays the same lick over and over" or that Michael Brecker was an improved, "cleaned up," John Coltrane. The young, white, male tenor saxophonist Alex Hoffman offered a notorious recent example of the effects of a jazz education based in a European tradition assumed to be the universal yardstick for all. Hoffman's Facebook page comment on Wayne Shorter's Carnegie Hall concert, "Fuck Wayne Shorter," went viral and elicited a firestorm in the jazz online community. In a later interview, Hoffman adumbrated a litany of characteristics that aligned Shorter with the body side of the Western mind/body split that would make even John Cage blush.[12] Hoffman lambasted Shorter for not demonstrating "perfect voice-leading over the course of many choruses" and for having a brash and harsh tone.

The sexism I felt from white men who assumed this yardstick deepened my desire to follow in the sonic footsteps of Ammons and Lateef even as these commentators kept putting forward their aesthetic values as universal.[13] Some of my fellow students began to describe my sound as "Texas tenor" or "old school" in a way that was pointing out my difference from the norm and suggesting it was "old-fashioned" or "not modern." The style based around Brecker and a European aesthetic tradition was not understood as

---

10 I place jazz competitions within a European pedagogical lineage. I have written on the intersection of European and African American traditions within jazz education in McMullen 2021a, 2021b, and forthcoming.
11 Email from Bowdoin student, July 10, 2020.
12 https://www.youtube.com/watch?v=8Etv2f1EpRU&feature=youtu.be. I interrogate Cage's view of the mind/body split in McMullen 2010.
13 I further interrogate this link of racism and sexism in white male jazz students in McMullen 2008, 2021b.

white, but as "modern."[14] A white saxophone lineage was proffered in other ways at UNT. At my jazz oral exam with my all white and male professors, I was asked what saxophonists I listened to. When I listed only Black players, many of whom leaned toward the avant-garde—Shorter, Henderson, Sanders, Shepp—I was asked if I listened to (white altoist) Jimmy Giuffre.[15] I found this white lineage persistently offered and defended. Thus, while I felt sexism from these men, I also felt pressure from them to align with a white lineage. But mostly I felt their desire to create and maintain a white lineage and to identify with it. I began to perceive white male resistance to identifying with Black male players as based in a discomfort about bringing Black men into their body. At a minimum, it seemed many white men felt conflicted about embodying Black male performance in ways that I did not. I've identified three entangled forces that I think steer white male jazz saxophonists away from "sounding Black": an allegiance with a European intellectual tradition; a preference for a European aesthetic tradition; and concerns about appropriating Black culture.

Young white students who come from segregated backgrounds (that is, the majority of the white population at a college) will assume a European intellectual tradition as simply reality unless they had some type of education that exposed them to other intellectual traditions. Alex Hoffman's analysis of Wayne Shorter's alleged shortcomings as a saxophone player came from his very Enlightenment-inflected ideas that privileged the mind over the body. According to Hoffman, Shorter's saxophone tone was "brash" and "harsh" and of a style where a "certain premium [is] placed on vulgarity. On an overemphasis on being *too* present in the moment." It is too embodied, "an emotional exhibitionism," rather than trying to "transcend" his body. Hoffman prioritized a disembodied modernism that separated great art from the vulgaris—dancing, yelling, stomping, expressing. This concern with expressing oneself too much, with too much "self" involved and not enough transcendence, is something I've connected with another musician, John Cage, and his assertion that he was transcending his self, when in fact, I argued, he was

---

14 As George Lewis has written, "coded qualifiers to the word music—such as 'experimental,' 'new,' 'art,' 'concert,' 'serious,' 'avant-garde,' and 'contemporary'—are used ... to delineate a racialized location ... within the spaces of whiteness" (Lewis 1996, 102).

15 Giuffre is literally in the North Texas lineage. He was a student there during the first ten years of the jazz program, when the college was segregated. For more on the origins of the UNT jazz program and Jim Crow segregation, see McMullen forthcoming.

trying to transcend his "disgusting" body, leaving his self even more reified as a great mind. While Hoffman may be an extreme example of this modernist lineage that separates and prioritizes mind over body, this distrust of expressiveness, linked to Blackness and the feminine, influences how jazz is taught in postsecondary programs. It entails an extreme distrust of losing oneself that has been linked to Blackness, the feminine, and indeed, to music.[16]

The concept of originality is another aspect of the European intellectual tradition that affects jazz education. John Murphy made a case for the "joy of influence" in jazz, connecting influence with creativity in an African American tradition. But anxiety around influence is the norm in a European intellectual tradition uncomfortable with the blur of time and of the individual. As I argued in my book, *Haunthenticity*, the European intellectual tradition depends upon boundaries between then and now, self and other.[17] The "true original," the great genius, is construed as the "self-made man," whose greatness rests upon how he has broken with everyone else and with the past. As such, there remains an anxiety about copying in the European lineage. Indeed, it can be construed as feminine as gestured in the comments made to me about myself and other women saxophone players cited above. Additionally, taking the vocabulary of other musicians is a way to acknowledge context, something the European white patriarchal tradition is loath to do.[18] In my view, this is why John Coltrane's use of symmetrical patterns has been taken up with such alacrity and infiltrated jazz saxophone playing often to the exclusion of more nonsymmetrical, idiosyncratic, context-based (related to the harmonic changes as well as alluding to other players) vocabulary.[19]

---

16 McMullen 2010 and the introduction in McMullen 2019.
17 McMullen 2019.
18 I am here referencing a strategy of whiteness, which is to remain unnamed and ahistorical. See Lewis 1996, Fiske 1994.
19 Symmetrical patterns can be developed by the musician and can sidestep the vocabulary—words and intonations—of previous players. It can be taken as stepping outside of history, narrative, language, and expressiveness. This fits the modernist idea to make it new and to be free from history. I take up the issue of symmetrical patterns versus contextual (allusive and harmonic) vocabulary in my forthcoming book. See Monson 2007, 294–95, on Coltrane's use of symmetry and its connection to spirituality, something I would argue gets lost within the subsequent pedagogy. Bebop vocabulary is the exception to the focus on abstraction. Bebop vocabulary, however, has also been broadly

It is useful to make a distinction between the European intellectual tradition and the European aesthetic tradition without asserting that these two can be fully or easily disentangled. In her interviews with jazz musicians, Ingrid Monson wrote that there was "no topic more certain to elicit firestorms of invective and counterinvective in jazz than the idea that jazz has both a white sound and a Black sound" (Monson 2007, 69). Yet, there is a widely recognized set of qualities associated with a Black sound in jazz. Prominent Black sonic signifiers in jazz include complex timbre, blue notes, a heterogeneous sound ideal, rhythmic intensity, and frequent use of polyrhythm.[20] Distinct white sonic signifiers are simpler timbre and a homogeneous sound ideal that manifests in ensembles sounding a note at precisely the same time, blending so that no one instrument will stand out, and a less percussive piano technique. This is not to say that all Black musicians sound one way and all white musicians sound another. As Monson notes, Lester Young, Johnny Hodges, Duke Ellington, and the Modern Jazz Quartet are just a few examples of Black jazz musicians incorporating sounds connected with a European aesthetic tradition, just as many white jazz musicians employ the characteristics of the African American tradition. Such examples do not preclude speaking of traditions of music making, their influences, and how musicians of all races are influenced by these traditions.[21]

---

formalized and abstracted. See, for example, Mike Steinel, *Building a Jazz Vocabulary*.

20 Samuel Floyd, Olly Wilson, and Albert Murray are several of the key musicologists who have articulated qualities associated with an African American musical tradition. Ingrid Monson reminds us that nineteenth-century descriptions of African American music focused on its harmonic elements; she argues for the ways that harmony is an important element of the Black jazz tradition (Monson 2007).

21 Please also see note 11 about jazz competitions like Herbie Hancock and Essentially Ellington. I make a distinction between tradition and race, as entangled as these two phenomena will be in the history of the United States. Thus, we can talk about the aesthetic traditions of African American and European music, traditions that anyone can investigate, study, and perform. Establishing a historic "sonic color line," as Jennifer Lynn Stoever argues (2016), is the practice of racism and racial hierarchy. In this chapter I am interrogating my connection to an African American sound, something I assert is fueled by what I hear in the music of Lateef and Coltrane that exceeds "race" but is also simultaneously and unavoidably influenced by the "sonic color line."

Jazz musicians of all races have been interested in a wide variety of music, and aesthetic borrowing itself is universal and unstoppable. A white person can be aware of racism, be anti-racist and still prefer Western art music to jazz or prefer jazz that incorporates many of the aesthetic attributes of Western art music like a simpler timbre or homogeneous blending. White people growing up in an aesthetic tradition that prioritizes simple timbres and homogeneous sound may continue to prefer this style in their adulthood. Many African American musicians going back to jazz's beginnings acknowledged a great love of classical music but were unable to pursue careers in the field due to racism. When it comes to the tenor saxophone, I prefer a complex timbre and in larger ensembles I prefer the heterogeneous sound ideal embodied in groups led by Charles Mingus or Sun Ra, but I also love the piano trio of Fred Hersch with more of the timbre of classical music with the creativity of improvisation from an African American tradition of jazz. These might be two sides of the timbre spectrum and my preference can fall anywhere in-between from simpler timbres of Mark Turner, Steve Lacy, and pianist Bill Evans to the more complex timbres of Gato Barbieri, Cecil Taylor, and Evan Parker. None of this negates either the study of tradition and influence or the social elements that support race and gender inequity.

I believe it is possible to enjoy different traditions without falling into unexamined racism, but it demands education and honesty from the listener. I am not arguing that these aesthetic choices are made in a vacuum separate from cultural influences. I am arguing that we need to account for the fact that people do have aesthetic proclivities that do not map onto their political positions or social awareness. That preferring "classical music," funk, jazz, or, conversely, not liking one of these styles does not need to be fully colonized by our social constructions of race and ways that we are identifying within those constructions. That said, racism is sneaky and ubiquitous, and it entails careful and continual examination in all areas of life, not least, in music. Within this I put forward that some white people may align themselves with a white lineage of jazz artists due to a preference for a European aesthetic tradition that does not preclude an anti-racist stance. This may be especially heard in the jazz piano tradition, which has plenty of practitioners, white and Black, who play often or exclusively with a touch more aligned with a European aesthetic approach.

A third reason I believe white musicians will avoid identifying with Black musicians is a fear of appropriating Black culture or appearing to appropriate it. To be influenced by jazz and to want to play jazz, however, is already to be reproducing sound that is coming from an African American tradition. To pinpoint which elements are Black and which are white and then to believe that it is appropriate for each race to play their own racial characteristics and not others underscores the irrationality of race divisions and reveals again that race is a system of power. Race as a system of power is different from cultural traditions, even as we will not be able to precisely delineate the differences between Black and white aesthetic traditions under the microscope, so to speak. To say that white musicians should sound white and Black musicians should sound Black also facilitates white musicians' and teachers' deferral of the "price" of American history. The "fear of appropriation" can be tantamount to a type of white fragility, an "apparently I can't say anything right so I'm not going to say anything" way to avoid the issue of race. One simply excuses oneself from the discussion because one can return to the majoritarian culture that is unmarked and "race-free." One problem, of course, is that in so doing, one does appropriate jazz, making the African American production of jazz invisible. My experience with white male jazz instructors in the classroom (I didn't have any white female instructors) was that we didn't talk about race because race makes "everyone" uncomfortable. As Toni Morrison has put it, "The habit of ignoring race is understood to be a graceful, even generous, liberal gesture," (Morrison 1992, 9–10). It is really a way to allow white people to remain comfortable. A white jazz musician will then simply connect with a white lineage of jazz artists to corroborate their nonappropriation of jazz. This is different from preferring and choosing a European aesthetic tradition while still becoming informed and engaging in the necessary racial conversations in jazz and the United States more broadly.

Thus, even as much ink has been rightly spilled on white appropriation of Black style, it is important to recognize all the ways that white musicians have consciously established a white jazz style and that this has not been an anti-racist project; nor has it succeeded in being nonappropriative if that was a goal. This is a wrinkle on Krin Gabbard's assertion that "it is more difficult to find white performers who do not imitate Black people than it is to find those that do" (Gabbard 2004, 19). While Gabbard is referring to the general basis of American popular music as rooted in Black musical traditions, and as such, I agree with his statement, at North Texas this knowledge of Black influence fuels attempts to establish a white lineage and history of jazz and trains musicians who avoid embodying Black musical sound (which is "too present," rather than modern, controlled, and measurable). A white inability or aversion to identify with a Black musician is deeply troublesome for what it says about our present and our future.

In my own experience, jazz was "saying something" to me, something I recognized as important. This does not exempt me from all the attendant racism I have embodied as an American. And: I can still go forward, attempting to learn and attempting to emulate and pass on what has been emulated and passed on before me. To hear this story and want to embody it you must identify with the storyteller. You need to take this human in and bring the message forward—a message that cannot be understood as apart from race but is also not delimited by race. Can this be done without taking a Black product and appropriating it into a white power structure through one's white body? As part of my love of jazz I am called to look more closely at my position in society growing up as a white female and how this subject position places me in relation to Black music.

White Female Hipness

Ingrid Monson pithily articulates the problem of white liberal racial stereotyping in her article on "white hipness," describing how "African Americans [have operated] as a symbol of social conscience, sexual freedom, and resistance to the dominant order in the imagination of liberal white Americans" (Monson 1995, 398). This "romantic version of racism," as Andrew Ross has called it, is part of a long history of white men associating a lusty cool with Black men and then taking it on themselves through racial mimicry, a phenomenon Eric Lott traced back to minstrelsy.[22] An idea of masculine Black cool has also been furthered by African American men, including perhaps most influentially Amiri Baraka, who has been critiqued for his denigration of the Black middle class and situating Black cultural authenticity in the Black male working class.[23]

Stories of masculine Black cool have done their patriarchal part to further sexism. At best, women are absent from these narratives. Monson writes that "through his scant mention of women, [Baraka] presents an idea of African American musical and cultural authenticity carried primarily through the activities of men." More often women are depicted as the bearers of strait-laced, middle-class values at odds with the cool male bohemian. This is seen in Black and white proclamations and definitions of cool, which malign both

---

22 Monson cites Andrew Ross (qtd in Monson 1995, 403). Lott 1995.
23 Monson 1995, 417.

white and Black women as standing for mainstream middleclass values and working to tame and domesticate men into this bourgeois, feminized ideal.

Thus, if women are routinely described as the buzzkills of Black cool so circulated in male culture, is there such as thing as female hipness, let alone white female hipness? Regarding Black female cool, Daphne Brooks argues (via Jayna Brown) that early Black women blues singers are centerpieces of Black cool that have resonated unacknowledged throughout the twentieth and into the twenty-first century (2010, 54–55).[24] In her article on Amy Winehouse, Brooks illuminates how Winehouse aligns with Black masculinity—Nas, Sammy Davis Jr., Ray Charles—but demonstrates that this hip Black "masculinity" in fact has unacknowledged roots in the performances of Ma Rainey, Bessie Smith, and even Mamie Smith. The long lineage of Black cool performed through white women as borrowers (Mae West, Sophie Tucker) and Black men is replete with Black women's unacknowledged and unremembered performances and voices. Brooks argues that these performances are caricatured in Winehouse's voice (though often via 1960s girl group sounds like the Ronettes) and in her performance of self (a type of racial mimicry influenced by Diana Ross's Billie Holiday-ish *Lady Sings the Blues* film character, among other stereotypes). Brooks argues that even if caricatured, Winehouse's performances nevertheless embody a history of Black sound that has come from Black women and their generative and sustaining role in American music (and its influence on the United Kingdom).[25]

---

24   Brooks writes that Mamie Smith was a "'a vaudeville chanteuse,' meaning that she had access to a robust range of cross-generic singing styles crafted, in part, from watching and listening to white female performers such as Sophie Tucker (the 'last of the red hot mamas') and (later) Mae West. These women were, as Jayna Brown astutely points out in *Babylon Girls*, absorbing the performance styles of Black women who worked for them, often times as maids (Brown 2008)" (Brooks 2009 and 2010, 47).

25   Thus, Brooks makes a case for Black women in the lineage of Black cool and for white women's appropriation of such cool. Ingrid Monson has also gestured toward the possibility of white female hipness. Eric Lott's description of white bohemianism as built upon an association of African Americans with "political liberation, emotional depth, [and] sensual intensity" does not, in Monson's view, "apply only to men, despite the fact that white men have predominated among those who have crossed the racial divide through music" (Monson 1995, 405). She mentions Latina gang members wearing zoot suits in a footnote as a possible source of female hipness that deserves more research and consideration. In sum, there has been some discussion of female hipness,

Brooks (and Brown) argue for a lineage of Black female hipness that would combine sexuality and a type of female cool—assertive, confident, competent—that I would argue does not derive from a mimicry of men. Indeed, Black women were the first popular entertainers, exploding onto the scene with the advent of race records just as records were becoming popular and instigating the beginnings of a mass media culture. Therefore, while white men had established a bohemianism linked to minstrelsy and then vaudeville, and projected this onto Black men, the cool of female Black performers like Rainey and Bessie Smith, I would argue, comes from real work toward attaining a type of confidence that could remain intact in the face of the brutal racism of the United States.[26] Thus, the cool of these women equates more to attaining confidence. White cool, as described by Lott and Monson is, in contrast, *performing* confidence. As such, it is the opposite of confidence. It is the difference between cool as a façade versus cool based upon gaining a true foundation for oneself to withstand the attacks of a racist and sexist society. As such, I would differentiate this confidence from "hipness" and link it to a tradition of Black feminist thought that has taught a type of self-sustaining confidence not dependent upon the evaluations of others.[27]

I believe it is only in the post–second wave feminist era that a bona fide white female hipness as a counterpart to white male hipness has emerged and it has developed to signal white female equality with white men. Like white male hipness, white female hipness ignores or objectifies Black women and takes the masculine cool associated with Black men onto the white female body, doing so in the name of (white) female empowerment and agency. A key example is early 1990s Madonna appropriating Michael Jackson's moves in *Express Yourself*, grabbing her phallus at the crotch and claiming Black cool like a white man. Madonna was praised as a model of female empowerment—claiming her subjectivity by appropriating the male gaze, being the one who desires rather than the one who is desired. She claimed this masculine subject position in part by appropriating the Black phallus in ways that previously had been the province of white men only.

Miley Cyrus's deployment of Black women's bodies to up her edgy sexuality factor in the 2013 Video Music Awards is another key example of white

---

but further investigation is needed to continue to shed light on race and gender constructions in American culture.
26 On cool as a protection or a façade as a strategy to survive racism in the United States, see Dinerstein 2017.
27 For more on Black feminist thought and jazz, see McMullen 2021.

girl hipness. In this case, Cyrus was making currency out of the Black woman herself, appropriating the "Black booty" as a prop in her post-Disney transition into the streets. As Tressie McMillan Cottom argued, Cyrus's use of full-figured Black women's bodies as symbols of "deviant sexuality" is a centuries long story.[28] What I think is different in our post–second wave era is Cyrus's use of these Black women's bodies to specifically assert her own agency like a white man. That is, in the lineage of Madonna, Cyrus is now making claims for her sexual agency and subject-as-opposed-to-object role via the objectification of Black women, placing herself potentially also in a lineage of Black male hip hop artists. Much like Don Imus's protestation that Black men call Black women "hoes" so why can't he, I believe Cyrus lays claim to the use of Black women's bodies because it is done, that is, Black men do it. Thus, Cyrus makes a statement of (white) female empowerment by aligning herself with the appropriative benefits of men without interrogating how these appropriative benefits are part and parcel of a racist and sexist society. By appropriating Black women, Cyrus chooses her side and objectifies based on her racial privilege, claiming this as feminist.

Both Madonna and Cyrus use a type of white woman hipsterism as a misguided feminist statement and a vie for authenticity. They deploy this hipness to escape the narrative that conscribes them to novelty, groupie, and amateur. White women are the poster girls of inauthenticity in American music that categorizes the Black, male, poor, blues artist as the pinnacle of authenticity.[29] Unfortunately, they counter this simply by attempting to have the sovereignty that white men have: the power to appropriate Blackness as a demonstration of their authority. White women's agency—claiming the phallus, their position as subject, owning their desires—is enacted through the unquestioned acceptance of Black cool: Jackson's Black, male, sexuality (in the crotch grab) and Black women's hypersexualized bodies that Cyrus deploys and controls as author of her video. Madonna and Cyrus are not performing racial mimicry, then, as much as they are performing gender mimicry, mimicking white men who appropriate Blackness in order to be authentic and cool. Rather than achieving real confidence, Madonna and Cyrus "perform confidence" through this lineage of the appropriation of cool.

---

28   https://slate.com/human-interest/2013/08/miley-cyrus-vma-performance-white-appropriation-of-Black-bodies.html.

29   For more on white female inauthenticity in music, see Coates 2003, McGee 2009.

In my practice of jazz, I can't step out of this history and ideas of Black authenticity and white inauthenticity, including white female inauthenticity. But I can, within a knowledge and continual recognition of that, proceed consciously down the path. I can acknowledge history and continually educate myself in it while understanding that I found some necessary, good, nourishing, and beautiful things along the way that I will practice. I can attempt not to perform confidence but actually gain confidence. And that can only come from the firm ground of honesty and knowledge.

Paying Dues, Jazz, and Repair

The phrase and metaphor "paying dues" was invented along with jazz itself, appearing in the early twentieth century and "first widely used by jazz musicians," according to the OED.[30] In 1962 Nat Hentoff defined the phrase in his book *Jazz Life*: "'Paying dues' is the jazz musician's term for the years of learning and searching for an individual sound and style while the pay is small and irregular." Hentoff understands the phrase as a struggle to find one's sound and style, which is a richer understanding than simply the idea of technically "mastering" one's instrument. But "paying dues" has an even more encompassing meaning in the context of African American history, a meaning most effectively mined by America's great interpreter, James Baldwin. In the same year that Hentoff defined paying dues, Baldwin presented a definition in his novel, *Another Country*, in which a Black female vocalist confronts a wealthy white woman with a truth about white Americans: "What you people don't know is that life is a bitch, baby. It's the biggest hype going. You don't have any experience in paying your dues and it's going to be rough on you, baby, when the deal goes down. There's lots of back dues to be collected, and I know damn well you haven't got a penny saved" (350). This larger context of "dues paying" and what precisely is paid for is missed in Hentoff's definition. Baldwin was the premiere expert witness on white ignorance and white inability to pay the "price of the ticket," the odd fear of freedom that hides behind the habit of dominance. This larger context of dues paying was a central component of Baldwin's philosophy and truth-telling, what he generously and tirelessly attempted to show America throughout his career. Ta'Nehisi Coates rearticulated this philosophy in his 2014 essay

---

30 https://www-oed-com.ezproxy.bowdoin.edu/view/Entry/58237?redirectedFrom=paying+your+dues#eid6087587.

in the *Atlantic*, "The Case for Reparations." Like Baldwin, who recognized this was a project for all Americans, Coates continually exhorts a collective "we," Americans of all races caught up in the fantasy of America. Coates calls upon us to wake from this fantasy: "Reparations—by which I mean the full acceptance of our collective biography and its consequences—is the price we must pay to see ourselves squarely."[31] The excellent news is that this ticket is, in fact, the ticket to freedom. The simple price is "the end of innocence," "[accepting] the consequences" of knowledge. And whereas Baldwin more often (and rightly) spoke to white people specifically, writing, "the end of innocence means you've finally entered the picture," Coates brings Americans of all races together in overcoming our not-seeing so that "we" can finally be free.

Within this more extensive understanding of paying dues, then, what is the price of the jazz ticket for a white woman? What needs to be added to the to-dues list? In short, my answer is to become a skilled jazz musician entails a more encompassing definition of "knowing what's happening" on the bandstand. Ida, the Black female vocalist in *Another Country*, tells the white woman, "Maybe nothing can be stopped or changed, but you've got to know, you've got to know what's happening" (292). If in jazz "you've got to know what's happening" on the bandstand in order to respond appositely, rather than habitually, this is not just about tritone substitution. Paying jazz dues includes a white jazz musician's interrogation of her role in sustaining a racist society. Paying dues is to commit to deep looking and deep listening rooted in honesty; to expand one's understanding of what jazz is and what jazz is teaching; and to understand that such work and practice is for *one's own* benefit, not something done for someone else because they are worse off. These dues are for all jazz aspirants and white musicians to pay their specific price in relation to the consequences of privilege and ignorance their white skin has afforded them.

If being a skilled improviser is the ability to respond eloquently to circumstances in the moment, to do this one must be able to clearly see and hear these circumstances and simultaneously grasp them within a historical context. Most jazz musicians currently learn how to do this with notes and chords and patterns and rhythms. Knowing this material helps the musician to respond appropriately, eloquently, and creatively, not rotely out of ingrained habit. This skill can be cultivated in terms of living in the United States, which means living within and as a part of our country's history. A

---

31   Coates 2015, 42–43.

French character in Baldwin's "This Morning, This Evening, So Soon" avers, "The happy people of your country who scarcely know that there is such a thing as history and so, naturally, imagine that they can escape, as you put it, 'scot-free.'"[32] This has been the central problem of the United States—the fantasy rooted in the "color line" that hides an honest look at ourselves.[33] I've attempted to do some of this looking in the first sections of this chapter by examining my love of jazz within a racist society where white appropriation of Black music is the norm and where notions of Black hipness perpetuate racism and sexism. These are some of the specific circumstances I encounter based on my subject position as a white woman that I must attempt to understand in order to respond eloquently and meaningfully moment by moment.

The price of the jazz ticket also includes understanding what it is one is paying for, what the value of jazz is. Like so many things, jazz's value deepens as one commits to it over time. Ultimately, jazz becomes a gift that one can accept and bring forward to the next generation. Engaging with jazz in such a way that grapples honestly with not only the formal and aesthetic elements but also the racial components and our own role within them is part of the wider project of waking up in America. It "represent[s] America's maturation out of the childhood myth of its innocence into a wisdom worthy of its founders" (Coates 2015, 48). Thus, along with the suffering of the hours of woodshedding and enduring one's own playing that doesn't measure up to where one wants it to be, all jazz aspirants have a lot more work to do. White musicians have their particular dues of waking up to whiteness (something they have learned to not see) and deconstructing the fantasy that prevents them from engaging fully in the world.

To consider jazz in such a way is to understand the music as a wisdom tradition. To bring a wisdom tradition into postsecondary education through jazz programs may seem like a tall order, but it is happening in institutions like the Berklee Institute of Jazz and Gender Justice, the University of Pittsburgh, and San Francisco State University.[34] Students who continue

---

32 Quoted in Tomlinson, 141.
33 Du Bois 2014 [1903].
34 I discuss these three programs led by Terri Lyne Carrington, Nicole Mitchell Gantt, and Dee Spencer in McMullen 2023. They are examples, I argue, of bringing the long tradition of Black feminist thought into mainstream education through jazz programs. I also discuss this phenomenon in McMullen 2021b.

to learn from a white male perspective that imagines itself as universal, that remains in its "innocence" and not-seeing, that conceives of jazz in its attenuated version that must avoid issues of race and gender, will be unprepared and undereducated, affecting their ability to secure employment or participate fully in a society that encompasses a broader view. They will be unprepared for the coming reality that they cannot escape history "scot-free." This will be a colossal failure of our generation of educators. Just as Baldwin counseled his fellow Americans years ago, the world is growing beyond white and, to supplement his analysis, male power. It is being dismantled from without, but also, in many cases, from within. That is, many men are ready to dismantle male power, not wanting to live in a world of narrow and monotonous gender norms. And more white people are preferring to be human, not only because they don't want to be irrelevant, but because they want to be free.[35]

"To encourage excellence is to go beyond the encouraged mediocrity of our society" (54). So wrote Audre Lorde in her collection, *Sister Outsider*. It was John Coltrane, Sonny Rollins, Elvin Jones, McCoy Tyner, Yusef Lateef, Sarah Vaughn, Ella Fitzgerald, Betty Carter, and so many other musicians who encouraged me to seek excellence through the sound of their commitment. Jazz spoke to me when I first heard the drum set played by the high school big band at my elementary school. I took up drums in beginning band while playing clarinet in concert band. I reached the jazz shores of Coltrane and Ornette only after college, buying my saxophone at a pawn shop South of Market in order to copy the breath of Yusef Lateef. I loved the music and the players who gave me the music. I identified with them like I had found a home, a wisdom tradition, a rich connection from one human who had accomplished something profound and breathed that into me as something to aspire toward, to conspire with, to be inspired by.[36] In jazz, I

---

35 That is, to "enter the picture." In 1984 James Baldwin wrote, "The people who think of themselves as White have the choice of becoming human or irrelevant.... For, if trouble don't last always, as the Preacher tells us, neither does Power, and it is on the fact or the hope or the myth of Power that that identity which calls itself White has always seemed to depend" (Morrison 1998, 812).

36 This chapter is making a connection between my breathing in the sound of Yusef Lateef, John Coltrane, and others and identification with them—recognizing a wisdom within their sound (made through their bodily efforts and their breath) that I attempt to learn and emulate. Ashon Crawley's important book *Blackpentecostal Breath* articulates his concept of Black Pneuma, which he describes within the history of Black Pentecostalism as "the capacity for the

continue to hear the sound of this commitment to the ones who came before and taught the meaning of devotion, to the ones who will listen in the future and learn; finally, it is the sound of obligation to themselves. It is the sound of confidence, not hipness. It is the wisdom in the sound, the breath sounding both in, as steadfastness, and out, as gift. Over and over until I expire, breathing in and out the gift of committing to something bigger, something more beautiful than the tedious and predictable ruts of capitalism, imperialism, racism, and sexism. My gratitude can only be expressed in my attempts to hear and to demonstrate that I have heard through my own sound. I recognize and resonate with the sound being given. I hear it. I humbly work to live up to the wisdom that is being passed through that sound.

References

Baldwin, James. 1993 [1962]. *Another Country*. New York: Vintage Books.
Barthes, Roland. 1975. *The Pleasure of the Text*. Translated by Richard Miller. New York: Hill and Wang.
Brooks, Daphne A. 2009. "Mamie Smith: A New Voice of the Blues." In *A New History of American Literature and Culture*, edited by George Marcus and Werner Sollers. Cambridge, MA: Harvard University Press.
———. 2010. "'This Voice Which Is Not One': Amy Winehouse Sings the Ballad of Sonic Blue(s)face Culture." *Women and Performance: A Journal of Feminist Theory* 20 (1): 37–60.
Coates, Norma. 2003. "Teenyboppers, Groupies, and Other Grotesques: Girls and Women and Rock Culture in the 1960s and Early 1970s." *Journal of Popular Music Studies* 15:65–94.

---

plural movement and displacement of inhalation and exhalation to enunciate life, life that is exorbitant, capacious, and fundamentally, social, though it is also life that is structured through and engulfed by brutal violence." He connects pneuma with the [holy] spirit, which is something I take up in relation to Terri Lyne Carrington's declamation that "jazz is a spirit" in my forthcoming book. Crawley writes, "Spirit—*pneuma*, breath, that which animates the body—is grounded in the necessity for sociality. Not only does Spirit give life, but that life is evident in how one leans toward others, how one engages with others in the world. We do not merely share in sociality; we share in the materiality of that which quickens flesh; we share air, breath, breathing through the process of inhalation and exhalation" (40).

Coates, Ta-Nehisi. 2015. "The Case for Reparations." In *The Best American Magazine Writing 2015*, edited by Sid Holt, 3–50. New York: Columbia University Press.
Crawley, Ashon T. 2017. *Blackpentecostal Breath: The Aesthetics of Possibility*. New York: Fordham University Press.
DiAngelo, Robin. 2018. *White Fragility: Why It's So Hard for White People to Talk about Racism*. New York: Beacon Press.
Dinerstein, Joel. 2017. *The Origins of Cool in Postwar America*. Chicago: University of Chicago Press.
Du Bois, W. E. B. 2014 [1903]. *The Souls of Black Folk*. N.p.: Millennium Publications.
Fiske, John. 1994. *Media Matters: Everyday Culture and Political Change*. Minneapolis: University of Minnesota Press.
Floyd, Samuel A., Jr. 1991. "Ring Shout! Literary Studies, Historical Studies, and Black Music Inquiry." *Black Music Research Journal* 11 (2): 265–87.
Gabbard, Krin. 2004. *Black Magic: White Hollywood and American Culture*. Piscataway, NJ: Rutgers University Press.
Hill, Marquis. 2020. "Nicholas Payton Looks to Direct the Culture." *DownBeat*, January 31, 2020. https://downbeat.com/news/detail/nicholas-payton-direct-the-culture.
Irving, Debby. 2014. *Waking Up White, and Finding Myself in the Story of Race*. Cambridge, MA: Elephant Room Press.
Kendi, Ibram X. 2020. *How to Be an Antiracist*. New York: Random House.
Leeming, David Adams. 1986. "An Interview with James Baldwin on Henry James." *Henry James Review* 8 (1): 47–56.
Lewis, George. 1996. "Improvised Music after 1950: Afrological and Eurological Perspectives." *Black Music Research Journal* 16 (1): 91–122.
Lopez, Barry. 2019. *Horizon*. New York: Vintage.
Lorde, Audre. 2007. *Sister Outsider*. Berkeley, CA: Crossing Press.
Lott, Eric. 1995. *Love and Theft: Blackface Minstrelsy and the American Working Class*. New York: Oxford University Press.
Mbembe, Achille. 2017. *Critique of Black Reason*. Durham, NC: Duke University Press.
McGee, Kristin A. 2009. *Some Liked it Hot: Jazz Women in Film and Television, 1928–1959*. Middletown, CT: Wesleyan University Press.
McMullen, Tracy. 2008. "Identity for Sale: Glenn Miller, Wynton Marsalis, and Cultural Replay in Music." In *Big Ears: Listening for Gender in Jazz Studies*, edited by Nichole T. Rustin and Sherrie Tucker, 129–54. Durham, NC: Duke University Press.
———. 2010. "Subject, Object, Music: John Cage, Pauline Oliveros, and Eastern (Western) Philosophy in Music." *Critical Studies in Improvisation/Études Critiques en Improvisation* 6 (2).

———. 2019. *Haunthenticity: Musical Replay and the Fear of the Real*. Middletown, CT: Wesleyan University Press.

———. 2021a. "Jazz Education after 2017: The Berklee Institute of Jazz and Gender Justice and the Pedagogical Lineage." *Jazz and Culture* 4 (2): 27–55.

———. 2021b. "The Lessons of Jazz: What We Teach When We Teach Jazz in College." In *Artistic Research in Jazz*, edited by Michael Kahr, 85–97. New York: Routledge.

———. 2023. "Improvisation, Pedagogy, and Black Feminist Thought: Alternative Knowledge Takes Center Stage." In *The Improviser's Classroom: Pedagogies for Cocreative Worldmaking*, edited by Mark Lomanno and Daniel Fischlin. Philadelphia: Temple University Press.

Monson, Ingrid. 1995. "The Problem with White Hipness: Race, Gender, and Cultural Conceptions in Jazz Discourse." *Journal of the American Musicological Society* 48 (3): 396–422.

———. 2007. *Freedom Sounds: Civil Rights Call out to Jazz and Africa*. Oxford: Oxford University Press.

Morrison, Toni. 1992. *Playing in the Dark: Whiteness and the Literary Imagination*. Cambridge, MA: Harvard University Press.

Morrison, Toni, ed. 1998. *James Baldwin: Collected Essays*. New York: Library of America.

Murphy, John. 1990. "Jazz Improvisation: The Joy of Influence." *Black Perspective in Music* 18 (1–2): 7–19.

Murray, Albert. 1976. *Stomping the Blues*. New York: McGraw-Hill.

Steinel, Mike. 1995. *Building a Jazz Vocabulary: A Resource for Jazz Improvisation*. Milwaukee: Hal Leonard.

Stoever, Jennifer Lynn. 2016. *The Sonic Color Line: Race and the Cultural Politics of Listening*. New York: New York University Press.

Tomlinson, Robert. 1999. "'Payin' Ones Dues': Expatriation as Personal Experience and Paradigm in the Works of James Baldwin." *African American Review* 33 (1): 135–48.

Wilson, Olly. 1983. "'Black Music as an Art Form." *Black Music Research Journal* 3:1–22.

Chapter Two

Three Reflections, with Epilogue

Steven Cornelius

A Dream

As I stand in a wooded glen, Ogún, the Yoruba god of iron and war approaches. His charred coal-black body radiates the heat and reddish glow of a forge.

Ogún looks at me through burning eyes. "Make up your mind," he says.

I already have.

"The answer is no," I respond.

Though daunted, I resist the orìṣà's presence and attempt to drive him away with the heat of my vision. There is surprising power in my focused mind. Ogún is reduced to a pile of ash on lifeless soil.

Yet moments later he reconstitutes. Ogún sizes me up. At first, he seems impressed by my resistance. Then he laughs at my impotence and confronts me a second time.

Again, I incinerate him. Again, he reconstitutes.

"Show courage," he scolds. "You know how to free yourself."

I do, but tell him I am done fighting.

Ogún calls me a coward. I understand this to be true.

Ogún feigns an attack. As he knows I will, I flinch. Then I lash back. I incinerate him a third time. This time I act. I quickly scoop the ashes into a tin can and begin to seal it shut.

Ogún's incarceration means my emancipation.

Before the seal is closed, however, understanding dawns. I stop, place the can on the earth, and turn away. Ogún reconstitutes. He allows me to depart.

This dream occurred more than thirty years ago, while I was living in New York City conducting dissertation-related fieldwork on the music of the Afro-Cuban religion Santería. As the above encounter suggests, my relationship with the Yoruba deities was both agitated and compulsory.

Drawn to, but unsettled by, the orìṣà and their activities, I wanted the impossible. I wanted to know them, to experience their manifestation and witness their world. But I did not want to be shackled by that world's rules.

Perhaps in part because of my experiences being raised in a liberal Catholic home and coming of age in 1960s psychedelia, I entered fieldwork open to a range of metaphysical experiences. I generally had no difficulty accepting the stories practitioners shared with me regarding their relationships with occult powers.

I witnessed many examples of possession trance. To me, some felt authentic, one even epiphanic. Most did not. That said, while I was drawn to the music, established solid friendships, and found the philosophy fascinating, I personally found much of the actual religious practice deeply disturbing (a sentiment I have never before revealed in my scholarly work). I was neither a religious aspirant nor an advocate.

I attempted to conduct my research in careful equilibrium while negotiating the labyrinthine pathways of Yoruba cosmology and New York's religious cultures. At religious ceremonies I sought to be invisibly present, inwardly anchored, and yet, experientially open. In personal relationships, I worked to learn as much as possible while neither becoming intrusive nor incurring debts I could not fulfill. In writing about socioreligious culture, I sought transparency but was also committed not to reveal things my teachers told me must remain private.

As to engaging with, and writing about, the orìṣà, in the end I was forced to rely on my own intuitions. Initially, I sought guidance from divination priests who encouraged me to share freely the information that came my way. They also warned me to pay attention to my intuitions. Certain topics may not be discussed. Should boundaries be crossed, the orìṣà would intervene, with significant consequences.

At times during my field experience, I was encouraged to participate in ritual life and to consider initiation. I was told repeatedly that all doors were open, and that insights and power awaited if I would only pass through. I did not. Santería's cosmology came out to envelop me, nonetheless.

The òrìṣà took abode in my psyche. I responded as if to mesmerizing, but unwelcome house guests who refused to leave. Initially, I was deeply troubled. But I grew to accept the situation as part of the "job." I attempted to digest both the òrìṣà's positive and negative aspects. In hopes of objectifying their qualities, potentials, proclivities, and manifestations, I used descriptive keywords to help guide my intuition. I also "played" the deities through bàtá drumming. And of course, I followed their activities in others while watching, and feeling the emotional qualities of, possession trances.

Eventually, some doors closed. Toward the end of my fieldwork, I was working on the analysis of a particular trance event involving Ọbàtálá, the father of many of the òrìṣà. This was to be the keystone chapter of my dissertation. But had I the right to discuss the event?

I wondered.

After writing some preliminary drafts, I sought advice from the temple's divination priests. Was I in over my head?

Curtail your involvement or pay homage to Ọbàtálá, who will protect you, they advised. Three painful events were foretold, but each could be easily mitigated with a simple act of fealty to Ọbàtálá. I chose not to act. Two predictions were realized within forty-eight hours.[1] The third foretold my death. I abandoned the topic.

Over the years, òrìṣà-based concepts have evolved in my mind. That process continues today. I associate Ṣàngǒ's lightning bolts with the thrilling illuminating power of intuition. I associate the crossroads of the trickster Èṣù with the decisions (so often poorly conceived) that open and close life's pathways. My òrìṣà are not gods to be worshipped but personifications of universal principles through which experiential possibilities develop, destiny forms, and shackles become attached or released. They continue to vitalize my thinking.

A few of the òrìṣà I conceptualize moderately well; others hardly at all. Some, I have no conscious relationship with whatsoever. Then there is Ògún, who twice approached me in the first months of fieldwork. Ògún will not be denied. He dwells within the occluded recesses of my soul life—in regions of fear, destruction, and wanton violence but also courage, fidelity, tenacity, and resolute honor. For me (though not necessarily for others), Ògún

---

1   As foretold, just hours later my father experienced a heart attack. Soon after, my home was robbed. Losses included my computer (holding a nearly completed dissertation), most of my backup disks, and almost all of my field recordings. Ọbàtálá awaited.

represents feral necessity. I witness Ogún within darkness, feel his penetrating gaze through verdant foliage.²

A Concert Review

An enthusiastic concert audience settles into the seats of the Toledo Museum of Art Peristyle Concert Hall. They have come to hear one of the first public performances of the Silk Road Project (January 2001), led by cellist Yo-Yo Ma. The venue is sold out. I am in attendance to review the event for the local newspaper. Having written about the art music scene in Northwest Ohio and Southern Michigan for nearly six years, I am looking forward to the opportunity to write about a "multicultural" music event.

Waiting for the concert to begin, I review in my mind a conversation from earlier in the week, when I spoke by phone with Mr. Ma. The concert, he said, will be a celebration, an exploration, and sharing of musical styles between peoples of Eastern and Western cultures. Boundaries will be mitigated; doors will be opened.

The program tells me that the first half of the concert features newly commissioned compositions by Asian or Near Eastern composers. Following intermission and closing the evening is standard Western concert repertoire: Ravel's piano trio. (I assume that the choice, a return to the audience's comfort zone, is rationalized because the middle movement is named after a Malaysian poetic form.)

Judging by the audience's unflagging enthusiasm, the concert is a rousing success. But I am mostly left cold. To me, the "Asian" music performances feel unripe and unsettled; the Ravel performance is inappropriately muscular. More problematic, however, is that the event feels not only culturally artificial, but musically out of balance. Mr. Ma's presence outshines and outweighs everyone and everything—the other musicians on stage, as well as the music itself. What I see is a performance that displays the power of fame (although I am sure this is not Mr. Ma's intention).

For most of the audience members, these tensions seem to have passed unnoticed (to confirm this impression, I mingled and queried during intermission), or are not relevant. They came to see Yo-Yo Ma, who was featured prominently throughout. I suspect that for many it made little difference whether Mr. Ma performed a program with Silk Road or the Dvorak cello concerto.

---

2   My experience of Ogún is hardly conventional. Indeed, my own deeply personalized relationship with the orìṣàs puts me firmly in the camp of the religious misfits described later in this essay.

I am stymied. How am I going to review this event? Should I discuss the uneven quality of the performances? The repertoire? The social possibilities and conundrums the concert presents? Musical icons? The audience? Or a myriad of other issues? In order to meet an 11:30 p.m. deadline, I will have about fifty minutes to write a four-hundred-word review.

After finishing my dissertation, I decided to distance myself from Santería. I stayed in contact with only a handful of people. It was nearly ten years before I attended another religious ceremony. (That was in Havana). For a few years I continued to perform the music, but never in a ritual setting. I had no desire to either encourage possession trance or actively associate with religious practice.

Although I briefly pursued musical connections in Ghana, I was mostly interested in working with musicians, and secular music, close to home. Almost immediately, after receiving the security of tenure from Bowling Green State University, an opportunity arose. I accepted a half-time position as classical music critic at the *Blade*, Toledo, Ohio's daily newspaper. The appointment was mostly to serve and document everyday musical life in Northwest Ohio, a culture made up of deeply committed regional artists largely overlooked by academic inquiries, and invariably ignored by the highbrow critics of major metropolitan newspapers. Not all was local, nor was all the work "classical." I wrote about struggling freelance musicians working territories hundreds of miles in circumference, regional barbershop choirs, the doings of Toledo native and jazz icon Jon Hendricks, contract negotiations at the Toledo Symphony, public radio programming strategies, and many other topics. Assignments occasionally reached west to Chicago, north to Detroit, and east to New York City. Twice, I wrote about university study-abroad trips I co-led to Ghana.

Passionate about teaching, I enjoyed writing for (and reaching out to) a general readership. My editors accepted nearly every story topic that I pitched. For feature stories, I usually had a couple of days to organize my thoughts.

For concert reviews, however, I rarely had more than seventy-five between the event's conclusion and the submission deadline. The Silk Road concert was a complex event that deserved a thoughtful and carefully nuanced response. Too complex. I was caught off-balance by what I had witnessed and was thinking, almost all of which seemed to conflict with the audience's ardent expressions of delight. Meanwhile, the clock to deadline was ticking.

In the end, I did not write about the search for common ground across cultures. I did not write about social parity. Nor did I write about the seductive power of star performers, and how arts organizations use that power to promote their seasons (and by doing so, too often compromise their missions). Instead, after spending precious minutes trying to work out these ideas (and present them gracefully) with limited space, I capitulated, mostly confining the piece to the basics: who, what, where, when, why, and how.

When I confirmed my submission with the copy desk editor, I was told that the page layout had been changed. The review's preassigned length (already unusually short) needed to be reduced by a little more than one-third. Someone (not a musician) on the copy desk would make the cuts.

The process was necessarily quick, and brutal. The composers' names were mostly eliminated. Cutting the already brief music descriptions made them even more inadequate. The piece went from being insufficiently conceived to being thoroughly disjointed. I was deeply embarrassed by the result. In the coming days, my readership (mostly through letters to the editor, though also through conversations) also expressed displeasure with the terse, chilly review. I considered responding with a follow-up essay, but new assignments and deadlines had already filled my schedule.[3] I moved on, knowing that similar issues would inevitably arise and that the broader ideas would eventually make it to print.

The Stroke

A silent and nameless witness to timeless infinity.
"I am."
With dawning self-consciousness comes relief, fear, and vertigo. All is precipice. I wake up.
"Have you been here long?" I ask.
"Three days," says Sharan, my wife, who sits beside my bed.
Confused, I try to sit up. It's not just the tubes that hold me down, my left side has no sensation; it is invisible to my mind's eye. I stare at an arm, which does not seem to belong to me. It is without sensation and will not move.
I struggle, but the ICU nurse tells me to lie still. I do not listen. Sharan reaffirms the order. I remember the ambulance and comply.

---

3   Although mine was only a half-time position, I was responsible for contributing about fifty thousand words a year.

"You cannot walk. Don't try to get up," says the nurse.

I know she is wrong. (She is not, I will discover in the following days.)

Sharan and I talk. She tells me we have spoken on and off over the past days. I do not remember.

I have experienced a right-brain stroke.[4]

I tell her I have just come back from T. S. Eliot's "still point." I tell her about witnessing the infinite.

It is silent, even to thought.

It is unbounded majesty.

It is beyond time.

I am shaken from, and also thrilled by, the experience. I desire to close my eyes and return, yet am afraid of evaporating into emptiness.

How long was I there? (Seconds? Forever?)

We make small talk. I tell her that my mind has no chatter, is Zen silent. I fall back asleep.

Flowing blood teaches me. It resounds from the deeds and experiences of my lineage. English blood. German blood. Roman blood. Greek blood. Primordial blood back beyond recorded history. My ancestors developed the blueprint for the body in which I now reside. I caretake DNA for future generations. Again, I experience T. S. Eliot's poetic voice: "Time present and time past [is] present in time future." We are all linked—through shared past, destiny, and mind.

Two days later, I remain in the ICU but am relatively alert for extended periods of time. A neurologist, with his resident intern and a half-dozen medical students in tow, comes to see me. He asks me how I am doing.

"Well," I say.

"Are you feeling depressed?"

"No," I respond.

He asks if I would like a prescription for depression.

"No thanks. I'm fine."

He begins speaking to the students, saying that depression comes with stroke and that he is going to prescribe an antidepressant.

Has he not heard me?

I try to protest, but nothing comes out.

They watch me struggle.

"Unusual to have strong aphasia with a right-brain stroke," he says to the students casually (and as if I am no longer present).

---

4   October 11, 2009.

Then he looks at me and says that I am making good progress and can expect about a 90 percent recovery.

This is worthless, but deeply troubling, information. What does 90 percent mean to a musician? Would he have been so cavalier had I been a surgeon?

Angered and offended, I want to tell him that I am left-handed but was generally ambidextrous when young. That I am a drummer. That my left and right brains are richly connected. That solving coordination problems is part of my daily work. That I have already been creating movement exercises while lying in bed. That I expect a full recovery.

I want to tell them that I have experienced the infinite, experienced T. S. Eliot's motionless dance. I know he is not interested.

I also feel like growling back something like, "I can speak just fine, thank you very much," but am paralyzed by my emotional vulnerability. My mouth is in knots; no words emerge. Reflected in the students' eyes, I imagine what they see, the broken shell of a man.

I am awash in humiliation.

Ours is a filtered world. Too often we experience what we expect (or are taught) to experience. We think and naively live within established pathways of thought. This is certainly true for everyday life, but it can also be true for trained professionals at work, including neurologists and this ethnomusicologist. The neurologist expected depression and saw it. But he missed the soft light emanating outward from my fragilely awakening inner life (perceptions likely to be dimmed if forced to take antidepressants).

I too, often fail to see clearly. Working on my dissertation in the mid-1980s, I thought about the things I was trained to consider. I thought about the group. I thought about social process and ways of being and acting. I sought order; I wrote about fit.

But a more accurate presentation would have embraced the religion's "misfits," an essential (and sizable) part of the simultaneously disjointed and integrated multiethnic and multinational social fabric that was Santería in the metropolitan area. Alas, only rarely did I discuss the idiosyncrasies of New York's diverse and recalcitrant Santería communities or the religious periphery from which individuals carved out and vitalized their own innovative interpretations of sacred meaning, musical style and efficacy, and ritual practice (as I would eventually do as well). Like the neurologist, I witnessed, but failed to perceive.

I also chose not to reveal my own lurching inner experiences. I wrote nothing at all about the many extraordinarily vivid dreams and emotions that pervaded my psyche. Again, I discounted the margins and stayed within self-imposed boundaries.

At my dissertation defense, a speaker expressed concern that the religion was insufficiently grounded in New York City for the data to be representative of Yoruba religious belief and practice, that too many ritual procedures were in flux, even missing altogether. I needed go to Nigeria, it was suggested.

In response to the critique, I argued that documenting an African diasporic religious culture taking root across ethnic and cultural lines in the New York metropolitan area was both relevant and timely because it represented social mores in flux and gave voice to underrepresented peoples. That was true, but my textbook response was simplistic, naive, and off base.

The speaker correctly sensed the dissertation's problematic condition but misidentified it, or so I believe. The problems with my work were ones of perspective and detail, not the religion's stability and maturity. It was not that the religious ideology was underdeveloped, but that my discussion of the multifaceted beliefs and desires of satellite practitioners (and transients) orbiting around the multiple religious communities' complex and oft-disputed social and sacred centers was insufficiently cultivated. To the project's detriment, I mostly discussed the conventional and its representatives. I focused on established groups and processes of conformity rather than on individuals' flexible and complex innovations within (but equally often around) those groups and processes.

Epilogue

Lying in bed at 3 a.m., I work on physical recovery from stroke. In my mind, I practice piano, mostly with left hand alone, but occasionally with both hands together. The melody comes slowly because it takes time to identify the proper finger, imagine the texture of each key underneath, exert the pressure required to push it down, then "hear" the tone.

As I engage, I discover something quite extraordinary. My left hand includes an extra digit between my middle and ring fingers. The phantom feels as real, and works as well, as the others. Without looking or touching, I cannot tell that it is not there.

I experiment. I reimagine the finger's placement. Now it is attached outside my pinky. Then I move it next to my thumb.

Is my entire left side equally mobile? I slide my shoulder down my rib cage. I am discovering, molding, and remolding the weakly constituted cognitive blueprint within which my entire left side seems to float. Fingers and toes, eye and ear, arm and leg are interchangeable, like Mr. Potato Head.

Stopping the exercise, I pay attention to my entire body. As I do so, left side awareness evaporates, occluded by noise from the right.

I marvel that my right side remains contained, does not drain into the hollow shell of the left.

With the stroke, aspects of death and rebirth seemed to unfold simultaneously. By every conventional standard I was profoundly broken. But inwardly, ethereal wonders seemed just beyond reach.

Before my stroke, I sought answers. Now, thirteen years later I am delighted with good questions. And if I pay careful attention, I discover better questions still.

Even today, a cursory nonvisual mapping of my left hand tells me that I have five fingers and a thumb. Wrong. But even in the most grounded minds, cognition is often inaccurate; personal proclivities may become ruts misguiding the wheels of thinking.

I found echoes of my phantom finger while writing these vignettes. Stories, ideas, and perspectives were easily taken up and juggled, shaped and reshaped, moved around for fit, and often deleted. Multiple perspectives seemed to accurately describe a situation, even when they conflicted.

So, how to conclude this essay? How do the preceding vignettes fit within a book focusing on intimacy in ethnographic fieldwork? That was a problem. After all, Ogún represents the antithesis of conventional intimacy. The concert review outlines my sense of alienation, confusion, and even outrage, in response to failing to meet a "fieldwork" challenge. The stroke remembrances tell of wondrous solitude, but still more of confusion and alienation. Nowhere to be found in these essays is there anything one might call intimacy, at least in the word's traditional sense.

That said, I believe there is always a kind of requisite intimacy between author and reader. Sometimes that relationship is explicit. It is always implicit, even in driest of tomes. Generally, we readers trust our authors to tell us the "truth." When we think they do not, we engage through disagreement, weaving in our doubts and (hopefully) seeking the author's perspective as we read.

In my better writing, which nearly invariably trends to the informal, one can easily sense the personality behind my words. This essay is my first excursion into foregrounding my own experiences to an academic readership, however. Here I have attempted to unveil *my* realities. Only in part, of course. Only as deep as I am able to dive with sufficient awareness to be relatively confident of what I am saying.

Chapter Three

Modulating Flawed Bodies

Intimate Acoustemologies, Chronic Pain, and Ethnographic Pianism

Mark Lomanno

Intimate Entanglements and Acoustemological Pivots

I could not play.[1] Had I not been so eager, I may not have been so careless as to play through the searing pain—that all-too-familiar, singeing sensation radiating back up from the piano keyboard through my fingertips. I already knew this throbbing pain when it reappeared after that first rehearsal in the Canary Islands. Pulsating from near my elbows, it would continually send out sharp jabs—back along my forearms to my hands and fingers, and up through my shoulders to my neck and temples—until the newly reinjured shreds of my tendons fused back together again. And then, back to the top.

I have been coping with that pain—the mark of chronic bilateral tendinosis—since my undergraduate days, when the tenuous balance of an ambitious practice routine, gig schedule, and multiple lessons per week was upset

---

1   I want to thank co-editor Sidra Lawrence for the invitation to contribute to this volume. This piece is as much my attempt to realize to her vision of what my work could be as it is to reflect the experiences about which I'm writing here. I'd also like to thank Veit Erlmann, Ryan McCormack, Marysol Quevedo, and Ellen Waterman for reading early versions of this chapter.

by a new instructor's approach that turned a few idiosyncratic elements of my posture and technique into a debilitating injury that has never completely healed. In the ten years between that injury and the rehearsal at saxophonist Enrique "Kike" Perdomo's home on the island of Tenerife, I had adapted, learned to ration my playing, to approach it more mindfully, and to practice self-care after more rigorous performances so that the injury would not flare up—or at least that minimal recovery time would be required for healing whatever damage I had done. (And then, back to the top.)

The reemergence of that injury, though, made it clear to me that the decade's worth of coping strategies was insufficient for this new challenge. I didn't know how to accommodate Perdomo's Petrof grand. That piano with a beautiful sound but impossibly hard action. Cramped into a small home studio with drum set, bass amp, and mic set up for the horn player. And a mixing board, computer desk, and photographer/friend up-for-the-hang. And the acoustics. As the sounds of my collaborators at their instruments reverberated around me—off the walls and up through the floorboards—I struggled to hear myself. I needed to hear myself. I kept pushing—down "through the keys," my teachers used to say. But the other musicians were closer to the piano's soundboard. The open piano lid was directing what I was playing straight toward Perdomo, one of my most important contacts. One of the few Canarian jazz musicians to have achieved success off the Islands. One of the main guys. It was his studio. His piano. His invitation to join in. He knew what was up. And would know instantly if I weren't up for that hang.

But what was I playing? I still couldn't hear. So, I dug deep. And pushed harder. And then, back to the top.

As I sat in my apartment in Tenerife, waiting—hoping—to heal from self-inflicted wounds at that rehearsal, I experimented with different postures, distances away from, below, and above the keyboard. In each case I carefully gauged which muscle groups were activated, trying to move away from the postures that caused my shoulders and forearms to tense up, all the while taking great care not to engage in the slightest the Fender Rhodes that Perdomo had lent me. I needed to heal fast: I was anxious about losing time for "productive research" in the Canaries, wasting the hard-won funding for finishing my doctoral degree. And about the second rehearsal, a date for which had already been set.

I developed a visualization routine and new repertoire of pianistic movements based not on previous training or an idealized sense of "how to play," but on my body. Beyond just my swollen forearms: an opening up from my legs, lower back, shoulders, and through my fingers. With this new mode of addressing the piano, I was playing no longer just "down through the keys" but also from back up through the floor under my feet. Rather than bracing my body while my forearms hammered down onto the keyboard, I found more healthy support in opening myself up to my body's movement and its energies channeled through my forearms.

I recorded that second rehearsal—managed with these new postures—so that I could assess afterwards. When I listened back, I heard what I played—and my voice, too. There were two sonic traces of this embodied, bioelectric circuit between the piano and me. Actuated at the surfaces of fingertips and keys, reverberating in opposite directions through the hammers and tendons, the kinetic energy was converted into two sets of frequencies—one conducted along the piano wires and the other on my vocal cords.

But I wasn't singing what I was playing. I was singing some of what I was trying to play. What I heard as a response to what the others were playing. What I had hoped I would hear back from the piano when I tried to play what I thought I wanted to. What I hoped was enough for them—but never too much for me. Well, for my arms. Just enough for me to think they had hopefully heard enough, because they might not say so. Enough to hang. Enough to write about. Enough to play again.

Listening back to the second rehearsal, I liked what I heard. I felt like I had just been through a full body workout. I don't like to work out; but I reveled in the feeling that I had worked that second rehearsal out through my *full body*. I was in touch. On the recording I was listening to myself be "in touch." As an improviser. As a pianist. As a participant observer hoping to have something to write about. I was in touch with the piano, with the other musicians, with my research project, and in touch with myself. Well, my body. My well body. My more well, hoping-to-cope body.

By repositioning myself—my body—I had at least achieved a more healthful, if not healthy, interaction. The cramped rehearsal space that I first tried to push myself into had become an intimate space for communion with my instrument and my collaborators. The same potential for injury existed—my vulnerabilities hadn't abated in the least—but this time we were more in touch. Opening up my stance at the piano bench had opened new possibilities for me, and so, for the ensemble.

In the moment, though, it also opened me up to a fair amount of ridicule. I didn't share my condition—or my pain—with the other musicians. They saw me stretching outside the studio before and during the breaks of the rehearsal. And they saw me—well, my legs and back—pitched diagonally and off-to-the-side at the piano. But they also listening to my playing. They listened approvingly, and said so. It looked strange (they said that, too) but it sounded more than good enough for that hang. (Eventually I'd go on to make a record with Perdomo of some of the tunes we rehearsed that day.)[2]

Still, I'd had to show them that something was off. My new, atypical postures at the piano exposed me. They knew something was up, saw I couldn't play normally, and asked. I blamed the studio's acoustics—carefully. Perdomo apologized, quickly moved to set up a mic, directed it at the piano's soundboard, plugged it into the bass amp, and then back to the top. That was as much of an issue as I was going to make of it. Besides, I hadn't learned the Spanish word for "tendon" yet.

They also *heard* that I couldn't play the piano "normally." I didn't quite catch everything—I had become accustomed to my contacts code-switching to Canarian Spanish when they wanted to put something past me—but there was more than one joke about my moaning at the piano while I straddled the bench.

Setting aside what I heard when I listened back to the recording—or what I thought I heard, what I told myself I heard, what I choose to write that I heard—in the moment, all they heard in that moaning was noise. And, thanks to the mic that Perdomo later put in the piano, it was amplified noise. I still wasn't singing what I was playing, so that added vocal track was in the way. And, unlike what came out of the piano, the singing didn't sound very good. Of course, I knew that they couldn't get one without the other. And I knew then that, when I would write about that playing, I couldn't write about one without the other.

Listening now—to those moments during the second rehearsal—I don't hear what they heard, though. I don't hear what I heard. So rather than trying to dig down deep into that moment so that I can hear myself in it, I am reaching for a more all-encompassing embrace of what I experienced by listening to it more openly: to approximate—to get closer to—it by playing at different paces and angles and engaging more senses. To feel more of that moment. And to feel more intimately about shared moments by bringing myself closer to—and putting my (self, playing, writing) in touch with—my partners.

While attention to embodied practices can reveal the intimate nature of interaction, attention to non-normative embodied practices—especially those impacted by pain—exposes the degree to which those who fail to

---

2   The record is *Celebrate Brooklyn Volume 2*, released in 2013 on Perdomo's 96K label.

account for their bodies rely on privileged perspectives through which they elect to ignore them. This privilege informs an ideal of "effortless mastery" in which considerations of everyday phenomena—not to mention the hypersensitivity to biophysical processes that chronic pain necessitates—can be cast aside in pursuit of a transcendent experience in which the performer becomes a disembodied conduit through which music travels unimpeded to the listener.[3] "Getting out of the way of the music" becomes a question of access and idealizes performances of those who choose to ignore bodily awareness in a way that those with bodies-in-pain cannot afford.[4]

So much of that dissertation fieldwork experience in the Canary Islands was about *feeling* things that I had studied. I was coming to know through my (hoping-to-cope) body how experience always preceded theory. How writing about experience is always an improvised translation. And how writing ethnographically is often hoping that I've written just enough for me and my interlocutors to feel again—to hang with—some part of what we felt in that moment.

What if we think of ethnography as not just building connections to bridge gaps of understanding but also as suturing ruptures and healing wounds? Improvising performance through pain models the kinds of conditions in which this healthful coping—this reaching for sensuous intimacy—can occur. In a way fostering intimacy—as an openness and vulnerability toward others—is a prerequisite for ethnographic work. Improvised performance provides inspiration for intimate actions in ethnography informed by "an ethics of intersubjectivity."[5] Playing with pain gets ethnography to move.

I am reaching toward a writing stance that captures the normally overlooked or silenced aspects of those rehearsals in the Canaries—those aspects of ethnography in which we press past pain, failure, or flaw. What trauma do we inflict on our bodies and ourselves as we neglect these vulnerabilities, these intimacies born from encounters that are not only always pleasurable?

---

3   On "effortless mastery," see Werner 1996. This fallacy of minimally mediated action—or low, bioelectrical impedances or coefficients of friction—is all the more apparent in interactions involving unequal power relationships. See Macharia 2019.

4   Nor those with bodies marginalized because of gendered, racial, or sexual norms.

5   Regarding ethnography, improvisation, and an "ethics of intersubjectivity," I'm thinking especially of the work of Omi Osun Joni L. Jones. See also Siddall and Waterman 2016 and Kozel 2017.

What is to be gleaned from the subtle moments in which we touch and are touched?[6] I am grasping for ethnography that not only incorporates vulnerability, pain, and non-normative conceptions of the body into its texts but also treats these conditions productively and holistically, realizing the dynamic potential for new approaches to multisensory scholarship that honors the highly contingent nature of embodied action and intersubjectivity. In short, I'm asking: How can improvising through pain at the piano bench connect intimately with the ethnomusicological work that follows it? What would writing that hangs with the processes, sounds, and interactions of these performances look, sound, and feel like?

I write like this not just to bridge the "yawning gap" between the two keyboards I use to get closer to my ethnographic work at the piano but also the gap between that work and *me*: to correct the falsehood that the presence of trauma and of coping, of feeling and passion, are anathema, inconsequential, or detrimental to the sound body work that I perform.[7] And the falsehood that my work and I exist separate from the communities around us. In the past I have gravitated toward writers like Moten, Mackey, and Weheliye because of their devotion to approximating the practices and aesthetics of writing jazz and improvised sound into the academic writing mix.[8] As my prior approach to the piano failed in the Canaries, so too have these citational practices in accounting for my experiences as pianist and ethnographer there. And so, to this mix I am adding perspectives from feminist scholars—most especially Omi Osun Joni L. Jones and Ellen Waterman, mentors whose guidance, support, and care have shifted my perspective on disclosing and working through trauma, the erotics of embodied performance, and the possibilities for holistic approaches to performance-based scholarship.[9]

In this chapter I don't just want to shuffle between keyboards, disciplinary approaches, and performative modes, though. Rather I am trying to coax these modes and interactions into each other to better expose the interplay that actually happens. I write like this because I have played, and read, and thought, and written; and loved, and hurt, and fucked, and moaned. All

---

6   Barad 2013.
7   See Sudnow 1981.
8   See especially Moten 2003; also Mackey 1987; Weheliye 2005; and Reed 2014.
9   Specific works by Jones and Waterman are cited throughout. I also need to mention again this volume's co-editor Sidra Lawrence, who introduced me to the work of Audre Lorde, Gloria Anzaldúa, and many other feminist scholars during our graduate studies at the University of Texas at Austin.

of these—the actions, the people, the postures, the texts, and the sounds—linger in me and my pain-filled body. Still. And, as anyone with chronic pain knows, because there's always trauma, it's never about eliminating pain but rather about stretching toward better coping. Here I'm stretching toward healing in writing by reflecting back on these encounters, working through the fear and hard lessons, and celebrating the joys of emergent, intersubjective, and citational kinships that continually renew my hope for coping.

Getting the Piano to Move

Second Chorus (1:37–1:53): Mindful, Repetitious Reaching[10]

"To hear the attacks is to hear the performer move."[11]

Pianism Archives All the Work

In the recording of the second rehearsal my voice intrudes frequently, especially during one particular piano solo—frustrated interjections marking a disrupted flow in the melodic line I was improvising. This moan functions as a sonic record of my laboring to negotiate the situation, accommodating all of its contingencies, including my body. Its intrusion amplifies the disjuncture in the performance—where my voice betrays the failed melodic line, my expectations for competent performance, and the differently abled body that produced them.

The pianist's moan—the noisy, non-normative utterances that violate their artistic voice—marks their performance as unmistakably embodied, connecting hands, fingers, and forearms to breath.[12] By attuning to these moans, somatic turns, and piano postures, we can revise and complicate the notion of "embodied competency": reintroducing alternate perspectives overwritten or ignored because of ableist conceptions of flawless,

---

10   A recording of Cedar Walton's "Bolivia" that we played at this rehearsal is available at http://www.rhythmofstudy.com/moanflow/, with tracks of each section referenced in the chapter and one of the entire recording. The timestamps correspond to sections of my improvised solo.
11   Shove and Repp 1995, 60.
12   See Sudnow 1981; Mackey 1987; and Lomanno 2017.

masterful performance.[13] We should be listening more intimately to the "telling inarticulacies," highlighting the translating labor that is and is not uttered, accounting for the traces of contact, and engaging intimately with the apparent failures and creative interactions they inspire.[14]

Pianist Keith Jarrett describes the audibly voiced labor entailed in his performance as "a wrestling match [in which] the piano is so stiff and unbending in essence that it takes all my effort to get it to sing. When we hear Bud Powell or Erroll Garner or countless other pianists grunt, squeal or moan, this is mostly the result of the effort to 'move' the instrument—to get it to translate a feeling not essentially 'pianistic' and phrasing not intrinsically piano-like."[15] Here he is alluding to the labored negotiation that pianism entails as a pianist attempts to move closer to their desired sound (and desired state of being-in-the-music) through and with the instrument. The presence of one voice brings the question of all voices to the fore.

Pianism Engages All the Senses

Resonating at the intersections of sound, dis/ability, gender, and improvised performance, the moan reveals phenomenological perspectives, new understandings, and critical interventions from emergent, embodied subject positions. Listening to, becoming-in-touch-with, and making space for our bodies in our work—adopting an acoustemology of intimacy—help to dislodge ableist conceptions of performance practice and further undermine the exclusionary scholarly practices that have marginalized differently abled bodies by writing out failure, "flaw," and pain.[16]

Part of being a pianist is quickly acclimatizing oneself to unknown instruments. While every pianist has their preference, for me avoiding pianos like the Petrof with "stiff" action is not just a matter of aesthetic preference but of well-being and well-articulated pianism. It's *pianism* because even "embodied piano-playing" isn't enough to encompass the range of comportments and

---

13   Titlestad 2004.
14   Mackey 1987, 252–53.
15   Jarrett in Doerschuk 2001, vi.
16   My understanding of acoustemology, especially as it relates both to ethnography and improvisation, is inspired mostly especially by Steven Feld. See. Feld 2015 and 2012.

somatic strategies I have to improvise and deploy because my body and the instruments I play are in flux.[17] Neither are fixed. Ever.

Pianism Draws the Musician into and down through the Instrument

About three weeks prior to that first quartet rehearsal, I had attended a concert by the other three quartet members. After the performance I played an impromptu duet with the bassist, Ruiman Martín, while the band packed up. We managed to fit in a few choruses of John Coltrane's "Bessie's Blues" before one of the hotel staff asked us to finish cleaning up so that they could close for the night.[18] Although I had known these musicians for more than seven months, this was the first time any of them had heard me at the piano.

The allure of playing *any* piano after months on the islands overrode any of my latent concerns about performing competently in that moment. Not knowing anything about the piano's tuning and action—or how those factors might impact my auditioning, or how much risk I was courting by jumping in—could not abate my desire to be with some of my interlocutors in this way. I had only about fifteen seconds to orient myself to the piano in the Bambi Astoria hotel lobby; and only then ninety seconds to successfully deliver the performance that eventually led to the formation of the quartet and an ongoing collaboration that continues today.

As a pianist, I am constantly having to learn other instruments, developing postural tactics to move each particular piano toward singing—to achieve an embodied pianism for and in that moment. Rather than an undifferentiated, always completed, embodied competence, I am continually and immediately re/learning at an instrument—both because of characteristic differences in the pianos themselves and because of the necessary, constant, self-reflexive, embodied awareness that working around and with my tendinosis demands. It goes without saying that different pianists have different pianisms, but for me one, singular pianism isn't enough: because of pain,

---

17 For more on jazz pianism, see Givan 2009; Moreno 1999; and Ziporyn and Tenzer 2011.

18 A video of this duet can be seen here: Mark Lomanno, "Un pequeño blues en el Centro Bambi-Astoria (Puerto de la Cruz)," recorded by Héctor González (March 27, 2011), http://www.facebook.com/video/video.php?v=10100368685677829/.

injury, and sensitivity to instruments, I need *pianisms*. Or maybe, more accurately: pianistic modes.

I'm not suggesting that the Bambi Astoria performance would not have succeeded had Kike's Petrof been there instead, but the difference in the two instruments—the two pianistic modes I needed to adapt to the contingencies of each situation—certainly problematizes the notion that the musician (ethnographer, writer, etc.) arrives fully formed and need only apply previously learned skills and ideas. In the translational shifts to ethnographic writing, accounting for the somatic modes through which acoustemological and embodied knowledges emerge is just as essential a citational practice as any acknowledgement of preexisting scholarship or interlocutor's contribution.

Pianism Amplifies Sounding Bodies

Keith Jarrett's collaborative, pianistic labor is not merely haptic—in the sense of interfacing only at the surface of the piano keys and his fingers. Rather, Jarrett's improvisational choreography at the piano bench includes sudden twists and turns, jagged and random limb movement, and a constantly shifting postural stance toward the keyboard. At times launching from the piano bench to full standing positions and at others ducking underneath the keyboard, Jarrett's unorthodox mode of keyboard address confronts audiences' expectations about bodily comportment in performance. Jarrett does not lose himself in the music so much as enter with the piano into "a particular performative state that has the intangibility commonly associated with an erotic object of desire ... a yawning gap ... [in which] the one and the other have lost their separate existence."[19] In describing the performance space this way Pedro Rebelo suggests that this impressionable intimacy between performer and instrument "is essential for the erotic to emerge."[20] The presence of Jarrett's physiological voice in his live performances—a significant source of critique and scholarly exegesis—heightens these associations with

---

19 Rebelo 2006, 33. This is not so much a transcendent loss of self, but rather a desire for a more intimate/erotic encounter with the instrument and the music produced through the encounter. See McCormack 2012.

20 McCormack 2012. Important scholarship on the construction of nonheteronormative masculinity and jazz performance implied herein includes Rustin-Paschal 2017 and Ake 2002.

the erotic.[21] To invoke Suzanne Cusick, Jarrett gets on his back when he performs.[22] Normative tropes about improvised jazz performance and the transcendent artist would expect Jarrett to surrender to the music. What draws so many into Jarrett's performances—and what draws out their emotional and vociferous reactions—is that Jarrett surrenders *to the piano*.[23] Seeing Jarrett literally get on his back at the piano violates the sexualized norms of jazz performance in a powerful way: by engaging in this intimate coming-together with his instrument Jarrett undermines the very notion of "effortless mastery" as described by pianist Kenny Werner. Jarrett's erotic wrestling with the piano exposes the performer's intimate coupling with the instrument-as-object as a prerequisite for engagement with "the music" and queers the phallocentric heteronormativity at the core of jazz performance and interaction in precisely the ways that Cusick outlines.[24]

Pianism Implicates the Listener, Too

By violating the norms of disembodied performance, Jarrett breaks his audiences' desirous flows, revealing the hoax of their autoerotic listening fantasies: the heteronormative dissenting of jazz listeners who can't get with the music because Jarrett's already there, and they are unwilling to go with him. The audible physicality of Jarrett's performance and his erotic stance of interpenetration with his instrument—of which the music is just one of

---

21   See Ake 2010; Carr 1992; Elsdon 2012; and Moreno 1999. Although Jarrett's is exceptionally loud (or at least exceptionally audible), the practice of subvocalizing while playing the piano is not an exceptional practice. In *Ways of the Hand* Sudnow demonstrates the pedagogical/autodidactic benefits, while a range of other artists, especially jazz pianists, can be heard engaging similarly. The critical attention to and reception of Jarrett's voice reveals a racially ambiguous conception of embodied pianism constructed on stereotypes and lingering tropes about the naturalized physicality of Black music-making. See Lomanno 2019.
22   Cusick 1994, 78.
23   Waterman 2008, 6–7. I owe Ellen Waterman additional thanks for her recommendation of Pedro Rebelo's work and dialogue about this chapter. In an email exchange about this passage, Waterman rightly pointed out to me that "this performative surrender … could be interpreted as [a gendered] act of mastery." Communication with the author. See also Rustin and Tucker 2008 and Provost 2018.
24   McCormack 2012; Werner 1996; McMullen 2016, 31.

the sonic traces—moves the audience toward voyeurism, perpetually blocking them off from satisfying their desire "to be 'in it.'"[25] Despite the transgressive potential in his performative erotics, Jarrett still very much desires this control over his audience: using his voice to berate audience members who violate his sonic space—who enter also into the "yawning gap" of his desired erotic state—is just as infamous as his moaning participation in it. From the perspective of the heteronormative jazzbro, Jarrett is an excessively vocal interloper who interrupts their getting with the music: Jarrett's clearly in it, and so, they can't be.[26] And, while for some the overt sexuality of his performances violates the intimate codes of jazz homosociality—that they all just can't share "in the music" together—Jarrett's censure of noisy audients reinforces the notion that he desires a monogamous communion with "the music."[27]

Meanwhile, the comments of Jarrett's longtime collaborator, drummer Jack DeJohnette, elaborate on the erotic relationship Jarrett has with the piano, wrestling toward intimate connection amid the yawning gap between pianist and instrument: "I think what Keith does with that instrument, technically and spiritually, when he reaches down ... he'll pull out some things on that piano ... he has a love affair with that instrument. I mean he knows its limitations, but if you take those limitations and stretch them ..."[28]

---

25 Rebelo 2006, 34: "To be 'into it' is to desire to be 'in it' or even to 'be it.' The ultimate desire is to diffuse the spectator and the spectacle and to become one." While this may be more pronounced when viewing his live performances, I'd suggest that, because of the audibility of his body this occurs across all modes of Jarrett's performances, including on studio recordings.

26 For "jazzbro," see Chinen 2013.

27 I would suggest that both Cusick and Jarrett are bypassing their instruments in problematic ways that Rebelo helps to point out. As my own experiences demonstrate, these keyboard instruments are clearly more than tools for achieving climax. Again, I thank Ellen Waterman for her suggestion of considering this performer-audient dynamic outside of jazz and the stereotype of the heteronormative jazzbro. The existence and prevalence of these normative listening practices of course do not forestall the possibility of different types of engagement with Jarrett's—or anyone else's—music. Communication with author.

28 Carr 1992, 147. See the same work at 46–47. Thanks to Aidan Levy, Kevin Fellezs, and Lewis Porter for their assistance in identifying and sharing this source with me.

Pianism Entails Risk

Getting this instrument to move can be debilitating. Jarrett's battle with chronic fatigue syndrome—and recovery from it—offers another example of a failing body that improvises through dis/ability. The lack of attention to this period in his life in the scholarship on his embodied pianism reflects multiple ways in which pain can be silent and silencing: in the same way that listening past the presence of Jarrett's physiological voice disembodies his music, so too does ignoring the painful moments of performance and the moments in which pain blocked performance. As Jarrett demonstrates in his "comeback" album *Melody at Night with You*, "a skilled improviser" gets the instrument to move in part by "an awareness of the palette of musical acts ... that is physically possible at any given moment."[29] In truly accounting for the body in performance, there needs to be accommodation for the skilled improviser for whom it is physically impossible to perform at a given moment—or over many moments.[30]

Pianism Exceeds Its Recordings

Given this wider view of pianistic performance, recordings—of whatever technology—remain inherently unfaithful, preserving "only a trace (a remnant) of a musical engagement" that "translates not only individual musical 'voices,' but their styles of engaging authority, their modes of expressive subjectivity."[31] Inasmuch as writing about those quartet performances in the Canaries without considering the collaboration, bodily engagement, pain induced by the Petrof's stiff action, and my recuperative measures seems unfaithful, I remain committed to folding in as many traces of those engagements as possible. Knowing at the time that I would be writing made excising such important elements even more disingenuous: because I will write I am thinking about my playing and my body in this way *while I'm playing*. These actions and ways of being are intimately entangled, and so "folding

---

29 Iyer 2002.
30 Recent reportage on the end of Jarrett's career emphasizes these points even more. See Chinen 2020. Alex Lubet's scholarship on Oscar Peterson's performance career after that pianist suffered strokes is also relevant here. See below and Lubet 2015.
31 Titlestad 2004, 157.

them into the mix" doesn't mean "teasing each one out," but rather "coupling with them more deeply."

"Fits and Starts": De/generative Conditions

Third Chorus (2:05–2:20): Intersubjective Gestures, Marked Moaningly

> "Creative capacity lodges thus in particular disciplined and desiring bodies, each with its own idiosyncrasies and possibly its idiopathies, and which is actualized only at the moment of performance. When we listen to jazz, it follows that we listen for a methodical and calculated engagement with musical possibilities at the borders of a performer's idiolect, at the ways he or she embodies a musical archive and can shape responses to interlocutors both present and implied."[32]

In the video recording of that impromptu performance at the Bambi Astoria Perdomo can be seen hovering just over my shoulder, actively participating by clapping and stomping out rhythmic accompaniment. Three choruses in, he shifts his attention to my hands-at-the-keyboard, watching—and then dancing along with—the outline of a melodic sequence I improvised that pushed us both on top of the time and the changes.

Listening and thinking back on these twenty seconds, I can perceive a discreet moment of a relationship developing through sounds and bodies.[33] First at Bambi Astoria and then at his home, Perdomo and I were coming to know each other through embodied action in sound, while I was also negotiating similar relationships with the pianos in each location. My throbbing forearms and the moans captured on the rehearsal recording were just two of the lasting traces of these encounters, inarticulate translations of these emergent relationships.

Despite the inherent infidelity of the ethnographic process, dis/ability, and pain complicate even further the translation of embodied performance

---

32 Titlestad 2004, 157. As Titlestad writes, performances include performer's idiolects—aspects of acting in the erotic space of performance that are not necessarily visually or sonically apparent but are present and definitional, nonetheless.

33 At 1:09 in the video Perdomo reacts approvingly to a harmonic superimposition played in my right hand (which I repeat because I sensed his new engagement in the moment). Attuned to each other, I transition into the aforementioned melodic sequence just after. See above, note 18.

practice to writing. For those performing-in-pain, revising performance practices and postures to move toward pain-free playing is a prerequisite for agency: viable subjectivity is dependent on embodied knowledge and improvisation. This isn't elective, merely desirous, or idealistic; it's imperative. Attention to bodies-in-pain exposes our reliance on functioning bodies such that to disregard that reliance—or the knowledge and privilege it produces—is to grossly overlook the means through which our work in all its stages and forms comes into being. As Lara Birk notes, "The able body is quick to delude its inhabitants into believing that they, as thinking, theorizing, scholarly subjects, are the sole authors of their thoughts. Pain, however, makes such illusions impossible. All ideas arise from within the walls of the body ... No idea or experience is free from the constraints of the absolute structures of skin, muscle, and bone."[34]

Pain fractures subjects-in-pain, causing them to externalize the pathophysiological aspects of their bodies. The pain in my arms prevents me from performing; I don't do that to myself. And I consider myself separate from (entangled with, impeded by) the pain, in part because I know—or can remember, or presage—myself free from that pain. Coping physiologically and psychologically with chronic pain necessitates constant wrestling with multiple conceptions of self (in and out of pain) and finding some temporary cohesion amid the ruptures.[35] Those-in-pain have to labor just to get their fractured bodies to move.

These hoping-to-cope modes for engaging with pain may be empowering (toward coping, agency, and/or intimacy) or debilitating (toward pain abated, loss of control, and/or disconnection). And yet pain from a wound or chronic injury can linger as the embodied trace—archived trauma—of intimate encounters. Pain signals haunt us relentlessly, affecting our actions and movements long after, whether or not they're perceived or perceptible by those around us as either idiolect or idiopathy. Whereas anxiety over self-harm can undermine the pain-filled subject's performance, so too can the outing of pathologized conditions that marginalize the subject within able-bodied communities, wherein musical competence, social belonging, and physical in/vulnerability are inextricably and hopelessly entangled with performative norms of "effortless mastery." This double bind of writing

---

34 Birk 2013, 396.
35 Because it is a chronic injury, thus far I have only been able to achieve temporary healing of my tendinosis. It's a wound that always foretells of future trauma. See below on pianist Michel Petrucciani's osteogenesis imperfecta.

ethnography faithfully while risking marginalization because of ableist bias begs the question at the heart of this chapter: how should the debilitating pain and essential coping strategies I improvised be manifest in my work? The moan audible on my rehearsal recordings calls attention to and revises my pianism as a sonic trace of my body laboring towards competence, belonging, and community. The conventions of ethnographic writing afforded me the authority to excise completely any trace of my pain and its affects: if I didn't write the frayed tendons and resultant failures in, they wouldn't exist. Including the moan, though, is not just an act of faith but a celebration of successful coping, and the more intimate understanding of my body-in-performance that emerged from it.

By interrupting idealized flows of transcendent performance, listening for pain and opening up to it in our ethnographies creates space for these silenced bodies, recodes pathologizing norms, and challenges notions of effortless, disembodied action. Whether I liked it or not, my moaning at the piano and stretching for long periods of time in between rehearsed tunes ruptured my already fraught persona as a competent participant-observer, signaling something "not normal"—and maybe pathological—about my (clearly laboring, never effortless, and debatably masterful) improvised jazz pianism, a performance practice very much evaluated on meeting phallocentric and homosocial expectations of mastery. Committing to writing this chapter—choosing to perform the idiopathic pain again in my ethnography—risks judgement and rebuke yet again, triggering traumatic anxieties over competence and belonging.[36] As when I sat down at the Petrof for rehearsal at Kike's, I am laboring to move (my) ethnographic writing not knowing what harm I might inflict on myself nor what new understanding might emerge from my de/generative condition.

Every embodied action—even those seemingly performed by one person—is inherently interpersonal, a collective choreography—a contact improvisation—in which we impress upon each other our attitudes and values about comportment, action, and personhood. Each musician in that Canarian quartet—and their instruments—were entangled in contact, with traces of each encounter on each of us as we compelled ourselves toward in/action. Frayed tendons in some cases; loosened, worn piano wires in others. These traces also figure into the highly contingent, improvised choreography about which any subsequent account—moans included—tells inarticulately.

---

36 Although the possibility of and hope for empathy and understanding exist as well.

Attention to those factors usually coded as extramusical—in this case, listening for pain among and beyond "the sounds themselves"—aids in teasing out and parsing these complex entanglements without overlooking or unraveling their constitutive interconnectedness.

Pathologies of Flawlessness: Fractured Pianisms That Moan

Fourth Chorus (2:34–2:49): Newly Emergent, with Failing Flow

> "Not long ago, in the midst of a jazz-quartet session in which I was participating, the recording engineer complained about what he called the 'radiator noise' the pianist made while playing, a hisslike sound that closely followed the pitches of his improvisation. After the engineer asked him to try to keep 'it' down, his performance became considerably stifled; eventually this supposedly harmless and even sensible suggestion by the engineer appeared to paralyze the creativity of an otherwise rather imaginative improviser."[37]

When I listen back to recordings of my playing, I can usually hear the tendinosis—in more than just the moaning. I can hear it in the wrong notes, awkward phrases, lines abruptly cut short, and as vocalized frustration. While the moan is a "telling inarticulacy," it can also tell many things inarticulately—exertion, ecstasy, frustration, calibration, engagement, desire, repulsion.[38] Just as abstractions of a pianist's "feel" and "touch" are associated with their artistic voice, hearing the moan—as trace of the physiological voice—as "noise" is a politically exclusionary act that exposes a disembodying move that ignores the intimate choreography of improvised contact between the pianist (and their fingertips, palms, joints, muscles, nerves, and so on) and the piano. Attuning listening practices to the myriad possibilities of the moan opens up the potential for connecting to our bodies, our musics, and others in more inclusive ways.

Especially because of the invisibility of some types of pain, confronting the stigmas that delegitimize the pain-filled subject requires some performance—a willful outing of oneself through verbal, somatic, or other act—that can add a level of risk to performance that often precedes and even

---

37 Moreno 1999, 75.
38 On "telling inarticulacy" see Mackey 1987.

prevents efforts "to move the instrument."[39] Listening to the performance of a pain-filled subject can tell many things—a spectrum of experiences all susceptible to mis/interpretation. Even the possibility that a painful moan might be misheard as musical incompetence rather than an improvised, embodied engagement with somatic difference is enough to keep some—myself included—from sitting down at the bench at all.

I'm suggesting an imperative to listen more attentively to the moans, radiator noises, and "extramusical" discrepancies that mark laboring bodies as they work to "move their instruments." The moan, then, marks these performers' labored attempts to resolve the internal and external dissonances of a subjectivity best characterized as an "ineffable whole."[40] Through looking to and listening for marginalized subjects as sounding, agentive bodies-in-performance, we can move closer to filling out existing canons and bringing about interventions that mark both these and pain-filled bodies as neither pathological nor exceptional.

Ethnomusicologist Alex Lubet has produced groundbreaking work on jazz, disability, and differently abled improvisers.[41] Considerations of physiological and psychological pain—especially as they relate to questions about debunking disembodied approaches to and conceptions of performance practice—remain largely undiscussed in Lubet's work, and jazz studies more generally. Whereas Lubet casts aside "sensory impairments or those cognitive, mental, or behavioral atypicalities often characterized as disabilities," I would suggest that there is greater need for attention to those categories that Lubet specifically passes over: not because they do or do not satisfy medically or academically sanctioned parameters of dis/ability, but because of the strategies that musicians have employed to overcome the socially imposed ontological fractures that these "atypicalities" can cause.

---

39 See Lawrence, this volume, and 2021; and Jones 2015.

40 This is a much larger topic vis-à-vis jazz studies, intersections of race, gender, and dis/ability, and normative conceptions of pianistic mastery. I am planning more work on this topic in the future, based on existing presentations I've delivered related to this work. In deference to the complexity of the topic and so as not to elide important differences, I have chosen to focus on examples in this section who are white, male pianists (i.e., identifying with similar racial and gender demographics as Jarrett). See also McMullen, this volume, and Rustin-Paschal 2017.

41 See, for example, Lubet 2015 and 2010. George McKay's work is also worth mentioning here; see especially McKay 2018.

Moreover, in disregarding case studies such as pianist Michel Petrucciani's osteogenesis imperfecta (also known as "glass bone disease") because they "seem to have no impact on their performance," I would suggest that Lubet is excising case studies essential to his investigations, in this particular case by implying that Petrucciani transcended his body in performance and that dis/ability that leaves no audible trace in performance is outside the realm of interest. It is at this juncture that pain emerges as a corrective to the narrative: the inaudibility and invisibility of (physiological or psychological) pain eludes Lubet's analyses. The ruptured tendons and broken bones that Petrucciani regularly suffered in performance had significant effect on his ability to perform and his overall well-being. His ability to cope with that pain, accommodate his dis/ability, and risk self-harm in order to "get the instrument to move" should not be overlooked.

While there are many examples of musicians-in-pain who can help fill out narratives on embodied jazz performance practice, pianist Jimmy Amadie warrants special mention. For Amadie, "coping with physical constraints" meant a thirty-year hiatus from public performance, during which time he underwent surgeries, physical therapy, and pain management. Developing a unique practice routine that minimized physical strain and a prolific career in education, Amadie worked over decades on an adaptive approach to music-making wherein he persevered through incrementally longer daily sessions and returned to an active performance career.[42]

Amadie's practice routine shows the physical danger associated with notions of "letting go of the body" in the search for effortless mastery. Like Amadie, in dealing with tendinosis, my pianism requires vigilance, a perpetual guarding against transcendent loss of (embodied) self. In listening to my playing, I can hear traces of past and present pain; however, while playing, I also have to maintain bodily awareness to guard against future pain, in the same way that Amadie did. Hypersensitivity to every finger movement, elbow position, level of muscular tension is all necessary to avoid self-harm. I can "get the instrument to move" without this mindful engagement but not without serious repercussions.

The masculinist ideals of jazz pianism dictate total command over the instrument: that willfully submitting the instrument and transcending bodily awareness is the precursor to effortlessly masterful music-making. Because of the bodily breaks and ruptures Michel Petrucciani suffered, his

---

42 The narratives around Amadie's "comeback" recording, *Live at the Philadelphia Museum of Art*, attest to this.

body was never the same after a performance. Petrucciani's body reminds us that all bodies bear the trace of performance encounters and that these performances are infused with our bodily presences. Lubet's suggestion that we don't need to get with Petrucciani's body—or Jarrett's rebuke of his audiences' noisy intrusions into his pursuit of intimate musical communion—are moves that choke off the emancipatory erotics of collaborative performance and emergent communities built through intersubjective intimacies.

New Disorders: Ethnographies of/with Pain

Fifth/Final Chorus (3:02–3:17): Revised, Reworked, and Well Attuned

> "Hence, to situate ethnography as a ruin/rune is to foreground the limits and necessary misfirings of its project, problematizing the researcher as 'the one who knows.' Placed outside of mastery and victory narratives, ethnography becomes a kind of self-wounding laboratory for discovering the rules by which truth is produced."[43]

As I sat at the piano at that first rehearsal, I knew that my arms would be sore the next day, that continuing to play could possibly do serious physical harm, and that, after all I'd worked through to be there to try to get that piano to move, I would not stop. Cutting short my first session in the Canary Islands, giving the musicians any reason to second guess the invitation they had extended, exposing recurrent personal issues with chronic pain—all of these were completely off the table. I sacrificed self-care in hopes of measuring up, trying to force my control over the situation, and "hanging with the guys." Willfully disengaged from my body, I chose to ignore that searing sensation I felt creeping up in my arms as the choruses flew by—that sensation I had already come to know as an aura of future pain, of everyday life and dexterity about to be disrupted, and, in this situation, possibly of ethnographic fieldwork undermined.

Pain fractures. Pain ruptures. Being-in-pain necessitates a modulation of somatic modes—new sets of postures for coping—undermining the stability and cohesion of the performing body/self. Pain—especially chronic pain—reminds us of the wound (present, past, and potential), the inherent vulnerability of the body, and the imperative to seek new, more mindful pathways

---

43 Lather, 2001, 482.

through the world.[44] For this reason pain isn't inherently destructive: pain postures that affect movement toward coping and connection can be generative, intimate, and intersubjective.

Exposing the ruptures, fractures, and flaws in disciplinary conventions and methodological assumptions—along with the pain that these conditions have caused—we should be wrestling to move our writing toward connecting with and making inclusive spaces for ineffably whole dis/abled performers, their knowledge, and the intimate kinships and communities that can emerge from such work. Though it greatly affected my ability to perform in those moments "in the field," the recurrence of my tendinosis changed my performance practice by opening up alternate frames of mind, engagements, and spaces for performance, including in writing about it afterward.[45] And, just as I adopted new pianistic postures for coping with the pain of my tendinosis, so too does writing about it and the associated, concomitant trauma require new postures and new perspectives.

Stretching ethnography toward intimate acoustemology is also a matter of opening ourselves and our work to the myriad entanglements of our own lives and bodies, finding then working out the knots and scar tissues of these intimate, intersubjective encounters. And coping with and through others. Acknowledging vulnerability is recognizing impedances—the cuts and wounds of our embodied interactions—as breaks to be sutured. Our vulnerabilities—the nerves, tendons, and intentional threads of varying tensile strengths that conduct our movement through the world—function as causal chains or pathways in which holistic intra/interpersonal action can occur. Connecting the postural mode of pain to others is a matter of developing new engagements and postures that embrace and work with these impedances.

Like our recollection of a live performance or appreciation of a recorded one, a frayed tendon is just as imperfect and unfaithful an archive of a musical encounter. But it is also an archive that bears a unique trace of such a coming-together. Fidelity in ethnography is not about one account but rather the messy suturing of many such failed archives. The reparative entangling that characterizes tendinosis—the healing that always foretells of a

---

44   Working through my process of wounding, coping, re-posturing, and reflection I would suggest that pain is not a posture; it's a postural mode.

45   Physiologically speaking, tendinosis is failed bodily repair that is disorganized, an improvised rerouting of cells that functions through revised, sometimes failing, biomechanical flow and movement.

future wound *and* our ability to cope with it—is a model for mindful, "good faith" ethnography, an affective loop (a repetition of solo choruses with difference) wherein vulnerability and interpenetration embrace the intimacy of emergent interactions.

For me, waking up pain free the morning after the "Bolivia" rehearsal is what compelled me along this line of thinking. My desire for continued work with these musicians necessitated new postural strategies that mitigated, coped with, or circumvented the pain-inducing conditions. Extending that process to ethnography seems natural since in that moment I was functioning in both capacities at the piano bench.[46]

The externalizing effects of pain, illness, and dis/ability provide deep insights that allow us to observe some aspect of ourselves as we might observe someone else; but also, recalling the more generalized meaning of intimacy as vulnerability, working through a more entangled sense of ethnography renders it more impressionable. Intimate work is work that is made by those open to being wounded.[47]

This is my attempt to better describe that very real—very intimate—connection between my forearm tendons and the piano wires of the Petrof baby grand that inspired this chapter. In addition to being connected at the moment of performance, both are governed by restrictions of tensile strength—the amount of force they can withstand without breaking apart. The tendon ruptures at between 50 and 100 megapascal, while the piano wire snaps at between 2600 and 3000.

What then is the tensile strength of ethnography? Its writings? Its practitioners? What are the limits to which we can stretch it open before it'll snap? And, because it *always* snaps, how do we cope with the fractures?[48] How do we heal after we've been broken? To persevere, forge new connections, and draw from our wounds the strength to move forward is to fashion new, more tightly entwined filaments, intentional threads even more resistant to breakage. These filaments conduct—with various levels of impedance—the flow

---

46 This is partly inspired by Sudnow 1981.
47 I'm guided here especially by the work of Gloria Anzaldúa and Jean Jackson.
48 In discussing this passage, my friend and colleague Ryan McCormack rightly points out that "thinking such ruptures as 'breaks' only reinforces a normative politics that values transcendent possibility over immanent knowledge production." However, I am suggesting that the value of the inevitably ruptured ethnography—or the ethnographer—does not lie in successful rehabilitation but rather lies *with* and *within* the coping process, including intimacy through writing and in communities of care. Communication with author.

of the moment and, while none are free of impedance, the layering (augmentation) of filaments—the repetitious weaving of ligatures—and their co-present, impressionable vulnerability opens wide the possibility of an articulated, intimate moment imbued with gestural and bodily excess. Through repetition we improvise new pathways around and across impedance. This move toward connection is one toward intra- and interpersonal intimacy.

Toward More Intimate Incorporations

For a long time, I couldn't write this chapter. And all the while I also couldn't improvise at the piano, even as I listened and relistened to field recordings of my having played. I was blocked. Though it wasn't physical pain that stopped me, there were physical symptoms: every time I tried to really get into it, my arm muscles would lock up. I was coping with the effects of trying to push myself into my work and my fingers had stopped moving at both keyboards.

I suspected that my process was so fraught with anxiety about exposing my chronic injury that I was moved to inertia and inaction. I lost myself in thousands of pages of reading trying to conceal myself and justify my pain behind an exhaustive list of peer-reviewed citations. I strove for an "effortlessly masterful" performance in which all the proper sources were perfectly sutured into the narrative, all the requisite scholarship carefully applied to this repeated performance of self-wounding. I hoped that you'd pay attention to the argument and not to me. Frustrated, unable to take it all in—or get it all out—in preparation for the third draft I printed the text out and cut it into pieces, moving them around on the top of the otherwise unused grand piano in my office, trying to find the right mix to align the resonant motives and get the chapter to sing. How could I bring you closer? Bring you "in it"?

Now that the chapter is written and I am starting to regain my voice at the piano—I realize that the reading was not just part of my writing process; it was part of a coping and healing process that revealed and dressed wounds well beyond what I've committed to print here. In theorizing intimate acoustemologies I turned my listening inward and applied my scholarly work to personal trauma I was only discovering as I tried to write. I reconnected with mentors, formed new kinships (through texts and in person), and eased into new professional relationships. Affirmed by these new connections, I found that by exposing my trauma (through texts and in person) I opened myself up to the possibility of healing more fully.[49]

All that reading about chronic pain, intimacy, and embodied performance practice also reminded me of the word "incorporate"—literally, the act of bringing into the body. Each in our own way and all together now we understand the risk and vulnerability entailed in bringing bodies close. (This heightened awareness of potential risk borne from proximity has long been known to the chronically ill, traumatized, and immuno-compromised.) The specific risks of self-harm I bring on stage or in the field because of my chronic injury are amplified yet again in writing my tendinosis back into my ethnographies. But those concerns speak to much more fundamental questions: What do I risk in bringing myself close with you? Can I control who is close to me?

And what about other bodies? Mindful that "in corpora actus" also can mean "putting bodies on one another" or even "bodies placed against one another," we need to allow for improvised contact and many different forms of more intimate listening as we bring this work into our bodies of scholarship and our student bodies. We need to listen to and listen for each and all of these bodies in the hopes of fostering closer connections.

Norms of "effortless mastery" in piano performance and ethnography—the effects of ableist ways of being and my desire to measure up and fit in—literally ripped my body apart from the inside. Brought about by trauma, reemergent tendinosis has been the mark of toxically masculinist perspectives in my pianistic and ethnographic work. Stretching toward healing at both keyboards brought forth pain and trauma I didn't know how to cope with. Healing meant imagining performance without retraumatizing myself,

---

49 In addition to those already mentioned I also have to thank colleagues Yvette Modestin, Kameelah Martin, Yvonne Chireau, and Micheline Rice-Maximin whose support and care go well beyond the work cited at the end of the chapter. For sharing their perspectives on indigenous and Afro/Canarian women and conversations about critical feminist perspectives on Canarian history, I would also like to thank Esther Alamo Sosa and vocalist Beatriz Alonso. Part of my healing journey has included new connections with children of/ *hij@s de* Oshun and Yemayá, as well as a personal relationship with the orisha Oyá. Part of the holistic approach to performance ethnography and intimate acoustemology for which I'm advocating includes spiritual practice. In addition to talking to Modestin, Martin, Omi Jones, and others about this emergent aspect of my work, I'm particularly indebted to the scholarship of M. Jacqui Alexander and Solimar Otero. See Lomanno, forthcoming.

another shift in postural modes. Continuing to reach out after you've been broken courts risk, triggers trauma, and exposes vulnerability.

Thinking back this was only ever about moving toward intimate connection. I knew I felt a connection between the burning, throbbing tendons in my forearms and the wires stretched out across the soundboard of that Petrof baby grand piano. I chose to play past the searing sensations of my forearms burning underneath my skin in an effort to reach my Canarian collaborators. When my tendinosis flared up after that first rehearsal, the pain was a stark reminder of the limits of my reach. Through more mindful approaches in my pianism, I was able to stretch those limitations toward more intimate interaction: finding improvised postures and emergent relations—to my body, the piano, and the other musicians.

Writing our sensations, vulnerabilities, and the risks of intimate connection into ethnography—augmenting scholarly voices with the physiological ones—compels us to embrace ethnography's inherent infidelity, opening up yawning gaps for listening to emerging, intra- and interpersonal entanglements. Our bodies fail. Our bodies hurt. Our bodies have flaws that, when exposed, make them and us vulnerable to even more pain. But our bodies heal. And hope. And connect.

References

Ake, David. 2002. *Jazz Cultures*. Berkeley: University of California Press.
———. 2010. *Jazz Matters: Sound, Place, and Time since Bebop*. Berkeley: University of California Press.
Alexander, M. Jacqui. 2006. *Pedagogies of Crossing: Meditations on Feminism, Sexual Politics, Memory, and the Sacred*. Durham, NC: Duke University Press.
Barad, Karen. 2013. "On Touching—The Inhuman That Therefore I Am." *Differences* 23 (3): 206–23.
Birk, Lara B. 2013. "Erasure of the Credible Subject: An Autoethnographic Account of Chronic Pain." *Cultural Studies/Critical Methodologies* 13 (5): 390–99.
Brooks, Kinitra, Kameelah L. Martin, and LaKisha Simmons. 2021. "Conjure Feminism: Toward a Genealogy." *Hypatia* 36 (3): 452–61.
Carr, Ian. 1992. *Keith Jarrett: The Man and His Music*. New York: Da Capo Press.
Chinen, Nate. 2013. "The Gig: Behold the Jazzbro." *JazzTimes*, July 13. https://jazztimes.com/features/columns/the-gig-behold-the-jazzbro/.

———. 2020. "Keith Jarrett Confronts a Future without the Piano." *New York Times*, October 21. https://www.nytimes.com/2020/10/21/arts/music/keith-jarrett-piano.html/.

Chireau, Yvonne. 2006. *Black Magic: Religion and the African American Conjuring Tradition*. Berkeley: University of California Press.

Cusick, Suzanne G. 1994. "On a Lesbian Relationship with Music: A Serious Effort Not to Think Straight." In *Queering the Pitch: The New Gay and Lesbian Musicology*, edited by Philip Brett, Elizabeth Wood, and Gary C. Thomas, 67–83. New York: Routledge.

Doerschuk, Robert L. 2001. *88: The Giants of Jazz Piano*. New York: Hal Leonard.

Elsdon, Peter. 2012. *Keith Jarrett's "The Koln Concert."* New York: Oxford University Press.

Feld, Steven. 2012. *Jazz Cosmopolitanism in Accra*. Durham, NC: Duke University Press.

———. 2015. "Acoustemology." In *Keywords in Sound*, edited by David Novak and Matt Sakakeeny, 12–21. Durham, NC: Duke University Press.

Givan, Ben. 2009. "Thelonious Monk's Pianism." *Journal of Musicology* 26 (3): 404–42.

Iyer, Vijay. 2002. "Embodied Mind, Situated Cognition, and Expressive Microtiming in African-American Music." *Music Perception* 19 (3): 387–414.

Jones, Omi Osun Joni L. 2015. *Theatrical Jazz: Performance, Àṣẹ, and the Power of the Present Moment*. Columbus: Ohio State University Press.

Jones, Omi Osun Joni L., Lisa L. Moore, and Sharon Bridgforth, eds. 2010. *Experiments in a Jazz Aesthetic: Art, Activism, Academia, and the Austin Project*. Austin: University of Texas Press.

Kozel, Susan. 2017. "Devices of Existence: Contact Improvisation, Mobile Performances, and Dancing through Twitter." In *Improvisation and Social Aesthetics*, edited by Georgina Born, Eric Lewis, and Will Straw, 268–87. Durham, NC: Duke University Press.

Lather, Patti. 2001. "Postmodernism, Post-Structuralism and Post (Critical) Ethnography: Of Ruins, Aporias and Angels." In *Handbook of Ethnography*, edited by Paul Atkinson, Sara Delamont, John Lofland, Amanda Coffey, and Lyn H. Lofland, 477–92. London: SAGE.

Lawrence, Sidra. 2021. "Sonic Intimacies: Performative Erotics and African Feminisms." *Senses and Society* 16 (2): 177–92.

Lomanno, Mark. 2012. "Improvising Difference: Constructing Canarian Jazz Cultures." PhD diss., University of Texas at Austin, 2012.

———. 2017. "Moan Flow: Chronic Pain, Intimacy, and Modulating Flawed Bodies." Presentation at the Improvisation and Mobility Conference and Festival, at the University of Regina, Saskatchewan, Canada.

———. 2019. "Wail: Radical Jazz Pianism and the Precarity of Black Breath." Presentation at the annual IASPM-US (International Association for the Study of Popular Music–US chapter) Conference, New Orleans, Louisiana.
———. Forthcoming. "Intimate Incorporations: Improvisation as Teaching / Teaching as Improvisation." In *The Improviser's Classroom: Pedagogies for Cocreative Worldmaking*, edited by Daniel Fischlin and Mark Lomanno. Philadelphia: Temple University Press.
Lubet, Alex. 2010. *Music, Disability, and Society*. Philadelphia: Temple University Press.
———. 2015. "Oscar Peterson's Piano Prostheses: Strategies of Performance and Publicity in the Post-Stroke Phase of His Career." *Jazz Research Journal* 7 (2): 151–82.
Macharia, Keguro. 2019. *Frottage: Frictions of Intimacy across the Black Diaspora*. New York: New York University Press.
Mackey, Nathaniel. 1987. "Sound and Sentiment, Sound and Symbol." *Callaloo* 30: 29–54.
Martin, Kameelah L. 2016. *Envisioning Black Feminist Voodoo Aesthetics: African Spirituality in American Cinema*. Lanham, MD: Lexington Books.
———. 2022. "'A Consort of the Spirits' or How to Cultivate Indigo, Conjured by Herself." *Langston Hughes Review* 28 (1): 1–9.
Maximin-Rice, Micheline. 1996. "Nouvelle Ecriture from The Ivory Coast: A Reading of Veronique Tadjo's 'A Vol d'Oiseau.'" In *Postcolonial Subjects: Francophone Women Writers*, edited by Mary Jean Green, Karen Gould, Micheline Rice-Maximin, Keith L. Walker, and Jack A. Yeager, 157–72. Minneapolis: University of Minnesota Press.
McCormack, Ryan Sawyer. 2012. "Outside of the Self: Subjectivity, the Allure of Transcendence, and Jazz Historiography." *Critical Studies in Improvisation* 8 (1). http://www.criticalimprov.com/article/view/1682/.
McKay, George. 2018. "Jazz and Disability." In *The Routledge Companion to Jazz Studies*, edited by Nicholas Gebhardt, Nichole Rustin-Paschal, and Tony Whyton, 174–84. New York: Routledge.
McMullen, Tracy. 2016. "Improvisation within a Scene of Constraint: An Interview with Judith Butler." In Gillian H. Siddall and Ellen Waterman, eds., *Negotiated Moments: Improvisation, Sound, and Subjectivity*, 21–36. Durham, NC: Duke University Press.
Modestin, Yvette. 2012. "The Whispers of the Ancestors: Development of a Black, Proud Panamanian Voice." In *Women Warriors of the Afro-Latina Diaspora*, edited by Marta Moreno Vega, Marinieves Alba, and Yvette Modestin, 123–39. Houston: Arte Publico Press.
Moreno, Jairo. 1999. "Body'n'Soul?: Voice and Movement in Keith Jarrett's Pianism." *Musical Quarterly* 83 (1): 75–92.

Moten, Fred. 2003. *In the Break: The Aesthetics of the Black Radical Tradition*. Minneapolis: University of Minnesota Press.
Otero, Solimar. 2020. *Archives of Conjure: Stories of the Dead in Afrolatinx Cultures*. New York: Columbia University Press.
Provost, Sarah Caissie. 2018. "Bringing Something New: Female Jazz Instrumentalists' Use of Imitation and Masculinity." *Jazz Perspectives* 10 (2–3): 141–57.
Rebelo, Pedro. 2006. "Haptic Sensation and Instrumental Transgression." *Contemporary Music Review* 25 (1–2): 27–35.
Reed, Anthony. 2014. *Freedom Time: The Poetics and Politics of Black Experimental Writing*. Baltimore: Johns Hopkins University Press.
Rustin, Nichole, and Sherrie Tucker, eds. 2008. *Big Ears: Listening for Gender in Jazz Studies*. Durham, NC: Duke University Press.
Rustin-Paschal, Nichole. 2017. *The Kind of Man I Am: Jazzmasculinity and the World of Charles Mingus Jr*. Middletown, CT: Wesleyan University Press.
Shove, Patrick, and Bruno H. Repp. 1995. "Musical Motion and Performance: Theoretical and Empirical Perspectives." In *The Practice of Performance: Studies in Musical Interpretation*, edited by John Rink, 55–83. Cambridge, UK: Cambridge University Press.
Siddall, Gillian H., and Ellen Waterman, eds. 2016. *Negotiated Moments: Improvisation, Sound, and Subjectivity*. Durham, NC: Duke University Press.
Sudnow, David. 1979. *Ways of the Hand: The Organization of Improvised Conduct*. Cambridge, MA: MIT Press.
———. 1981. *Talk's Body: A Meditation between Two Keyboards*. New York: Knopf.
Titlestad, Michael F. 2004. *Making the Changes: Jazz in South African Literature and Reportage*. Pretoria: University of South Africa Press.
Tucker, Sherrie, et al. 2016. "Stretched Boundaries: Improvising Across Abilities." In Siddall and Waterman, *Negotiated Moments*, 181–200.
Vallone, Mirella. 2014. "The Wound as Bridge: The Path of Conocimiento in Gloria Anzaldúa's Work." *Revue Electronique d'Etudes sur Le Monde Anglophone* 12 (1). https://doi.org/10.4000/erea.4135/.
Waterman, Ellen. 2008. "Naked Intimacy: Eroticism, Improvisation, and Gender." *Critical Studies in Improvisation* 4 (2). https://www.criticalimprov.com/index.php/csieci/article/view/845/.
Weheliye, Alexander G. 2005. *Phonographies: Grooves in Sonic Afro-Modernity*. Durham, NC: Duke University Press.
Werner, Kenny. 1996. *Effortless Mastery*. New Albany, IN: Jamey Aebersold Jazz.
Ziporyn, Evan, and Michael Tenzer. 2011. "Thelonious Monk's Harmony, Rhythm, and Pianism." In *Analytical and Cross-Cultural Studies in World Music*, edited by Michael Tenzer and John Roeder, 145–84. Oxford University Press.

Recordings

Amadie, Jimmy. *Live at the Philadelphia Museum of Art*. TP Recordings, 2013. Compact disc.
Jarrett, Keith. *The Melody at Night with You*. ECM Records 1675, 1999. Compact disc.
Perdomo, Enrique "Kike." *Celebrate Brooklyn II*. 96K Music, 2013. Compact disc.

Chapter Four

Performing Desire

Race, Sex, and the Ethnographic Encounter

Sidra Lawrence

I called him to tell him that I was going out of town for work. He met the car, a small minibus full of travelers, which was sitting parked on the side of the road in the center of town. The midafternoon sun meant that the streets and shops were busy, full of people shopping, working, and sitting gathered in small groups in the shade of trees and shopfronts. I was sitting in the back seat on the driver's side when he arrived. He climbed in the driver's door, stuck his head and shoulder around the seat, and placed a stack of folded money in my hand. He told me to use the money to buy phone units and call him while I was away. I thanked him but was embarrassed. I knew that everyone in the car had seen what he had done. I knew they would see him giving me the money as a sign of intimacy, an exchange that normally takes place between a man and his girlfriend.

Sitting here today, my phone rings. I look over and see that it is him, but I do not answer. I've been avoiding his calls since I returned to Fielmua a few weeks ago. I don't feel that I can explain my need to remain distant, to untangle myself from our relationship. I don't think that I can clearly express my need to be free from his controlling regulation, the arguing, and the shadow that he casts over my daily life here. And so, I ignore the call, knowing that he will assume that I have perhaps met someone else, someone who will not permit me to see him. This is the reason that will satisfy him, the only one that will square up to his internal logic. But even knowing this, I can be sure that my distance has caused him some shame, and for that I am sorry.

⁂

In this opening vignette I recall a brief ethnographic moment that highlights how relationships are performed under the gaze of a culturally informed viewership. The exchange that took place in this moment opens up layers of ethnographic knowledge. Like ripples in a pond, one moment tells us about the performance of intimacy, the political economy of sex, and cross-gender public interactions. The following narrative explores the connections between the researcher's body, gender, and race as a meaningful component of ethnographic experience. I see this work as a means to more fully understand the ways in which relationships and erotic subjectivity structure knowledge production. Embedded in this story is a portrayal of power as a negotiable field of action. I suggest that since relationships are filtered through a publicly mediated interpretive lens, the quotidian details of ethnographic exchanges reveal much about culturally informed ideas about the erotic, desire, and intimacy. My interest in sharing this story is primarily to expand the ways in which we consider the erotic relevant to ethnographic knowledge and to reimagine what constitutes erotic experience. Though the story is framed through the details of my personal experience, I focus predominantly on the public perceptions of a relationship and the culturally located meanings it engendered more than a detailed account of interpersonal interaction. This story is, of course, partial, and there are many exclusions that I do not consider germane to my primary arguments.

I never intended the relationship to become what it was. I met him in July 2008.[1] Years later, after several periods of ethnographic research in the small rural town on the border of Burkina Faso and Ghana, I recall our relationship with a mixture of emotions.[2] From the time I met him in 2008, through living there in 2009 and 2010, and returning again in 2012, 2014, and 2016, our interactions have undergone a significant transformation. In my mind our relationship resists easy definition because so many of our interactions

---

1 I have decided not to include his name in this document and will refer to him only by his pronoun.
2 I lived in Fielmua conducting research in July 2008, from August 2009 to August 2010, again in July and August 2012, from June through September 2014, and from December 2016 through January 2017. During this period, I studied the local dialect of Dagara in order to facilitate communication.

have been characterized by tension and conflict, and yet I feel affection for him, as well as gratitude, because our relationship animated questions for me that I hadn't thought to ask. And what I learned about ethnographic methods by discovering what lies beneath speech and prioritizing sensory experience fundamentally altered my approach to the field (Minh-ha 1989; Stoller 1997). As I retrace our memories the lines of our shifting friendship define many of the contours of my knowledge and experience of Fielmua.

When I began my research project, I was searching for female *gyil* players; the gyil, an eighteen-key gourd xylophone, is usually played by men and is associated with male spaces and men's work.[3] Informed by postcolonial and African feminist theoretical models that disrupt universalized narratives of female empowerment, I was devoted to dismantling the monolithic construction of the African female subject. Theoretically informed of the problems and dangers of representing African women through "Western eyes" (Mohanty 2003, 17–43), I was prepared to focus on the individual lives of Dagara women. What I was less prepared for was the relationship that I developed with him and the shape that it would give to my work.

I have found that the theoretical frame of erotic subjectivity has been useful in analyzing this story because it not only offers the possibility of deeply interrogating relationships as embedded within power structures but also reflects the ways that relationships generate a constant negotiation of fields of power. Erotic subjectivity animates the political dimensions of sensuality as an epistemological position. Anthropological accounts of erotic subjectivity are numerous and range from explorations of intimate encounters as meaningful to ethnographic experience to accounts that describe the institutional implications for discussing such experiences (Kulick and Willson 1995; Markowitz and Ashkenazi 1999; Wekker 2006). Additionally, anthropologists have investigated the ways that queer subjectivity structures both ethnographic methods and epistemologies (Lewin and Leap 1996; Gill 2010; Allen 2012). In 2015, the *Journal of the Anthropological Society of Oxford* devoted an entire issue to the subject of sexual harassment in the field. Each of these works has demonstrated that the erotic orders knowledge and encompasses a wide range of experiences, from desire to violence.

---

3   The gyil (plural, *gyile*) is found in the Upper West Region of Ghana and in the neighboring countries of Burkina Faso and Côte d'Ivoire. There are a number of regional and ethnic variations on the gyil and its repertoire, as well as the specific social significance of performance; in all communities the gyil is played almost exclusively by men.

Locating erotic subjectivity within culturally grounded parameters directs us to increased understandings of how power is deployed and negotiated, how it intersects and bears down upon people in a multiplicity of ways.

My interest in erotic subjectivity in ethnomusicology emerged during the early years of processing my ethnographic work in Ghana and trying to find ways to locate my subject position within the context of my research area. I found that I had a problem when it came to the topic of the erotic in ethnography. I had so many experiences in the field that I internalized as extremely important to shaping my knowledge and understanding of my research but that seemed to lack a home in my written accounts, and I didn't have an adequate model for naming those experiences.

The two broad categories that I often find useful when discussing erotic subjectivity are violence/subjugation and desire/love. These categories emerged out of the range of everyday experiences that I was having in the field that spanned that spectrum as I sought to figure out how they structured my knowledge and how to name them in writing. Some of those experiences were easier to label as erotic because they fit inside the western commonplace usage that aligns the erotic with sexual desire or arousal or even with forms of violence, abuse, and exploitation that emerged because of my gender and sexuality. Others seemed to fit a definition of the erotic that was expansive, one that prioritized the sensory and revealed the connections formed, connections that were often intimate but not sexual, but that ordered so much of what I know. It is this area of the erotic that propels my interest deeply, because there are so many erotic experiences that do not reside on the poles of violence or sexual desire, and in seeking out descriptive modes to give voice to these experiences, I believe that we open up increased possibilities of ethnographic knowledge. Additionally, I embrace a configuration of the erotic that draws from scholars who incorporate shared physical, emotional, and spiritual connections, the sensual aspects of knowing, and the political dimensions of desire (Lorde 1984; Alexander 2005) and those who suggest that anthropologists/ethnomusicologists proceed from analytic frameworks that recognize sensory perception as crucial to the organization of experience (Stoller 1997; Hahn 2007). This expansive configuration also allows me to resituate the erotic within my larger research project because it affords the possibilities for looking at how Dagara women love each other and build intimacies and why that framing might revise the ways that we describe ethnographic encounters.

My research methodology, based on postcolonial feminist theory and feminist anthropology (Spivak 1988; Stacey 1988; Minh-ha 1989; Abu-Lughod

1990; Behar and Gordon 1995; Mohanty 2003), was designed to address methodological concerns that fundamentally challenge what constitutes knowledge in terms of both ethnographic data and representation. My methods rely upon relationship building, sustained everyday interactions, and lived experience as the most effective modes of research. My focus on everyday actions, solidarities, and strategies of resistance used by women brought about ethnographic interactions that were strongly grounded in the quotidian. This focus on the everyday oriented all of my interactions, as well as what I consider relevant to an ethnographic study. By not separating the ethnographic experience from the material that informs our studies, we call into question the presumption of disciplinary knowledge.[4] It is a commitment to more fully understanding the process of knowledge production that motivates an excavation of human relationships. By focusing on one such relationship and incorporating the lens of the erotic, I aim to portray a complex portrait of ethnographic encounter.

My relationship with him became part of a web of interactions as various individuals in the community responded differently, often projecting desire onto us. I often felt discord between the interiority of emotion and the public performance in which we were taking part. My personal struggles with the tensions between us, my desire to understand and interrogate his seemingly conflicting motivations, and my efforts to learn locally appropriate modes of interaction were crosscut by third-party interventions. Examining the web formed between us and "the community" (also composed of variously motivated individuals) reveals a nuanced portrayal of desire and conflict. Investigating the expectations, roles, and ideological filters that produced and informed our relationship lends insight into the performance of the erotic and provides a model for exploring the racially gendered body as a repository of ideology.

In exploring aspects of this relationship, I hope to dislocate presumptions about dichotomous power differentials between the researcher and the people with whom she works and instead investigate the complex, sometimes contradictory navigation of human relationships. How can these entanglements

---

[4] This is one example of an opportunity to challenge hegemonic modes of knowledge production and consumption that regulate and compartmentalize "legitimate" forms of knowledge and experience. By distinguishing between valuable or authorized speakers, utterances, or contexts, we empower and reproduce existent power structures. These challenges have been taken up in feminist scholarship/activism by writers, artists, and thinkers who question such frames as language choice, narrative style, and publication space.

provide critical insight into ethnographic knowledge and into the power hierarchies that are both reinforced and confronted through relationship building? "All relationships are agreements about distribution of power, agreements negotiated in varying degrees of intimacy" (Cusick [1994] 2006, 71). Our negotiations provide an example of the complex terrain of power distribution. In our interactions, the locally constructed categories of race, gender, and class were fixed, but their manifestations were not. These categories are given additional meaning through the ideological framing around the geopolitical distinctions of global North and South. I suggest that through a look at our everyday interactions the construction of categories of belonging in Fielmua is shown to be both stable and made real through performance. In this case, the performance of desire exposes the mechanisms that inform gendered and racialized subjectivity.

Navigating the terrain of desiring and being desired, as well as the culturally specific terms through which desire is produced, directs us toward a relationally constructed understanding of subjectivity. Field research becomes a process not only of getting to know another but also of relearning ourselves. The ways in which we experience ourselves as gendered, sexualized subjects must be reexperienced, reexplored, and reconstructed as we seek to connect with others and to learn how they live within their bodies. Negotiating these parameters is always a relational process. Other scholars have shown how conflict, as well as passion and everyday choices in relationships, can have important implications for anthropological knowledge (Newton 1993; Wekker 2006). Thus, the choices that are made when revealing shared moments between people are not arbitrary; they point us to other ways of knowing.

I have chosen particular narrative techniques that reflect a nonlinear, reflective, interpretive reality rather than a linear presentation of events. This is based on a desire to balance cultural critique with a way of writing that resembles the conflicting and the contradictory, the emotional and intellectual tensions of life. As other writers have noted, this is challenging, because the act of breaking something apart to analyze it replicates the very power structures that are being critiqued (Cusick [1994] 2006, 76–77; Minh-ha 1989, 48–49). Both Suzanne Cusick and Trinh Minh-ha liken certain modes of inquiry and analysis to gendered forms of violence. To "speak nearby instead of speaking about," as Minh-ha suggests, allows a way of "speaking that does not objectify, does not point to an object as if it is distant from the speaking subject or absent from the speaking place. A speaking that reflects on itself and can come very close to a subject without, however, seizing or claiming it" (Chen 1992, 87). I was further influenced by Michelle Kisliuk's ([1998] 2001) evocative "performance ethnography," in particular, the way that she demonstrates the interpretive and performative engagements of field research; and by writers who blur the lines of fiction and ethnography, who call into question what constitutes anthropological knowledge and who choose story telling as a narrative technique that allows the reader to move with individuals as they navigate the complexities of their lives more fully, because the story is not required to have critical distance (Fernea 1965; Abu-Lughod 1993; Lortat-Jacob 1995; Chernoff 2003). All of these ethnographers wove their stories into what can be called "critical ethnography" by selecting the stories and revealing a situated, yet detailed, picture of the lives of the people they know and seek to represent. Like these authors, I grapple with the representational politics inherent in narrating shared experiences.

The story that follows does not belong exclusively to me. Representing the web of interactions between everyone involved is challenging because I am retelling these experiences through my own interpretive lens. I would like to therefore be clear that the narrative style is a crucial choice because it allows for personalized language that keeps present my interpretive voice. As I retell parts of our story, I punctuate the prose with interpretation and interjection or pause and reflect as one does in life. This creates a shift in narrative register that mimics the experience of ethnography in which one has an experience or a conversation but then creates a translation to interpret the various meanings attached to what was said or done. This story is partial and incomplete, and it reflects a condensed version of years of experience. Telling it now also represents my memory of experiences as they happened and should be understood as a pointillistic account of lived reality rather than as a linear narration of events as they occurred.

I hope that sharing this partial story will facilitate a fruitful dialogue about erotic subjectivity, culturally and racially coded bodies, and mediating relationships in field research. By seeking out an interpretive framework that challenges a unilateral model of power, I hope to utilize an analysis of sensory ethnographic experience (Minh-ha 1989; Stoller 1997; Hahn 2007). The body stores memories and knowledge, and too often we rely upon verbal communication to construct our mutual realities. To "write the truth the body has been terrorized into keeping silent" (Jones 2010, 10), I suggest that we acknowledge ethnographic authority in the contours of lived experience.

The Story

Looking back, I wish that I had seen then what I more clearly see now. Some days I regret the choice to become his friend, and I punish myself for not being more aware of the broader context of our friendship and the implications it would have for my work. The other day I attended a women's microfinance organization meeting, and I saw his wife. I looked at her for a moment and was overcome with a sense of guilt; though she knew about the friendship and was involved in the effort to convince me to be his girlfriend, I cannot truly know how he held our relationship over her head, what she might have felt, and what I was blind to. This is me, projecting my emotions onto her, of course. She has never expressed any of this to me. But in my imagining of how I might have hurt her I can see the mistakes that I made, as well as why I made them.

When I met him, I was at the beginning of my research project. It was a period when I had few friends in the area and was grappling with my heightened visibility in a rural town in West Africa. He was among the first people who introduced themselves to me, and then he made a sustained effort to build a friendship. Meeting him brought me into a world where I had a name and stopped being just the white woman. I had no pattern to my days then. I wanted to work with women but had little idea how to build those friendships. Women seemed difficult to access, private, and closed off. They moved together and spent most of their time working or in the house. Choosing to conduct a project without a research assistant or a clearly demarcated agenda of formal interviewing or surveying meant that I was, at that point, just trying to become familiar with the community, build relationships, learn the patterns of people and the layout of the town.

Men were the easiest people to meet. They were in public, were more openly friendly, and often spoke more English. In those early stages, men played an important role in helping me get my bearings, introducing me to people, showing me around, and explaining various aspects of life. At the time, I spoke very little Dagara, and he spoke almost no English. The day I met him I was making a phone call at the phone box in the market square, the only place at the time to make a phone call. I was feeling the pressure of the project, the loneliness of isolation, and the frustration of what felt like a rudderless series of days. I knew that I looked visibly upset and that even if people couldn't hear what I was saying, I would appear to be acting unusually. I didn't care. He rode over to me on his motorcycle and said, "Don't cry." Looking at him, in that moment I was happy. He offered to show me around town on his motorcycle, and I happily agreed. It didn't even occur to me how it would look to people or that people would even notice. At the time, I was so unfamiliar with my own visibility, the power of gossip and rumors in Fielmua, or the strangeness of seeing us together.

He was good-looking and charming, and even thought we couldn't communicate very effectively with each other, I could tell that he was funny. It grounded me to have him as a friend, to know someone's name. He introduced me to his friends, showed me what the town looked like after dark, and taught me how to look at Fielmua as a place where people lived and created lives. Field research is always a process of coming to see—what appeared to me initially as a series of pictures of people I didn't know, whose lives I couldn't fully recognize, and whose motivations were opaque became clarified. When I returned to Fielmua the next year he anchored that trip by introducing me to the first woman who became a close friend and by opening up my world beyond the doors of my house.

The community's perception of our friendship was overwhelmingly couched in class-based terms that are also racially encoded. Like many people in rural Dagaraland, he is a farmer. He is also a successful business owner who trades batteries and sugar across the border of Burkina Faso. In this community, his heightened status as a business owner with some disposable income is counterbalanced by his lack of formal education. Illiteracy became a primary marker of his articulated sense of identity, and I repeatedly witnessed him confronting a sense of exclusion based on this diminished status. My own status as a white American woman pursuing PhD research heightened the public perception of our status differentials. Our seemingly close friendship provoked constant questions, surprise, and on some occasions disdain. My status as an educated "outsider" reads differently to different people but carries with it a clichéd notion of power, prestige, and money linked to well-ingrained ideas about the inherent distinctions between the global North and the global South. I think the broader community expected me to socialize with formally educated men and women rather than businessmen or farmers. In fact, people often expressed what they felt was his inability to contribute to my project by sharing anything valuable.

The tensions expressed about our friendship are, I believe, a product of the authorization of the elite voice in Fielmua that extends to the ability to communicate cultural values. I did not fully recognize his interpretation of our status differentials; instead, I experienced his sometimes-unexpected proclamations about what he hoped to gain from me. His actions in this regard were uneven. For example, he would adhere to local customs regarding gift giving and other forms of public social exchange. He would never have let me pay for a bottle of beer, because it would run counter to his sense of masculinity and appropriate action. On the other hand, he could easily be provoked into chastising me for not buying him a car, a reflection of his misguided sense of my status and financial capacity. This type of behavior is common enough to be recognized as a product of social notions regarding life on the "outside" but also as a product of the localized interpretations of the performance of status. In this context, the signifiers of wealth are incredibly important, as is displaying those signifiers publicly. One does not hide the status of wealth but displays it publicly. It is this performance of status that elevates an individual and separates him or her from the lower classes. He expected me to behave in this way and also to enable him to behave in this way. Though I was not giving him money, people thought that I was, and that raised his status, even moderately.

Another dimension to the class discrepancy between us frequently emerged when he was angry with me. He sometimes vented his frustrations about literacy-based discrimination toward me by accusing me of preferring other people who were of higher status. This angered and hurt me, but my protests against this were rarely heard. He couldn't see that his status was insignificant to me. But because this was what he expected, he would project this onto me.

Our relationship often provoked this class-based discrimination, but he also used the relationship as a platform to mediate his frustration with being discriminated against. Although I interpreted our friendship as personal, I quickly realized that the entire community was invested in our relationship and that he was using the relationship to garner status for himself. For example, when we first met, I spoke very little Dagara, and he spoke almost no English. However, after years of friendship I am able to communicate in Dagara, and he also is able to speak a substantive amount of English. Now when he sees me with formally educated men or women, he speaks to me in English, demonstrating his ability to communicate "on my terms" and through an expressive mode recognized as a status marker. In fact, the visibility of our friendship had already served as a means of directing the community's attention to him in new ways.

This relationship took on more complicated dimensions as community members interpreted our interactions through the framework of an intimate relationship. In Dagaraland, men who are polygamists and monogamists alike commonly have girlfriends. Men and women do have platonic friendships but seeing men and women together in public usually provokes rumors about sexual relationships. My heightened visibility and outsider status make me extremely vulnerable to such rumors, and when he and I began spending time together in public, the presumption was that we were engaged in an intimate relationship. People even began to call me his wife/woman.[5] Though I was annoyed by this practice and tried countering those claims, truthfully, I heard many of the same rumors about anyone with whom I was spending time. I really couldn't be with men at all without people engaging in gossip, and it was clearly fruitless to spend all of my time trying to prove that I was not sleeping with someone. These rumors carried far, including prominent male members of society calling professors of mine in the United States to report me. Since I was subject to such personal scrutiny I learned to live with the gossip, understanding it as part of daily life, and moved on with my work. If it pleased people to talk about me in this way, then I tried not to listen. A close female friend, a wonderful and generous woman who spent much time helping me learn to navigate daily life, was once told that I was having an affair with her husband. I was horrified, because their family was so foundational to my life, and they are both dear friends. She cleverly remarked that if that was the case, then she was happy, because she would soon be traveling to America. Though she reacted with humor, she could have done otherwise, and I was upset by the exchange. She advised me, wisely, that if I wanted to spend all of my time listening to what other people had to say about me, then that would be the only thing I would have time for all day. I tried my best to ignore such talk and to proceed with my own best judgment.

Despite this public perception of our relationship, his behavior toward me did not immediately resonate with my own model of male sexual interest. There were conflicts in his behavior toward me that I was not initially fully able to interpret. For example, he would typically send one of his junior brothers to pick me up at night to bring me to a bar to sit with him and his friends but would be sure that we did not take the main road. I noticed this right away but didn't fully grasp that he was trying to avoid people seeing our interactions. I also didn't immediately understand the performance of status being played out between him and his juniors. Retrospectively, I can see that, like most of the relationship, his display was more for the benefit of his peers and juniors than for me at all. For men, the capacity to "send" a junior to bring someone, something, or to run an errand on their behalf cements their social positioning and articulates a hierarchy of status. Age is an extremely

---

5   In Dagara the word *pɔg* means both "wife" and "woman."

important determiner of status that crosscuts with gender and educational levels. His anxiety about class was relieved, at least temporarily, by his capacity to retrieve me via a junior.

At other times, though, he would pick me up and take me to town, to the egg stand, or to watch TV at the pharmacy. These seemingly routine activities were opportunities to show me off or, rather, to show off that we were together at all. It was the juxtaposition in his mind between what people saw as an unusual friendship and the naturalness of the friendship itself. Though I could clearly see that this was part of his motivation, I was also benefiting from our arrangement not only because I was learning rapidly about the layers of the town's social categories and interactions but also because he introduced me to what life looked like on a day-to-day basis. Sitting with him and his friends at night I heard conversations about topics that I would never have thought to ask about, and in observing their interactions with each other, I gained invaluable insight into male social ritual, language patterns, and the negotiation of minute status differentials.

In my experience, the Dagara rarely make definitive declamatory statements that line up with behavioral patterns. Since they tend to favor indirect modes of communication, observation of repeated actions and daily verbal exchanges is a more effective means of ascertaining the values and experiences of life in this area. Though I was somewhat naive about the implications of our personal interactions, I chose this mode of education, knowing that I was learning something that otherwise could not be learned. And of course, though it sounds facile, we enjoyed each other's company. He was funny; he made me laugh. If he was in a good mood, he told stories and jokes, he reminisced about his life, and he was generally pleasant company. We were at ease with each other even when we didn't know each other that well, and this was comforting and reassuring to me.

As I was getting to know him, a neighbor told me that he was married. I asked him to introduce me to his wife, and he denied being married. I was annoyed and hurt and then also became suspicious of his motivations. Shortly after, I met his wife and mother by chance while walking home one day with a Dagara female friend. As we passed his house, his mother was sitting in the front yard shucking corn, and she called over to us. She began calling me his wife and greeting me enthusiastically. His actual wife, whom I recognized but had never met, then came out and shook my hand. She spoke in Dagara to my friend, instructing her not to reveal that she was his wife. She then said in English to me that she was his sister. I raised my eyebrows, and she said again, "Sister," and patted her chest with her hand.

I interpreted this attempted deception through the localized construction of racialized sexuality as it intersects with perceptions of privilege. Like many people, he had a predetermined idea about white women based on local rumors and the media. This idea included a certainty that white women were not only monogamists but also exceptionally volatile and were likely to resort to gun violence if they suspected infidelity. I believe he was motivated by wanting us to have a relationship that would be ruined if I knew he was unavailable. I also think there is a perception that white women are both status markers and symbols of mobility and affluence. It is common to hear men speak about white women as embodying idealized beauty and elevated social class. I cannot be certain about why his wife chose to participate in this deception, but I suspect that he told her that they could only benefit from me if I thought he was single.

Breaking through this deception was a process of sustained effort that eventually resulted in his telling me that he was indeed married, though for a few months, he perpetuated this lie insistently, including involving his friends and mine. Getting past these initial constructions of difference significantly changed our relationship and allowed me to get to know his wife on different terms. Being able to speak to her openly provided me with opportunities to ask her more direct questions about their relationship and also allowed me to sit with her and talk about our families, our lives, and ourselves. I am grateful that we have moved past the deception, but I continue to struggle with the effect that public perception of my relationship with him has had on his wife.

The political economy of sex in Fielmua (like many other places) dictates the exchange of sex with material gifts or money.[6] Although he did not regularly buy me gifts, aspects of our relationship mirrored this framework. For example, not only did he always pay for food and drinks, he would send his junior brothers to my house with eggs, tea, mangos, chickens, and other small gifts. The idea of sexual exchange is often critiqued in the west as prostitution—a position that implies the absence of exchange in western sexual relationships. Though the politics are presented differently, and the materials exchanged might not be the same, the idea that sex is a mode of expressing personal intimacy in western relationships and is exclusively an exchange-based one in African cultures serves only to assert a sense of difference and

---

6   This is true in other parts of the world as well. Gloria Wekker (2006) offers an excellent and extended discussion of the political economy of sex in Afro-Surinamese women's culture.

superior moral positioning over African subjects. So, though I draw attention to the exchange norms in this area, I do not wish to imply that this is a distinct or unique feature but rather that certain material objects and money are usually exchanged. Since I was receiving those objects, it is worth noting that that exchange became part of the performance of desire in this case. I began this essay with a brief vignette in which he handed me money to buy phone credit. This is the precise type of exchange that demarcates intimacy and thus contributed to public perception.

While this mode of exchange points to intimacy, it is also important to note that gift giving is also common in other types of relationships among the Dagara. For example, any two people can give each other a gift as a gesture of respect; common among these types of gifts are eggs, bread, guinea fowls, chickens, goats (larger animals are more significant gifts), groundnuts, cloth, or other useful items. Bringing people gifts when you visit their home is common and appropriate, as is returning from travel with gifts. Rarely will you travel without people asking, "What did you bring for me?" It is also not uncommon for visitors to give money to relatives, as well as other household items. So, while gift giving often points to intimacy, it is not necessarily an overt indication of a sexual relationship, just a close one.

The idea of exchange, though not necessarily sexual, certainly does mark out sexual relationships. Women expect to receive money, soap, lotion, and other beauty maintenance items from their sexual partners, as well as phone credit, clothes, and other personal items. While these gestures are indicative of a sexual relationship, they are also common among another category of Dagara male-female relationships, that of the sɛn. The sɛn is a category of relationship between men and women, married or not, that entails giving gifts, sharing food, and helping each other in mutually beneficial ways. The category is somewhat joking and playful but is a socially acceptable mode of friendship for men and women. Relying upon this indigenous category of friendship, I tried to embrace our relationship in this new category and then was also free to give gifts to him and his family. It was my hope that by sharing with his wife (masked initially as his sister) I would be able to counterbalance rumor and perception with the respect implicit in the gift. By pivoting around gift giving, I intended to transition into a locally grounded framework, one that made me more comfortable.

Although there were many positive aspects to this relationship, I will not idealize it. Although difficult at times, it was always a negotiation of boundaries. He wanted us to have a relationship that fit squarely within Dagara social norms, but I also have boundaries and expectations for a relationship and for my work. Our friendship made it difficult for me to interact with other men from his social class. He would either approve or disapprove of my other relationships and interactions and would make his feelings known either way. The more friends I made, the more jealous he became, and he would erupt in anger and accuse me of injuring him. At times these arguments were extremely hurtful as I grappled to understand what rule I had violated or the appropriate way to respond that balanced the context with my own needs. I sometimes found that he was intentionally provoking me publicly in order to perform his status and reassert control of the interpretive frame of the relationship. Not only was I uncomfortable with those interactions, but they were not appropriate within localized Dagara social norms. We both wrestled with wanting to be friends but had personal parameters that determined how we functioned happily in relationships.

Over time we both compromised and mediated our expectations of the other in a way that has resulted in less volatile interactions. By coming to know each other and navigating these boundaries, we both became more than the products of our pasts and more than the public perception of who we should be; through building that friendship, we both were shown to be complex, flawed, vulnerable, and sometimes contradictory.

Eventually, the toll our friendship took on me became very difficult for me to bear. His anger and jealousy provoked arguments with other people in the community whom he perceived as being too close to me. I found his behavior increasingly troublesome and stifling, and I felt trapped by the ways in which the community perceived us. Protesting against being called his wife was pointless, and I could see that the only way to get away from this situation was to distance myself entirely. I realized that by my doing that he might experience a sense of shame that he was unable to maintain the relationship or continue to benefit from it in any way.

One evening in the summer of 2014, I was sitting outside with a male friend at a drinking spot when he arrived. Though I had tried to avoid being near him, I felt that getting up and leaving would be more inappropriate, and so I decided to stay and behave casually, greeting him and his companions. After some time, he got up, came over, and began stroking my hair, which was pulled back into a ponytail. He started saying, "n pɔg, n pɔg" (my wife, my wife), and then began touching my face, even leaning down to kiss my cheek. I recoiled, tried moving my face from his hands, and asked him to stop. He didn't react but went back to his conversation with his friends. I was seething, embarrassed, and angry. Touching a woman's hair or her face in public is unthinkable, especially if she is with another man. It presumes an enormous amount of intimacy. The public display was intended to posture toward his friends and my male friend more than toward me.

After he left, I asked my friend directly how he could sit quietly when I was visibly uncomfortable, even to the point of crying out for him to stop. I felt so violated; realizing that I had hoped my friend would protect me made me feel vulnerable. My friend explained that he was merely seeking a reaction; had he offered it, it would have provoked an extended dispute. By not reacting at all, he had sidestepped the conflict. Though I later saw my friend's reaction as thoughtful and reasonable, I was still left with a sense of sadness—sadness for the loss of what once was an important friendship, sadness that he felt compelled to treat me as property, sadness that I felt he was more concerned with public perception than with anything else. Yet I remain grateful for the important role that he once had in my life and for what I learned from our moments together. He attuned me to how to pay attention to relationships as modes through which to gain insight into cultural knowledge. I became more thoughtful about embodied ways of knowing. In research, as in other areas of life, relationships are not one-dimensional, linear journeys from one place to another. It's possible to learn as much from loss and confusion as it is from love; those categories need not be understood as separate and distinct.

Reflections

Although the primary focus of my research is women's musical lives, I found that it is impossible to theorize musical performance without a deeper knowledge of both men's and women's gendered subjectivities. By opening up a space in my writing and in my life for understanding Dagara men's experiences, I found that gender is not the only regulatory parameter that guides people's lives and choices.

He pointed me to a more nuanced perspective on class-based masculinity and status, as well as authorial privilege. Our relationship animated the constructions of racialized sexuality and illustrated gendered performances of desire. Learning his boundaries for transgressive behavior gave me critical insight into how gender is made real as a regulatory parameter for Dagara women. Though his understandings of my whiteness structured his interactions with me, many of our conflicts were the product of disagreements about appropriate and transgressive behavior. Those transgressions point to the ideological differences that we brought into the relationship.

I continue to have anxiety about his wife's perception of our relationship. My discomfort also reveals on some level my own perception of polygamy and whether or not I feel comfortable participating in a relationship with a married man. Informed by an African feminist perspective, my research on practices of polygamy in Dagaraland recognizes the multiple and varied experiences within these social conditions. Many Dagara women embrace polygamy as a strategy of resource sharing and collaboration. Cowives are frequently close friends who utilize the framework to ease labor distribution and form female-centric networking opportunities. Cowives also form bonds of love and commitment to each other that are nuanced and enriching. I simultaneously recognize that many Dagara men use the practice of polygamy to threaten, displace, or harm their wives. The experiences within the framework of polygamy depend heavily on individual behavior, but choice-making capacity is skewed toward male privilege. My unease around these issues reveals an unsettled conflict in my intellectual grappling with power asymmetry.

At various times we were both hurt by the other's behavior or through misunderstandings that resulted from a lack of insight into the other's unarticulated expectations. I was, in fact, unaware at certain points of my role in displays and negotiations of local power asymmetries. Relationships that form in the field are often portrayed as a replication of power asymmetry in which the ethnographer is always the more privileged party. I believe that this construction is in part reliant upon inherent notions of difference between the people with whom we work and ourselves. This model also obscures the negotiation of power in all relationships in all locations—field research often heightens the visibility of those negotiations because people bring in potentially disparate ideological parameters. Locating points of sameness has long been a technique of feminist ethnographers working to challenge the dichotomy of self and other (see Abu-Lughod 1990). Collaborative anthropologists propose a challenge to power asymmetry through the creation of intersubjective space (Lassiter 2005; White 2012). I suggest that thinking about power as multidirectional and negotiable moves us away from models of power asymmetry that focus on the field researcher's position as the exclusive site of subjectivity. Instead, we can move toward demonstrating intersubjectivity through representing connections formed, as well as multiple perspectives on those connections and their meanings.

Additionally, a focus on everyday relationships as a space of power negotiation destabilizes the tendency to rely upon broad categories of belonging. My relationship with him helped me to more clearly understand the intersecting local categories of identity that he was negotiating and that situated him within his community. Though individual identities are produced through social categorization, they often defy the simple logic of such categories. As Lila Abu-Lughod points out, focusing on individuals and our daily interactions with them "trains our gaze on flux and contradiction; and the particulars suggest that others live as we perceive ourselves living—not as automatons programmed according to 'cultural' rules or acting out social roles, but as people going through life wondering what they should do, making mistakes, being opinionated, vacillating, trying to make themselves look good, enduring tragic personal losses, enjoying others, and finding moments of laughter" (1993, 27). Retracing memory and experience provides an opportunity to think about how individuals engage with cultural codes, as well as where they depart from them. My relationship with him reveals both the cultural expectations of how the erotic is performed and instances of contradiction, where his or my behavior deviated from the norm; thus, the relationship also shows the boundaries of negotiating the erotic in these circumstances. Demonstrating emergent forms of knowledge and the conflicting realities of human life reveals the nonlinear structure of human engagement. Conflict is fruitful analytically because moments of tension represent ideological or perceptive differences that point to multidimensional understandings of appropriate and transgressive behavior.

I argue, too, that we require greater scrutiny of ethnographic encounters, including those experiences that have informed our awareness of context, meaning, and interpretation. Here, I ask what happens when we misstep? What do we make of those experiences that under later review were misguided, not fully thought through, or simply mistakes? Just as conflict can be a fruitful source of knowledge, so too can vulnerability and fallibility. The hermeneutics of vulnerability will perhaps yield new layers of ethnographic knowledge not previously revealed. In making ourselves vulnerable and in looking deeply and with thoughtful consideration into those vulnerabilities through an interpretive framework, I hope that we broaden not just what we know but what we consider to be knowledge. These are not just personal stories; these are truths that open up possibilities to ways of knowing and experiencing shared encounters.

The purpose here is not to criticize choices made by ethnographers but rather to encourage sharing details in order to achieve greater levels of insight into cultural exchanges. As we seek to decolonize representation, a scrutiny of ethnographic encounter will dislocate the uneven critical lens placed on the ethnographic subject. Recognizing exchange as a multidirectional process entails a willingness to admit the limits of our vision, as well as moments of expansion. Retracing memories and experiences provides an opportunity to reflect upon the process of coming to know. Exploring field research in all its messiness—the mistakes, missteps, tensions, and connections—potentially disrupts power imbalance, or at least calls into question authoritative knowledge. I have gestured here toward a model that interrogates power through the examination of how categories of belonging are created and maintained through the performance of desire. A more complete analysis would weave in other perspectives on these events as well (see Mongosso and Kisliuk 2003), offering a polyphony of voices that represents textually the types of dialogues and differences that occur in life.

As I have shown, though we are individuals, we interact through a web of public discourse, including the histories through which our bodies are assigned meanings. It is our challenge to represent those entanglements and the ideologies that constitute them. It is my hope that by sharing this information we can theorize new ways of bridging the gaps between research and life and discuss modes of representation that reflect the relationships we form, in all their complexity.

References

Abu-Lughod, Lila. 1990. "Can There Be a Feminist Ethnography?" *Women and Performance: A Journal of Feminist Theory* 5 (1): 7–27.

———. 1993. *Writing Women's Worlds: Bedouin Stories*. Berkeley: University of California Press.

Alexander, M. Jacqui. 2005. *Pedagogies of Crossing: Meditations on Feminism, Sexual Politics, Memory, and the Sacred*. Durham, NC: Duke University Press.

Allen, Jafari. 2012. "One Way or Another: Erotic Subjectivity in Cuba." *American Ethnologist* 39 (2): 325–38.

Behar, Ruth, and Deborah A. Gordon, eds. 1995. *Women Writing Culture*. Berkeley: University of California Press.

Chen, Nancy N. 1992. "Speaking Nearby: A Conversation with Trinh T. Minh-ha." *Visual Anthropology Review* 8 (Spring): 82–91.

Chernoff, John Miller. 2003. *Hustling Is Not Stealing: Stories of an African Bar Girl*. Chicago: University of Chicago Press.

Cusick, Suzanne G. [1994] 2006. "On a Lesbian Relationship with Music: A Serious Effort Not to Think Straight." In *Queering the Pitch: The New Gay and Lesbian Musicology*, edited by Philip Brett, Elizabeth Wood, and Gary C. Thomas, 67–83. New York: Routledge.

Fernea, Elizabeth Warnock. 1965. *Guests of the Sheik: An Ethnography of an Iraqi Village*. New York: Doubleday.
Gill, Lyndon. 2010. "Transfiguring Trinidad and Tobago: Queer Cultural Production, Erotic Subjectivity and the Praxis of Black Queer Anthropology." PhD diss., Harvard University.
Hahn, Tomie. 2007. *Sensational Knowledge: Embodying Culture through Japanese Dance*. Middletown, CT: Wesleyan University Press.
Jones, Omi Osun Joni L., Lisa L. Moore, and Sharon Bridgforth, eds. 2010. *Experiments in a Jazz Aesthetic: Art, Activism, Academia, and the Austin Project*. Austin: University of Texas Press.
Kisliuk, Michelle. [1998] 2001. *Seize the Dance! BaAka Musical Life and the Ethnography of Performance*. Oxford: Oxford University Press.
Kulick, Don, and Margaret Willson, eds. 1995. *Taboo: Sex, Identity and Erotic Subjectivity in Anthropological Fieldwork*. New York: Routledge.
Lassiter, Luke Eric. 2005. *The Chicago Guide to Collaborative Ethnography*. Chicago: University of Chicago Press.
Lewin, Ellen, and William Leap, eds. 1996. *Out in the Field: Reflections of Gay and Lesbian Anthropologists*. Chicago: University of Illinois Press.
Lorde, Audre. 1984. "Uses of the Erotic: The Erotic as Power." In *Sister Outsider: Essays and Speeches*, 53–59. Freedom, CA: Crossing Press.
Lortat-Jacob, Bernard. 1995. *Sardinian Chronicles*. Chicago: University of Chicago Press.
Markowitz, Fran, and Michael Ashkenazi, eds. 1999. *Sex, Sexuality, and the Anthropologist*. Urbana: University of Illinois Press.
Minh-ha, Trinh T. 1989. *Woman, Native, Other: Writing Postcoloniality and Feminism*. Bloomington: Indiana University Press.
Mohanty, Chandra Talpade. 2003. "Under Western Eyes." In *Feminism without Borders: Decolonizing Theory, Practicing Solidarity*, 17–43. Durham, NC: Duke University Press.
Mongosso, Justin Serge, and Michelle Kisliuk. 2003. "Representing a Real Man: Music, Upheaval and Relationship in Centrafrique." *Emergences* 13 (1–2): 34–46.
Newton, Esther. 1993. "My Best Informant's Dress: The Erotic Equation in Fieldwork." *Cultural Anthropology* 8 (1):3–23.
Spivak, Gayatri. 1988. "Can the Subaltern Speak?" In *Marxism and the Interpretation of Culture*, edited by Cary Nelson and Lawrence Grossberg, 271–13. Urbana: University of Illinois Press.
Stacey, Judith. 1988. "Can There Be a Feminist Ethnography." *Women's Studies International Forum* 11 (1): 21–27.
Stoller, Paul. 1997. *Sensuous Scholarship*. Philadelphia: University of Pennsylvania Press.

Wekker, Gloria. 2006. *The Politics of Passion: Women's Sexual Culture in the Afro-Surinamese Diaspora*. New York: Columbia University Press.

White, Bob W. 2012. "From Experimental Moment to Legacy Moment: Collaboration and the Crisis of Representation." *Collaborative Anthropologies* 5 (1): 65–97.

Chapter Five

Thick Descriptions

Catherine M. Appert

This essay contains descriptions of sexual harassment and references sexual assault.

Shortly before 2 a.m., I reach my limit, overcome by one, or two, or fifty touches too many. My awareness resets at every squeeze of my thigh, every touch on my shoulder that becomes a caress in its slow, silent recession of skin from skin, dropping downward to light upon my back, my hip before pulling away in a brief respite. Begin again. The tacit timer clicks along, my body tensing as I wait for him to wrench it back to zero; still, I startle at the pressure of his hand reattached. I'm alert to where he is at every moment, to people's eyes on us, to the way he claims and directs my body, pulling me here and there until we move like conjoined twins connected not just at the hand but at the shoulder, arm, and hip; linked—no matter how many times I make myself small and pull away.

Ethnography is haunted by stories left untold. Lines of prose thicken into images of life, of being there, of presence narrated into truth only through absences and unspoken moments. Experience splinters in the writing, where thickness redacts as much as it reveals. I am pulled to invert this thickness, to throw the unseen into relief. To read the gaps, to recognize the fictions; to hear what's not said, what can't be named. To imagine what becomes of scholarship—to the publishable account—when description reveals what it is meant to conceal. To speak that which in turn becomes unsayable.

He had picked me up nearly twelve hours earlier. Emerging from the hotel, I glanced right and left, my eyes initially passing over the ▮▮▮▮ parked across the way, expecting a silhouette ▮▮▮▮▮, realizing his was the lone car on this sandy expanse passing as a road, drifting toward him. A man sitting outside the neighboring restaurant took my hesitation as an opening, hurling greetings that intruded on the midday quiet; I paused in the abandoned road, torn between a spectacle of rudeness for the interlocutor ahead and my resistance to the stranger behind. In those seconds of indecision, he looked past me to the car. Oh, you're with a man—he said, returning to his careless squat in the shade of a striped awning.

███. I climb in and we drive to ████████ and in a constant stream of words he tells me about his projects, about how ███. We turn off the highway onto sandy roads, his voice rising above resounding layers of metal, the thunder of clanging shocks, the delicate clinking of my earrings. He tells me ██. I wish I could record the conversation, knowing there's no way I will remember everything. But we've only just met, and so I merely listen.

Arriving at the venue where he will perform tonight, ████████, we greet a group of men—████████████, ████████████. We sit among them, scraping plastic lawn chairs across uneven tiles to cluster around one of many tables tucked under a metal roof that borders an open courtyard with a covered stage in one corner. He orders me a Fanta, though I would have asked for Coke; beads of sweat roll down the glass bottle to coalesce in a puddle on the plastic tablecloth. The men make tea, boiling loose, dry green leaves, adding sugar and sprigs of fresh mint, pouring it back and forth between shot glasses until a froth forms on the top, passing the glasses around and refilling them until everyone is served. I decline, saying I usually only drink the first, bitter round, and they laugh—whether at what I've said or how I've said it, I can't tell. The tea's familiar rumble and swish advance like clockwork under waves of chatter that overcome and then recede from the voices inside and the half conversation of a woman on her phone in the courtyard.

I settle into the long-familiar rhythm of voices and boiling water and pouring tea, letting my attention slip away until language becomes noise and I could be in any living room or studio with new acquaintances or old friends all performing the same predictable ritual, passing cups around in an order determined by a complex and unspoken nexus of age, gender, and position, refilling and passing them again. Over the years I've come to distinguish the first, second, and final round by the shifting balance of tea, sugar, and mint, from a parching yet somehow pleasureful bitterness to a cloying lightness that sticks in my mouth until I choke it down, hoping beyond hope that the fresh mint added at the last minute will spare my stomach, eventually learning to decline without offending.

Hours later he'll tell me that here, finally, is the first round I was waiting for, and I'll take it, assuming they've started over with a new box of tea, only to gag on its sweetness and wonder if I've somehow confused my ▮ vocabulary, or if he is playing with me.

I take in the space, jotting short notes on my phone to jog my memory later. Murals cover the walls, familiar folk art like I've seen in ▮. Primary colors, red, green, yellow, and black, swirl together into landscapes of round huts and gnarled trees as stationary as the stick figures that move among them. To my left, the wall reads ▮. To my right, ▮. In the courtyard's bright patch of sun, women rehearse for a dance performance at ▮, and I watch them for a while, my body tilting like a flower toward the sun, lured by the familiar movements I'll never join. Their bare feet mark rhythms on tile; their voices signal transitions and entrances. By the time the drummers arrive the women, like me, are already drenched in sweat.

He is a gregarious man; he tells stories in ▮ and ▮ and repeats them in English for me; his slight hesitation and narrowed eyes make me wonder if he understands when I dutifully respond in my native tongue. He does voices and impressions, recounts direct speech, tells of getting informed on in ▮ for ▮, traveling to ▮ for performances. At his tacit insistence I abandon ▮ completely, slowing and quantitizing my speech with careful breaks between words, avoiding contractions, policing my tongue until the measured weight of this alien English silences me. He tells me about his new radio show; he's just changed stations ▮ because ▮. He insisted they buy him a new microphone—Show Mic 58, a leading vocals mic. For backup, he says, they could have an SM-57. Because many people prefer the sweet melodies of a woman for backup rather than a man. So that's a woman's mic ▮.

A mango drops on the metal roof with the force of a gunshot, and sunlight breaks through. I jerk back, startled.

As the conversation continues into the afternoon, he begins to grasp my thigh, or to grab loosely at my hand, hanging down between our seats. He transfers credit to my phone though I don't need it. He leans close to show me pictures, of ▮▮▮▮▮▮▮▮▮▮▮▮▮▮▮▮▮▮▮▮▮▮▮▮▮▮▮▮, of ▮▮▮▮▮▮▮▮▮▮, of ▮▮▮▮▮▮▮▮. Every image is prefaced by a touch.

In a haze of smoke from burnt paper and the leaves mixed with seeds and dust and nicotine and tobacco, he calls me ganja lady, although I've abstained. He responds to the question in my raised eyebrow, saying sometimes just breathing the smoke can affect you more than smoking. I silently wonder if this is wishful thinking.

The afternoon wanes; the courtyard fills with shadow and sound and movement and people, a cheerful and expansive sociality buzzing from corner to corner. Alone in a sea of connection, I send a text message across an ocean, searching for someone to tell me to do what I already know I should. She responds that she loves me, she prays I'm safe, but she cannot—cannot hear this, cannot help me, can only not, not in this moment, maybe not in any moment ever. Her curt explanation, a blunt disclosure of recent survival, sends a shock wave through me, disrupting the closed circuit of tension in my mind and body. Across thousands of miles, her pain and my fear of pain collide and recoil.

Violences resonate across oceans, blurring ethnography and life; outsiders linked by an emic perspective on what it is to *be* (women) there or here or anywhere.

We sit for hours, until ▮▮▮▮▮▮▮▮▮▮▮▮▮▮▮▮▮▮▮▮▮▮▮▮▮▮ rain begins to sound against the metal roof like an automatic weapon chasing us into the dark, airless space of the interior structure, where bright murals give way to the dreary spoils of a pillaged thrift store. Evergreen forest at twilight (photo printed on canvas). "▮▮▮▮▮▮▮▮▮▮▮▮▮▮▮▮▮▮▮▮," reads a dystopic space scene; as my eyes adjust to the light, galactic shadows give way to tableware, artfully arranged on an infinite background. An oil painting of a steepled church in a meadow completes the collection, its gilded frame an incongruous gleam of glamour in the cheerless room. ▮▮

I'm pressed so hard against the side of the couch ▮▮▮▮▮▮▮▮▮▮▮▮▮▮▮▮▮▮▮▮▮▮▮▮▮▮▮▮▮▮▮▮▮▮ that I am sitting at a slant, my small bag the only space between us, his legs spread wide and a foot of tattered cushion stretching away on his other side. The drumming of the rain

██ mutes external sounds until all there is this, us, resonant bodies, a noisy quiet.

When it stops, we go outside for the soundcheck. On the wall above the speakers a cat perches, tense and still.

I retreat inside, settle into a ragged armchair whose exposed foam padding is riddled with holes suggestive of what creeps and crawls within. I press myself down, the high back shielding my torso, the deep seat enclosing my thighs, the leather wings framing my ears, dulling but not escaping his voice as it blows in from the courtyard.

[Writing these notes the following day, here is where I break].

Fuck this fieldwork and fuck this dude and his wandering hands that never wander so far as to belie the ambiguity of his movements and give me an indisputable something to contest, to push back against. I'm sitting here holding out for a few images and a colorful performance description, the kind that spice up my work and delight colleagues at conferences. And fuck them too, and this insistence on audiovisual documenting when words on the page must ultimately be enough; and when we were taught to position our microphones and cameras, where were the directions about how to position our bodies; when were we ever told how certain bodies are already positioned, (im)moveable, vulnerable, in service always to the data we collect, the scholarship we produce?

I had convinced myself to just stay until he performed, that otherwise the whole day, the hours of unwelcome touches and secondhand smoke, would truly be for nothing. But surely nothing about ████████████████████████████████ is worth those endless minutes earlier tonight where we left the club, driving to the middle of nowhere, arriving in the pitch black of a power outage and entering the implied silhouette of a house ██████, ███████████, with someone I thought to trust because he is a friend of a friend of a friend, my body rigid with fear it threatens to violently expel and I'm frozen holding in tears and vomit wondering where I will burst first, standing with my hand on my phone to call—who, when everyone I know is hours away?

In this somber courtyard, the sudden and unexpected silence of the courtyard bears down on me. I could leave, but no taxis patrol ████████'s dark sandy streets, full of his neighbors and kin, the shopkeepers who gave him candies as a child, the street food vendors who went to primary school with his mother.

And fuck me for questioning my own perception because his brother showed up and ultimately *nothing happened* beyond hours and hours of grasping at my body like a woman at a market stall on an endless search for the perfectly ripe mango.

We use the word "friend" to describe those who become interlocutors through arbitrary connections; nothing more than a step across a sunny street renders the man behind a stranger and the one ahead a friend. In a dark alley, that unmoored step would be laughable if it weren't so terrifying. Description enacts these fictions of friendship, thickening acquaintance into something that masks the extractive and transactive nature of fieldwork, corrects and flattens its power imbalances. But the fiction of friendship also redacts power as it renders particular bodies susceptible, catches them up in transactions to which we've somehow always already consented by initiating an ethnographic relationship. Friendship, not preceding ethnographic experience but rather invented in description, masks the institutionally produced conditions of fear under which we work and which are its redacted double.

Inside the house, his brother awaits; they ▮▮.

We head back to ▮▮▮▮▮▮▮. I take in the transformed space, jotting mental notes, finding refuge in research, in the cataloging of details. ▮▮▮▮ music plays above the clinking of bottles and the chatter and flirting of the crowd. There are more men than women, many more. ▮▮.

I've been wondering all day who Emu is, or what the word might mean in ▮▮▮▮▮▮▮. Now, surveying the club from my seat in reassuring proximity to the main door, I see painted over the entry to the inner room the words "Emu Lounge" curving over a black outline of an emu bird, and I laugh to myself, or at myself. Sometimes to discover is to forget what we already know, to miss what's right in front of us. Some things are exactly what they seem.

We immerse ourselves in language, customs, relationships; our learning aims to erase or render unsure what we already know. But this touch on the small of my back, this hand resting on my knee, is not a discovery of ethnographic experience. It is known without being sought, learned in unwilling immersion. Its familiarity is that of high school teachers, of college professors, of senior faculty in hotel room parties when I am still a student, of colleagues at conferences all these years later when surely, I thought, I've aged beyond. Layered inscriptions of dominance that entrain the body since childhood to silently avoid or survive but never challenge.

Spent, I think about my students, how I have hoped to teach them differently, even as the crushing weight of institutional pressure to produce still threatens to override my own sense. I think about the article I'd hoped to write, the larger project I'd planned to carry out. I think about what will happen later when he insists on driving me home.

Shortly before 2 a.m., just as his set is about to begin, I plead a sick stomach, tell him my ride is outside. He looks at me with disbelief, powerless in this exact moment to hold me.

What is it, after all, that we describe through ethnography? Where do we abandon fact for fiction, detail for gloss; when do we shield the subjects of description? I could tell you where the venue was, what it was really called, that the forest was neither evergreen nor at twilight, that it wasn't painted on canvas. When such fictions fall short, when they can't protect us or them, what must be redacted and who does that redaction protect? How to articulate this inaudibility, to let the holes and silences speak, to dwell in the unvoiced, the unsaid, the unrevealed? We might look *for*, instead of *past*, the gaps in description, read them not as gaps in experience but gaps in what can be said. We might, as I have done here, render them visible, invert ethnographic redaction, return to the negative of the moment of encounter and refuse to develop it into an "ethnography" whose presences emerge only through strategic absences and muting.

Arrived at ▮▮▮ hotel in the dark and quiet, I pass two men smoking on a patio outside their room. One greets me with the same smile he wore yesterday when he said he'd like to take advantage of my husband's absence and asked for my room number; I know him by his missing tooth and ▮▮▮, ▮▮▮▮▮▮▮. I walk on, feeling his eyes on my back, sure he's counting the doors between us. In my room a flying cockroach the size of my hand perches on the curtains; I recoil, stare at it for a moment, defeated, wanting it gone but hesitant to open my door again to the night and the men seated not twenty meters away, watching me. Tears mix with the limp flow of the shower pattering gently on tile as I wash the smoke out of my hair and the shame off my body, lathering over and over until the bottle is empty. I send a text saying how great it was to meet, how sorry I am I had to leave. The bodies of the roaches I've flipped over and left to die twitch in grotesque synthesis with my still crawling skin. Slower, smaller, smoother, until I finally sleep.

Chapter Six

Entering the Lives of Others

Entangled Intimacies, Trauma, and Performance

Ama Oforiwaa Aduonum

Moving from silence into speech is for the oppressed, the colonized, the exploited, and those who stand and struggle side by side a gesture of defiance that heals, that makes new life and new growth possible. It is that act of speech, of 'talking back,' that is no mere gesture of empty words, that is the expression of our movement from object to subject—the liberated voice

—bell hooks

Sɛ woankasa wo tiri ho a, yeyi wo ayi bɔne

[If you don't talk about your head, you get a bad haircut]
—Ghanaian Akan proverb

Bloomington-Normal, Illinois. June 5, 2020. My friend and I are on our morning walk on the Constitution Trail. We are discussing many topics, including aging and exercising, hypertension, music, Black Lives Matter, the police. We spend a long time talking about the protests following the killing of George Floyd, Breonna Taylor, Ahmaud Arbery. I tell him that true to the Ghanaian Akan saying, ɔhohoɔ ani tuatua hɔ kwa, "The visitor's eyes do not perceive," as a female Ghanaian immigrant it took me decades to understand the effect of race relations on Black bodies. Like some Africans who come to America, I tell him, I was very naïve and oblivious to discourses on race, racial politics, and anti-Blackness, and how those affect Black lives in America. I saw, but I did not see. I tell him that my journey, most of which involved Black women, had been long and fraught with tension and misunderstanding. He asks, "What was it like for you?" He asks for specifics, for some key moments on that journey. I pause. I reflect.

As a Ghanaian Akan female scholar, performer, and a mother living in America, my body is on edge. The effects of white-body supremacy that live and breathe in my own body, the result of my experiences as a Ghanaian woman living in America, have me trauma ghosted, that recurrent or pervasive sense that danger is around the corner, or something terrible is going to happen.[1] I police what I say to white people, upholding their emotional patriarchy (Armah).[2] Our Ghanaian Akan Elders say, *Nea ɔwɔ aka no suro sonsono*, "She who has been bitten by a snake is afraid of a worm." From my initial experiences and interactions in this country I am cautious about what I say to Black women, whose trauma has confronted me. Like many Black mothers, I too fear for my son's life. When my son starts to jog during a walk, my heart skips a beat, and I am tempted to ask him to walk instead. I scan the area to see if any white person is watching him. When he pulls his hoodie over his head, I want to ask him to pull it back down. His question, after the murder of Philando Castille, haunts me, "Will they kill me too when I grow up, Mama?" Does my fear for my son's life and this shared trauma with Black mothers indicate that I have finally arrived in America,

---

1 According to Resmaa Menakem, "white-body supremacy" is a term that describes how the white body is elevated above all bodies. The white body is the ostensibly supreme standard against which other bodies' humanity is measured. The attitudes, convictions, and beliefs of white-body supremacy are reflexive cognitive side effects, like the belief of a claustrophobe that the walls are closing in. These ideas have been reinforced through institutions as practice, procedures, and standards. https://medium.com/@rmenakem/white-supremacy-as-a-trauma-response-ce631b82b975. "Trauma ghosted" is the body's recurrent or pervasive sense that danger is just around the corner or something terrible is going to happen any moment. (See Menakem 2017, 8).

2 According to Emotional Justice Institute founder Esther Armah, "emotional patriarchy" is a system that prioritizes, privileges, centralizes the feelings of white men no matter the cost or consequence. Some of these consequences lead to brutality on Black bodies, many times, death. https://www.theaiej.com/emotional-justice.

that I have more in common with Black women than what I perceived to be the case when I first arrived in America? Disconnections and connections. Can trauma disconnect and connect simultaneously? If silence is a symptom of trauma, could performance restore speech, inching toward emotional justice (Armah) and healing?[3]

This essay examines my connections and disconnections with women of African descent, our trauma, and the transformative power of performance. I explore our entangled and diasporic intimacies. Through these encounters and through my performance art piece, *Walking with My Ancestors* (2019) I explore (1) how histories of enslavement and colonialism, language, religion—and hairstyling—generate connections and disconnections between me and those who share that history and (2) how performance serves as a site of protest, recovery, and healing.

Tears They Cannot Stop! Entangled and Diasporic Intimacies, Transatlantic Imaginations, and Trauma[4]

Our Wise Ghanaian Akan Elders say, ɔnantefoɔ sene oni ne ɔse asɛm, "The walker knows more than her mother and father." First as a student, then as researcher and performer, I have walked with women of African descent during my sojourn in the United States. With Black female students at Fisk University, with the Urban Bush Women, and with other African American women in different contexts I have built relationships and learned about their lives, especially through music and dance. But ɔnantefoɔ na ohunu amane, "The walker also suffers," and some of these walks were crosscut and

---

[3] According to Esther Armah, "emotional justice" is a visionary framework for racial healing that centers the well-being of global Black people developed over a decade across cities, communities, and continents. This framework does three things: (1) It explores how a legacy of untreated trauma due to systemic injustice from global histories of enslavement, colonialism, and apartheid shapes how we learn, lead, work, build and love as global Black and white people; (2) it interrogates emotions as structural, as a key component to creating and upholding systemic injustice; and (3) it centers global Black people and our healing, our emotionality and our interiority; it engages global white people to do their work of dismantling. Emotional justice has four pillars: Racialized Emotionality, Emotional Patriarchy, Emotional Currency, and Emotional Economy. https://www.facebook.com/emotionaljustice.

[4] Alluding to Dyson 2017.

enabled by legacies of slavery and colonialism, by issues of gender, race, and culture, and by conflicts in personality, location, field situation, and language. Furthermore, my identity as a Ghanaian female scholar muddled, but also facilitated those interactions. For example, my journey as a researcher with an all-female vocal group fell through because I used the wrong terminology when discussing my topic with them.

> Sweet Honey in the Rock
> Mothers, aunties, sisters
> I lost you at conception
> A miscarriage
> Missing an opportunity to connect
> Aaa
> *Obi nkura nanka, nnyae nanka, nnyae nkose, "Meḥnunie a anka"*
> One does not have the opportunity, dismiss the opportunity to declare, "If I had the opportunity"
> I did
> We could not gather

Some encounters developed into enduring relationships; others were short-lived. My experience with Black students at Fisk University, my work with Urban Bush Women, my brief walk with an American woman at Gorée Island, and with local Senegalese women there, were characterized by connections and disconnections. Our histories, language, gender, religion, and legacies of slavery and colonialism connected and disconnected us, sometimes concurrently. The journey was long, involving uncertainty, self-doubt, low self-esteem, loneliness, friendship, laughter, joy, and mourning.

Misconstruing Fisk

Like many Africans who travel to the United States, I came on a student visa in the late 1980s to attend college.[5] I majored in Western classical voice.[6] Like many Ghanaians with whom I grew up, before arriving I did not know

---

5   See Apraku 1991, Arthur 2000, and Mwakikagile 2006 for other reasons why Africans leave the continent for the United States.

6   Upon completion, I attended graduate school. Later, I was able to find an employer who petitioned for the immigration services to admit me as a permanent resident under the third preference category of the immigration law.

that Black people lived in America. I did not watch much television, and my Elders didn't talk about Black Americans; so in spite of my high school education, I knew little about the Atlantic slave trade.[7] Even though I read and even saw a production of Ama Ata Aidoo's *Dilemma of a Ghost* (1964) in which Ato, a Ghanaian Fante man, brings from America a Black woman as his wife, that did not create for me a historical awareness of slavery and white supremacy.[8] Like Ato's family members in Aidoo's play, I accepted the ongoing Eurocentric narrative that, despite evidence to the contrary, the United States is "a white man's country" ([1964] 1971, 12). So, when I arrived at Fisk University in Nashville, Tennessee in 1986, I was shocked that it was a predominantly Black institution.

Some of the students at Fisk made fun of my accent, my clothes, and my Afro hairstyle. Disconnections. Not yet sure they were Americans, I wondered if perhaps they came from parts of Africa that I did not know about. I did not have the courage, the understanding, or even the American English accent to ask such questions. Many of the students, including my roommate, denied her (their) ancestral connection to Africa and claimed rather a Native American or West Indian ancestry. Some of the Black students, at the time, echoed the Tarzan-inspired racist stereotype that Africans lived in trees and did not wear any clothes.[9] I felt simultaneously the pressure to conform while trying to remember who I was and to be myself. Being myself, though, came with some repercussions.

In Ghana everyone looked like me and spoke the Ghanaian languages I spoke, or if not, at least understood my English. But arriving at Fisk, though almost everyone looked like me, they were clueless about the Ghanaian

---

7   See Agenti 2007, Holsey 2008, and Osagie 2000 for the African silences surrounding slavery.

8   The Fante are an Akan group located on the coast of Ghana.

9   I was not the first African to attend Fisk University. According to Walter L. Williams, the "university attracted Africans in the 1870 and 1880s" (1980, 229). Many of these students were sponsored by faith-based organizations like the American Missionary Association, a Christian abolition group that helped freed Blacks in the South after the Civil War. The organization sponsored five Africans to Fisk. Those later settled in Sierra Leone as missionaries. In fact, according to Williams, the *Fisk Bulletin* demonstrated great interest in African missionaries by remarking that "African students forcibly illustrate the vital relations which the Christian education of the Colored people of the South [sought to] sustain the civilization and evangelization of the Dark Continent" (1980, 229).

languages I spoke, and when I spoke English, I was asked to repeat it again and again. So, I just did not speak. Silenced. The different hairstyles that I was used to—corn row, Afro, braids, *dansinkran* short cut, scarves, were not common.[10] I felt alienated, alone, depressed, and sad. Disconnections. Our histories were entangled; our aesthetics were entangled; our cultural experiences were entangled due to centuries of "nursing at the tits of white supremacy."[11] I was not aware of any platforms to discuss these issues. *Ah! ɔhɔhoɔ asɛm yɛ awerɛho*; "The visitor is pitiful!" Even today, this initial experience continues to define how I interact with African Americans.

> Fisk University
> Black female students
> Brown-skin girls
> I was your sister across the Atlantic
> Separated by histories of racialized slavery
> Colonialism
> Terror
> Distance
> Longing
> Entanglements
> The white-body supremacy that lived in your bodies
> Lived in mine
> Our trauma
> Dis/connections
> We were deprived of Lorde's intimacies

Due to my experience at Fisk, for a long time I shut myself off from all Americans, and Black American women in particular. I did not allow myself to experience the full richness of African American culture. While the experiences with women at Fisk University were important for my broad initial introduction to American racial politics, to finer-grained colorism in the Black community, and to the politics of hair within those realms, it was my interaction with another group of African American women that helped open the platform to engage with those issues. Urban Bush Women would become my bridge.

---

10 In the late 1960s and '70s, especially as it coincided with Independent Movements in Africa, the Afro in America was associated with the "back to Africa" and Black Power movements.

11 Pamela Hoff, "African Radicalism" Zoom discussion, June 2020.

Connections and Disconnections with Urban Bush Women[12]

I first met the founder of Urban Bush Women, Jawole Willa Jo Zollar, in 1997 when I was a graduate student at Florida State University. A petite Black woman with a powerful presence, during our first chat she learned that I was Ghanaian and told me about her trips to Nigeria and Mozambique. She also told me about Urban Bush Women (UBW), her Brooklyn-based dance company, gave me numerous pamphlets and other information, and invited me to a performance. After more conversations and a mutual decision that I would work with her company for my dissertation research, I accepted Zollar's offer to participate in the company's first Summer Institute for artists held at FSU, which involved workshops, dance classes, discussions, and games. On the first day, when I walked into a room full of mostly Black women, I almost screamed, remembering my experiences at Fisk, "Ahhhhhh!!!!" Ghanaian Akan Elders say, *Nea ɔwɔ aka no suro sonsono*, "She who has been bitten by a snake is afraid of a worm." Will they leave the room like my roommate did at Fisk? Will they say I smell? I wanted to leave. Maybe if I don't speak, they won't hear my accent and notice that I come from Ghana. But unlike at Fisk, the fifty or so participants at this workshop—from Brazil, Cuba, Haiti, and the United States—these women had an expanded knowledge of Africa and referred to it as the motherland, the ancestral land. Connections. Many of the participants wore Afros, braids, and locks. Some wore dashikis and a few used African names. They even asked me the meaning of some Ghanaian names: Kofi, boy born on Friday; Ama, girl born on Saturday; Adwoa, Monday girl; Kwabena, Tuesday boy. For a moment, I was disturbed by what could be the reducing or essentializing of Africa—the Afros, the dashikis—styles that many continental Africans don't wear. Disconnections. However, these reservations diminished when I came to critically understand these things as a way of "performing the African diaspora" or a "diasporic intimacy" that

> does not promise a comforting recovery of identity through shared nostalgia for the lost home and homeland. In fact, it's the opposite. It might be seen as the mutual enchantment of two immigrants from different parts of the world or as the sense of the fragile coziness of a foreign home. Just as one learns to live with alienation and reconciles oneself to the uncanniness of the world around and to

---

12 Part of this section is from Aduonum 2011.

the strangeness of the human touch, there comes a surprise, a pang of intimate recognition, a hope that sneaks in through the back door, punctuating the habitual estrangement of everyday life abroad. (Boym 1998, 501)

We danced to Senegambian drumming and call-and-response singing; we also danced the Cuban rumba, Brazilian fightdance capoeira, and moved to the music of Haitian Vodou and Cuban Santería. Victor Turner's "utopian vision of world community based on mutual respect and enjoyment of cultural differences, exchanges of feelings as well as of ideas, and the increasing ability of people to experience and re-experience each other's cultural identities" (as paraphrased in Schechner and Appel 1990, 1) was celebrated in this space. Performance would create a space to share our diasporic intimacies. Connections.

Oh, how I danced! "You from Africa?" they asked, "Yes!" But soon my comfort gave way again to my persistent naïveté when I made a comment that offended: a light-skinned participant cut off her hair during the third week of the workshop. I asked, "Are you trying to be more Black?" She frowned and walked away. Our entangled histories.[13] Though I had learned about the fraught notion of "passing," about the brown bag test that had been prevalent, and about the fine-toothed comb test, I was still oblivious to how traumatic and sensitive these topics were for African Americans.[14] Workshops on "Undoing Racism," panel discussions, plays, dancing, and other readings helped with that. By the end of the four-week session, I realized why I had offended her. I apologized. But I was still "arriving in America."[15]

---

13 John Arthur perceptively acknowledges that "African-born and American blacks are divided by history, and by a lack of understanding and appreciation" (2000, 81). See also Yoku Shaw-Taylor's discussion about this issue (2007). Brown bag/paper bag test, an element of the color complex, was a ritual once used by some Black fraternities and sororities to discriminate again darker-skinned blacks. The fine-toothed comb test was used to discriminate against Blacks with coily and curly hair.

14 During the final week of the institute, my modern dance class had the opportunity to learn *Batty Moves*. In a line, together with a group of young and older Black women, I moved my butt like I did not care. According to Edward T. Hall, "humans are tied to each other by hierarchies of rhythm that are culture-specific and expressed through language and body" (1976, 64), so I did not care.

15 My metaphor for the initial steps to understanding and embodying white-body supremacy.

When I observed rehearsals and saw a performance of Urban Bush Women's *Batty Moves*, in which African American dancers shook their buttocks freely like I had done back in Ghana, I could see what I had not seen during my early years in America.[16] It was a platform to perform our diasporic intimacies.

A four-beat Senegambian rhythmic break cued a section in which four dancers came onstage with gyrating hip movements, to a mix of Senegalese *sabar* and Haitian Ibo rhythms.[17] The tempo picked up within the section and climaxed with another rhythmic break that led into a song. The seven dancers wore black tank tops, matching bike shorts, and UBW shirts tied around their waists and knotted in front.[18] Their costumes hinted at what they intended to do—kick butts! In the next section, they all moved upstage to sing the "Big Mama" song, accompanied by a groovy New Orleans second line rhythm, the type that is heard during funeral processions.[19] What was so engaging and exciting about this section was the way in which each dancer elaborated on the song by inserting her own lyrics, until she arrived at the point where the others joined in. One of the dancers performed her version of the song in a hip-hop rhythm:

> I'm an African American
> Of the Seminole tribe
> My legs are big and my hips are wide
> I am big and strong but I am sweet and shy
> Back home they call me "coffee" cuz I grind so fine

The other dancers sang their versions of the song, sharing their African American heritage but also emphasizing their other identities—Seminole, Bajan, Cuban, and Nuyorican—to illustrate both individual and collective identities as women of the African diaspora. The group answered each solo

---

16 The performance included three dances: *Transitions* (1996), *Bitter Tongue* (1987), and *Batty Moves* (1995). *Batty Moves* was commissioned by the Philadelphia Dance Company and premiered in 1995.
17 Sabar is both an instrument of five to seven drums and a music and dance rhythm from Dakar. Ibo is a rhythm associated with a Haitian deity of the same name.
18 The seven dancers were Dafinah Blacksher, Michelle Dorant, Carolina Garcia, Dionne Kamara, Kristin McDonald, and Amara Tabor-Smith.
19 According to Junior "Gabu" Wedderburn, former UBW musician and collaborator on the project, "Big Mama" means "big butt mama" (2009).

with a refrain, "Wooo Big Mama, Big Mama, yeah, yeah," and the segment ended with a funny adaptation of "Old McDonald Had a Farm"—which I was not familiar with. The line "with a quack-quack here …" was humorously transformed into "Big Mama here, Big Mama there, wooo Big Mama you're everywhere."

I enjoyed how each performer shared her own personal voice and movement. I was fascinated by the combination of sensuous movements with athleticism, and the blend of slow and brisk motions. I was particularly enthralled by the Africana sensibilities in the movement vocabulary and music, and in the integration of music and dance. The emphasis on live drumming, with its use of different timbres, created dense texture; the different rhythmic patterns interlocked, overlapped, and clashed, creating polyrhythms and syncopated patterns that caused excitement. All these stirred me and made my "memory walk," as Yarimar Bonilla (2011) describes it in her research with labor activists in postcolonial Guadeloupe where she participated in a "form of […] political and historical walking." The Creole slogan for these events, according to Bonilla, is *fe memwa maché*, which literally means to "make your memory walk" or "take your memory on a walk." The phrase refers to the process of thinking back, scanning your memory for past events; when something or someone causes you to recall something, they are making your memory walk.

One of my memory walks occurred during the part of the dance where performers defined themselves by singing individualized versions of the "Big Mama" song. I was reminded of one of the childhood games that we played in Ghana, at nine and ten years old. I would proudly stand in front of my playmates and authorize myself.

> I am Ama Oforiwaa
> ɔhɔɔha Náná
> I, member of the Kwahu people
> Those who are known to stretch their money
> We are teased for being stingy pɛ-pɛɛ
> La!
> …
> I can drum, I can sing, and I can dance
> I can also shake my buttocks like this

Later in *Batty Moves* came the "Warrior liberation butt solos." In a semicircle formation facing the audience, the dancers gyrated and rotated their hips and buttocks, swinging, rolling, and shaking in tantalizing, even aggressive ways. One of the dancers stepped into the half-circle to perform her version of a good butt shake. She isolated her buttocks by "freezing" her torso, then she jiggled her butt to the left, to the right, then circled it in a back-and-forth motion. Another dancer stood on both hands with her legs wide apart in the air; she kicked her legs to the beat of the cymbal. With a taunting look on her face one more dancer stood in place and rotated her hips slowly in circles while getting lower and lower. A different dancer went down (with back toward the audience) on slightly bent knees and back, humping and grinding, while her fellow performers cheered her on. Another dancer rotated her butt toward the audience, then while still stepping and jiggling as fast as the drumroll, she danced toward her mates (one after another), who responded in kind. Finally, all seven dancers turned to the audience with more strutting, gyrations, and rotations. The section climaxed with the chorus "Big mama in the house, y'all." A pair of temple blocks, sounding the clock sounds, signaled a belligerent final call, "It's funky up in here, y'all!" Hm. It was sweet *pa-pa*![20]

My memory walked to the times in Ghana when we had our butt-shaking contests. My sisters and friends were very good at these contests because they practiced a lot. I too practiced. As I remember it in my own memory walk, to jiggle well, my sisters instructed me to

> hold torso still
> shake body
> from hips down
> It is what is beautiful that is shown
> OR
> walk with slightly bent knees
> back bent, buttocks stuck out
> shake butt with each step
> jiggle, step, jiggle, step
> *wé-lé, wé-lé, wé-lé, wé-lé*

I felt connected with the Urban Bush Women dancers and felt those movements in my own body's memories as if I were onstage with them, authenticating myself in front of my peers. These memories and connections were very crucial to me because of my initial experience here in the United States. Performance became a site of healing.

---

[20] Urban Bush Women dancers were not twerking. See Kyra D. Gaunt's article on twerking (2014).

But there were differences. In Ghana, we jiggled because we wanted to make a statement about the beauty of our buttocks, and because it was fun. It was fun for the UBW dancers as well, but they also jiggled because they wanted to make a statement to the Western dance world and the dominant US society about the beauty of their buttocks and their bodies. According to Zollar,

> When I first started dance training I was moving unselfconsciously and very free. After I went to college to major in dance, I started tucking and pushing and trying to hide my body, in particular, my abundant gift from Africa; then I would go to African dance classes or out to parties and move, groove, and work my whole body. Then I would go back to my modern and ballet classes and start squeezing, tucking, holding, and apologizing for my body. I finally decided that enough was enough. That, in fact, I would find a way to bring the two ideas together to celebrate the traditional African culture that honors the movements of the hips, breasts, shoulders, hands, feet, thighs, and head, as all are important expressive elements in dance. (1998)

One dancer, Marjani Forté, a UBW dancer, explained her interpretation on *Batty Moves*.

> Batty Moves! I can pretty much guarantee that, unless they were thin, every black female dancer has had issues with her body. Batty Moves is one of those things that outright, in-your-face, challenges the myopic notion of beauty. We do it with a sense of reclamation like, "This is my body and look at how fabulous I am in it. I can do all this stuff that you said I could not do or that you said I shouldn't do because of how I am shaped. I am a dancer with breasts; I am a dancer with thighs, so what?" It says that "I am a dancer and I work; this is my body at its best potential or going towards its best potential, so I am working my body; I am stretching; I am doing the things to fine-tune my instrument, but not to make it look like something that it's not." I think that that is important. For audience members, it says, "Embrace who you are. Embrace your fullness; embrace your power." (2009)

The butt encoded defiance, and memories of pain and trauma for the dancers. Theirs was an act of remembering in which they represented their sentiments as Black females in dance, an act that also signaled their journeys toward affirmation and acceptance; while mine was an act of remembering that took me back but also brought me home in my body.[21] My memories and theirs intersected, overlapped, crisscrossed, and interlocked in the performed moments of dancing. Together we connected, constructed, and traversed a middle ground, emphasizing the fluidity, reciprocity, and density of that interaction. *Batty Moves* was our "space of encounter" (Averill 2004, 101), our "site of memory" (Nora 1989, 7), and, in a way, our "collective autobiography" (Turner 1990, 9). The power which comes from sharing deeply any pursuit with another person, the sharing of joy, whether physical, emotional, psychic, or intellectual, to form that bridge between the sharers that can be the basis for understanding much of what is not shared between them and lessens the threat of their difference (Lorde 1984, 56), was realized in this space. Layered dis/connections.

I was never told to "tuck in" because I never took ballet lessons. Neither was I told to lose weight in order to dance. I danced because I had a body. Even though I had been in the United States for about ten years, I was not aware of these references. However, after hearing about these experiences, my memories are colored by their memories and they have become my prosthetic memory (Landsberg 2003, 2004), and part of my tapestry of memory. Any time I see *Batty Moves* performed, I smile, but I also empathize and extend solidarity to the dancers. The UBW dancers and I were separated by histories of slavery and colonialism, just as I was from students at Fisk University, yet that did not matter. *Batty Moves* and its performance allowed us to connect through others' memories, reinforcing Obioma Nnaemeka advice that "as people of African descent, our attention should not be solely on how blacks in Africa and those in the African Diaspora are related to each other, but also how they relate to each other" (1997, 377).[22]

Urban Bush Women
My bridge
Ghanaian Akan Elders say
Enam dua so nti na ahoma aduru soro
It is because of the tree that the rope reaches the sky
I felt your movements in my body's memories
Jiggle, step, jiggle, step
wé-lé

---

21 See Babatunde Lawal, Okot p'Bitek, Caroline Card and others about the use of buttocks in African dances.
22 See Arthur 2000 and Mwakikagile 2006, in particular, for a discussion on the relationship between American Blacks and continental Africans.

We connected
Diasporic intimacies
Through our bodies
A transnational community
Of butt shakers
Entangled intimacies
Butts!

Urban Bush Women and *Batty Moves* performance took me a step closer to my walk through American racial politics, racialized trauma, and other intimacies.

Scales of Memory in Senegal

My walk with UBW took me to Senegal, a place that inspired the creation of their piece *Les écailles de la memoire—The Scales of Memory*. When I arrived in 2009, I was by then an established professor in America at Illinois State University, having lived and taught in the United States for many years.[23] But I was also a Ghanaian Akan from a matrilineal society that traces inheritance through the female line, one in which, traditionally, the "wife retains her own clan (lineage) identity and name" (Rattray 1929, 22), one who speaks Akan Twi, Ga, and some French, exposed to traditional Akan philosophical thought by way of hi-life music, *Ananse* stories, different games, and teachings from Elders. I wore layers of identity, morefold than W. E. B. DuBois's "double-consciousness" or the two-ness for which Bernice Johnson Reagon suggested a straddling strategy. Striving for integrity I straddled multiply, sifted, and wove together my identities. As a Black African, I considered myself primarily an insider, a status that I still believed would afford me easy access to teachers.[24] Like Jacqueline in Mariama Ba's *So Long a Letter*, I believed I "should have been able to fit into Senegal" (1981, 42), because it is another Black and West African society. But Africa is very diverse, very big, and separated by languages, religions, local cultures, histories, and varied

---

23 My father and mother saw the need and taught us traditional music and dance. Growing up in postcolonial Ghana in the 1970s, I was schooled via a Western curriculum where English language was the mode of instruction (see Gyekye 1996). I have also lived, been educated, and worked in the United States of America for many years.

24 See Akbar 2012, Burnim 1997, Gwaltney 1990, and Oriola 2012.

encounters with the colonial legacy. I in fact did not fit in. Experiencing these disconnections in a Black African country was even more unsettling than what I experienced with the Fisk University women, the more so because I had thought I was at "home." I quickly concluded, though, that as a Ghanaian female in Senegal, "insider/outsider" categories are not simple. Some of my walks in Senegal were rewarding; others were challenging, frustrating, and exhausting, reminding me daily of the many shades of "at home-ness" (Gallinat 2008, 10), not fully in, and not fully out.[25] Senegal revealed experiences of belonging and mistaken assumptions about belonging that I had taken for granted.

I arrived in Dakar one January morning. A taxi dropped me at my new residence.[26] Though the majority of Senegalese are Muslim, my host family was Christian. My hostess lived with her husband and two children. She was a woman, a wife, a mother, and a Black African like me. Connections. But we were also different. She spoke Wolof and French; I spoke Akan Twi and English. As I chatted with her, I realized the French I had reviewed months prior and had felt confident about before getting to Dakar was actually not that good. I sensed her careful performance of the legacy of French colonial assimilationist etiquette, while I struggled by contrast with different layers of English colonial legacy. She had straightened hair; I had locked my natural hair. She wore a wedding ring; I did not.[27] This was my initial experience of what Senegal was to become for me. I went to bed thinking about how to manage these layers of dis/connections.

I also learned very quickly that being a woman did not necessarily guarantee me a connection to Senegalese women. If who we are, as "gendered and sexual persons, affects how we respond and how others respond to us, even in non-sexual contexts" (Whitehead and Conway 1986), then our gendered identities have more impact on our field experiences and the production of knowledge than we acknowledge.[28] Thus, as a woman, I assumed that most

---

25 I liken this feeling of "in-between-ness" to what Ghanaians call a "wayfarer," or *saman twetwe* (roaming ghost), and recalls anthropologists' "liminal" state where one borders or lingers before reaching a definitive state, a threshold (see Turner 1977).
26 My room had a single bed with a wardrobe, a dresser, and a mosquito net. I did not think I needed the net until a mosquito serenaded me in my ear.
27 I had lost mine and after a while did not believe in them. One should not be marked or tagged. It should be in the heart and mind.
28 Many authors have documented their experiences as women in the field, exploring issues of political intimidation, robbery, intimacy, sexual

of my research and interactions would be easier with women and that I would connect easily with women. But the layers of disconnections challenged those assumptions. Many of the women had relaxed their hair and/or wore weaves. Many had bleached skins, like the Ghanaian women who continue to bleach their skins. Gaps. Unwanted connections. I felt uncomfortable with that blatant performance of desiring whiteness. These encounters provided opportunities for questioning, destabilizing, and reimagining insider/outsider labels and opened up ever-changing statuses to new significations. The alienation I experienced while conducting research at Gorée Island, and the unmooring I felt at times, could only be remedied by embracing ambiguous and ever-changing labels that rejected dichotomies. I straddled. Several of the encounters challenged my sense of belonging and defined how I proceeded with my study, underscoring the notion that "fieldwork at home never simply equates to insider research."[29] I pondered, "What damage do limiting categories do to our encounters?" Ironically, it was actually Senegalese men who extended a welcome "home" to me once they learned that I was Ghanaian. But these gestures were superficial. I still felt like an outsider, invisible, lonely and did not have any lengthy or deepened conversations.

Surprisingly, instead, I connected easily with American tourists, and especially African American women. This was interesting because for a long time in America, as noted, I had struggled to connect with African American women. Yet, in Senegal, our experience in America connected us. I spent one day with an African American lady who had traveled to Senegal to conduct research on the Wolof language, which brought some joy and ease. It did not matter that she was much younger and single (as it might have mattered with a Senegalese woman). Being able to have a conversation about something familiar and making references to and talking about experiences in America were calming. America, a land thousands of miles across the sea, a land to which enslaved Africans, our ancestors, were taken, a land whose history is connected to this island, was our bridge. Dis/connections. We were two Africans with different histories, linking up on a slave island via experiences in America. She and I talked about the similarities between the brutalities on Black bodies in the streets of American cities, and the brutalities in the former dungeons for enslaved Africans, the Long March by enslaved Africans through tunnels and woods, and on the slave ships. We talked about the similarities between the dungeons and the modern prison industrial

---

harassment, and assault. See Moreno 1995, Green et al. 1993, Newton 1993.
29   Zhao 2017, 189.

complex that incarcerates Black bodies. We talked about our experiences as Black women in America, the sensory knowledge stored in our bodies —the invisibility, the constant pressure to conform to white standards of beauty, the disregard for Black women's voices and their contributions. Connections. We were

> Sojourners
> Connecting through our search for answers on an island that imprisoned our enslaved ancestors
> In a language tied with oppression and disenfranchisement
> Dislocation and loss
> Legacies
> Both nursed at the tits of white supremacy
> Ghosts of slavery and colonization
> American experience
> Connect us
> Linkages
> Through entanglements

This encounter, though brief, became an inflection point for my connection with African American women over the years, as I found more grounds to connect.

Performance: Unpacking Diasporic Intimacies and Histories toward Resistance and Healing

When George Floyd was brutally killed by a white police officer, I cried. The Akan say, "When you go to someone else's funeral, cry" (for yourself because you don't know what your funeral would be like). We also say, *"Wote sɛ obi abɔgyesɛ rehye a, sa nsuo si wo deɛ ho,* "When you hear that someone's beard is burning, place water by yours." So, I cried for my son, my daughter, and myself. *Bueeeeeiiiiiii! ɛna-é! Agya-é! ɔbenten-é! ɛno-é! ɔdeyeɛ-é! Asomasi-é! yéé! Hmm* ... I could not sleep for days and stayed in bed in a mental state that I could not shake off. Anxious. I was afraid. I thought about the daily aggressions my son and daughter experience. I had really arrived in America. I pored over a section of my solo work, *Walking with My Ancestors,* in which I recite,

"Will they kill me too when I grow up, Mama?"
How can a mother protect her
Son, daughter from hate? (*Walking with My Ancestors: Cape Coast Castle*, 2019)

How do mothers of Black children sleep? Do they sleep? How do they cope? How do they heal, attend to untreated trauma when another Black man is killed, opening those cuts in the souls again and again? Akan Elders say, *Agyanka hunu afunsie a, na ne werɛ aho*, "When an orphan sees a cemetery, she becomes sad."

Listen
Bueeeeeeiiiiiiii …
Ah!
The *agyanka* orphan is pitiful
Mmm….m
Their souls, memories, wounds, pain
Run so deep
Moaning they cannot stop
Dr William Smith's racial battle fatigue
Dr Joy DeGruy's post-traumatic slave syndrome
Tears like waterfalls
Aaa, Sweet Mother
You are *ɔbaatan*
Black Mother
ɔbaatan na ɔnim deɛ ne ba bɛdie
It is the mother who knows what her child will eat
Do you know what your children will eat
Eh! Na wo bɛ yɛ dɛn?

Owuo begya hwan
Who will death spare
Owuo ne yɛn reko, ɔpatafoɔ ne hwan
Death is in a fight with us, who will mediate
Du-é!
Owuo nim adeɛ kyɛ
Death does not know how to share fairly
Du-é!
Mmm…

Sweet Mother
How you go sleep when your children be killed

> How you go chop when some of your children no fit chop
> How you go happy when many of your children be killed
> Tears you cannot stop
> The joys of motherhood

"Walking with My Ancestors"

Walking with My Ancestors: Cape Coast Castle (2019) is a solo, multimodal performance piece I created about a mother's search for guidance from the spirits of her Ancestors in the former dungeons for enslaved Africans.[30] The piece, which evolved from my TEDx Normal Talk,[31] is based on original, firsthand research I conducted in the Ghanian former dungeons.

The resulting performance piece takes the audience on a ritual journey that includes dance, music, and drama and leads to revelation, reconciliation, and rebirth. I mean it to offer fresh perspectives on the experiences of the nameless and forgotten enslaved Africans who languished in the dungeons and to demonstrate how today's racial and cultural problems connect with truths of our shared and painful pasts. It provides a platform for deepened conversations about identities, trauma, immigration and migration, border crossings, homeland and diaspora, and the "ghosts of slavery." Ultimately, *Walking with My Ancestor*s is a story I tell about adversity, hope, resilience, emotional justice, protest, survival, and healing.[32]

---

30 *Walking with My Ancestors* was originally produced by Don Shandrow of Coalescence Theater Project and co-directed by Kim Pereira and Don Shandrow.

31 Aduonum, "Walking with My Ancestors," YouTube video, https://www.youtube.com/watch?v=56WTvTyyLsY.

32 Kelsey Watznauer previews the play's performance with the following in the Bloomington-Normal, Illinois, *Pantagraph*: "In Cape Coast Castle, she takes a ritual journey with the dead and discovers truth and peace in her effort to answer that core question. While the play depicts the story of her return to Ghana, 'Cape Coast Castle' also tells 'the core of the immigrant story' and the third space—'the place where an immigrant is not quite part of this country, not quite part of the country that they are from, but they're a hybrid.' She tells the story of coming to terms with her life in America and her roots in Ghana, finding revelation, reconciliation and renewal along the way." ("From Ghana in Chains: Award-Winning 'Walking with My Ancestors' comes to Bloomington" [September 12, 2019]). An audience member, Ted Miller, president of the Washington State Community Theatre Association said, "*Walking*

Figure 6.1 Ama Oforiwaa Aduonum being shackled, Cape Coast Castle, Ghana. Photo by Ben.

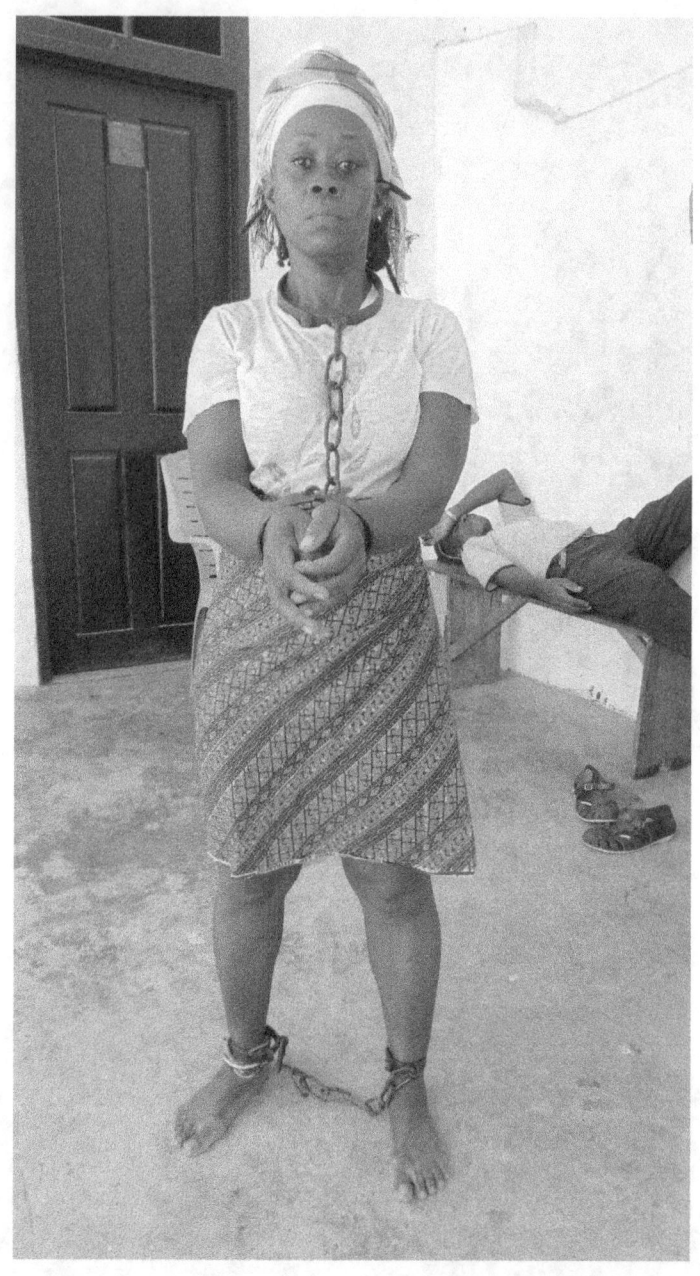

Figure 6.2. Ama Oforiwaa Aduonum shackled, Cape Coast Castle, Ghana. Photo by Ben.

Walking with My Ancestors is in six parts. *Nsateaa baako ntumi mpopa animu*. "One finger cannot effectively clean the face." So, I use multiple artforms—song, dance, drama, with drumming, the playing of various handheld instruments, storytelling, and silence to convey my message. I employ Senegalese and Beninois lullabies, songs of Ghanaian Akan warrior associations and Ewe traditions, and African American spirituals, such as "Wade in the Water" "Motherless Child," gospel music "Precious Lord," and movement vocabularies from the Zulu *ndlamo*, Brazilian capoeira, Ghanaian *agbeko* and *asafo*, Senegalese *lenjen*, and Haitian vodou. I use different Ghanaian languages and proverbs to capture the various messages explored in the piece. Combinations of these contribute to my ways to protest, "overcome, contain, resist, reveal, avoid, relieve and hide from suffering in its varied (trauma) guises" (Thompson 2009, 77). There are no scene changes. I leave the stage at the end.

The performance begins on a dark stage with two rehearsal blocks and a pair of Ghanaian *atumpan* drums; the high-pitched drum is to the right of the low-pitched drum. One of the rehearsal blocks has an iron slit bell and an *asalato* on it, and two wicker rattles on the ground by it. The other rehearsal block has a basket with fruits and a Ghanaian *atɛntɛbɛn* bamboo flute; next to the box on the floor is a Ghanaian *adenkum* stamping tube. As I enter the stage, a bright white light is projected onto me and follows my path. I am holding a calabash of water—a symbol of cleansing, dressed in a white top and a long white skirt with white beads around my ankles and wrists. Six white handkerchiefs are tucked into my skirt around my waist. I am wearing white because it is the color that Ghanaian priests wear to enter the spiritual realm and communicate with the Ancestors and Gods. The color is preferred because it is fragile, penetrable, transparent, and vulnerable. I walk downstage toward the audience, raise up the calabash, and recite a few words. I purify the stage by sprinkling some water to my left, to my right, and in front of me, each time calling on *Twereduampɔn Kwame, Ototroponso Ahuntahunu* Supreme Being, Ancestral spirits and various Akan Gods with song. I invoke the spirits and the audience into the ritual space to partake in and bear witness to the performance. I take a sip of the water to show that it is safe to consume, then I spray it toward the audience and set down the calabash. I walk upstage right to the set of talking drums, pick up

---

with My Ancestors is a powerful theatrical voice in our difficult conversations about race in America today, connecting the audience to the cries for equality and justice" (Email correspondence, July 6, 2019).

two L-shaped drumsticks, look up, and play the following to summon the spirit of the *Tweneboa* tree for guidance and protection. I recite each line in Akan before I play.[33]

Tweneboa Kodua
Wo kɔɔ baabi a, bra
Tweneduro
Wokɔɔ baabi a bra
Merefrɛ wo: yɛse bra
Akokɔ bɔn anɔpa
Akokɔ bɔn nhemanhema
Meresua; momma menhu
Meresua; momma menhu

(Tweneboa Kodua
If you went somewhere, come
Tweneduro tree
If you went somewhere, come
I am calling you; they say, "come"
The cock crows in the morning
The cock crows early morning
I am studying; let me know
I am studying; let me know)

I end the call, pause, lay down the drumsticks, pause; then I walk away from the drums downstage, stand behind the calabash filled with sacred water. I look out at the audience a few seconds, and then tell my story about the event leading to my son's question.

July 6, 2016
We are [at] a stoplight
On the corner of Clearwater and Veterans Parkway
Heading north on Veterans in Bloomington, IL
Burger King is on our right
It is about 5:30 pm
The radio broadcasts the shooting death of
Philando Castille
Alton Sterling was shot dead the day before

---

33 I borrowed the text from *Ayan*, a text by the late Kwabena Nketia (1969). Tweneboa, tweneduro is the tree from which the pair of Ghanaian atumpan drums are carved.

My son asks
Me so me nyin a wɔ mo beku me
Will they kill me too when I grow up, Mama

My muscles tense
Heart sinks
Eyes twitch
I
Am afraid

I think about my life in America
Black female professor with a PhD
At a predominantly white institution
My experiences
Hm!
…
Torn to pieces
…

I raise up both arms in desperation and ask.
Who will advocate
Intervene
Help a Black female professor at the intersections
Help a mother to understand
Cope with aggression
Fear?
…

How can I raise a young man to be fearless, when
I
Am afraid

"Will they kill me too when I grow up, Mama," and "How can I raise a young man to be fearless, when I am afraid?" anchor the entire production. They address the collective trauma of Black women and seek strategies toward healing. As a site of memory, resistance and healing, this performance allows me to reenact, share, and relive those memories. It allows me to tell my story, and in telling the story, gives "voice" to the fears of many Black and Brown mothers. Storytelling gives power back to me, the teller, to redefine and assert the value of our lives, to have agency, and to affirm our humanity. Through storytelling, I collaborate with the audience to imagine our future.

It is my way of seeking the faith that James Baldwin projects: "It is necessary, while in darkness, to know that there is a light somewhere, to know that in oneself, waiting to be found, there is a light. What the light reveals is danger, and what it demands is faith."[34]

I continue by humming, "Laale muloo," an Ewe song that is performed to summon and bless Ancestral spirits. Seated, I accompany the song with the 12/8 *agbeko* pattern on an *atoke* bell. This song leads to parts 2 and 3 of the piece where I share my experiences and dialogue with the spirits in the former dungeons. In parts 4 and 5 I discuss the experience and trauma of African Americans in this United States and connect that to the daily hostilities my children face.

> I want to tell you about your descendants
> Black people
> Your beloved offspring
> They inherited your scars
> And were never meant to survive
> Incarcerated, raped, pickled
> Chopped, shot, hanged
> Strangest fruit
> Forced to eat their own genitals
> Burned and sold as souvenirs
> Haunted and hunted
> Hmmmm….
> Delectable black bodies
> Still incarcerated
> …
> I think about my daughter
> My son
> The daily aggressions they face
> Born a crime[35]
>
> How can a mother protect her
> son, daughter from hate? (Aduonum, *Walking* 2019)

By this time, I have sung several spirituals and "Precious Lord" by the grandfather of Gospel music, Thomas Dorsey. Also, by this point in the performance, I have performed a plethora of movements from warrior dances

---

34   Baldwin 1964.
35   Borrowed from Trevor Noah, *Born a Crime* (2016).

Example 6.1 Ghanaian Ewe agbeko bell pattern.

to portray anger, victory, and celebration. The verse ends with "Black Lives Matter!" with my right hand in balled fist, a Black Power symbol, and I kneel on one knee to evoke Colin Kaepernick. Then I rise, with the balled fist, and run around the stage singing a victory song of the Asafo warrior group in Ghana. I also perform excerpts from the Ghanaian Agbeko warrior dance. I sing in each of the sections and perform different dances. My arms flail up and down, to the sides to show frustration, resilience, and strength. I strike a karate pose, a boxing pose to exhibit resistance and defiance, and exhibit different facial expressions—scorn, sadness, fear, pity, and happiness. I scream and shout to express frustration, anger, and fear. I wail and sob to evoke empathy and express sadness. I whisper to console and caution. I also remain silent at key points during the performance as a form of resistance. Untreated and hidden trauma pours out of my body. Finally, at the end the piece, I deliver my son's question again, "Will they kill me too when I grow up, Mama?" I answer with a Beninois children's song, *Iro Ye, Nou ka ye manao*, translated below.

> My dear children
> What can I give to you
> I have nothing to give you
> I am going to pray for you
> Your life will be happy
> Till eternity (Aduonum, *Walking with My Ancestors*)

ɔba nyansa foɔ yebu no bɛ na yɛnka no asɛm. "The wise child is spoken to in proverbs, but not in plain language." Toward the end, I share the lessons learned from this experience, using several Akan proverbs including, ɛnyɛ toa pɛ nti na ahoma sɛn ne kɔn. "It is not the wish of the gourd that the rope hangs around its neck." Life is full of entanglements, some of which we cannot control; however, while they hang around "our necks," we can manage them and continue to live and resist them in any opportunities that present themselves. Sɛbe, sɛbe, fɛfɛ na ɛyɛ fɛ, nti na ababaawa tu mmirika a, ɔsɔ ne nufu mu, ɛnyɛ sɛ ɛbɛte atɔ ntira. "It is because of her beauty/fashion, that is

Figure 6.3 Ama Oforiwaa Aduonum in *Walking with My Ancestors: Cape Coast Castle* (2019), Normal, IL. Photo by Illinois State University Photographer, Lyndsie Schlink.

why the beautiful Black woman holds her breasts when she runs, not that they will drop off." I end playing a beautiful melody on the *atɛntɛbɛn* bamboo flute to bid the Ancestral spirits farewell and send them back to their slumber. *Go mu brɛbrɛ, brɛbrɛ, brɛbrɛ, brɛbrɛ, brɛbrɛ, brɛbrɛ.*

At the end, I had shared my son's question, my fears and those of Black mothers, my loneliness as a Black female professor, talked and testified, reflected on them, massaged them, and connected them to experiences of other African Americans, especially mothers of Black children. Having massaged and scorned the white-body supremacy, claimed that shared trauma that lives in our bodies, and those diasporic intimacies that connect us, I exit the stage.

If silence is a symptom of trauma, could performance restore speech, toward "emotional justice" and healing? If untreated trauma shifts and shapes how see and interact with each other (Armah 2020), then I will learn to shift how I live and interact with people of African descent; I will continue to love my son, my daughter and teach them to be proud of who they are, and live

Figure 6.4 Ama Oforiwaa Aduonum in *Walking with My Ancestors: Cape Coast Castle* (2019), Normal, IL. Photo by Illinois State University Photographer, Lyndsie Schlink.

boldly, for nothing is possible with fear. I will love others more justly and continue to unlearn the ways that are harmful to us. In the prophetic words of hip-hop icon Kendrick Lamar, we are "gon' be Alright!"[36]

Conclusion: *Between the World and Me*[37]

In the car with my son, recently, I asked him again to share with me how he feels when he learns about the murder of another Black person. "Am I next?" he replied without hesitation. My heart sank. My muscles tensed. Eyes twitched. He continued, "Because it seems in America, white people have not learned to accept Black people and to question their fear of Black people. But they have to deal with their fears just as we have to deal with ours." Hearing my son, I realized that for us to create an authentic intimacy, we

---

36 Kendrick Lamar, "Alright," *To Pimp a Butterfly* (2015).
37 Ta-Nehisi Coates, *Between the World and Me* (2015).

must be connected in some way through our bodies, to "enter into the lives of others" like Emma Goldman recommends (1934). Our Ghanaian Akan Elders say, *etua wo nyɔnko ho a, etua dua mu,* "If is in someone's body, it is in a tree!" You don't feel it. They also say, *Aboa nkaa wo da a, wode wo nan ne wo nsa na ɛprɛprɛ no.* "If you have never been bitten by an animal you toy with it with your feet and hands."

"The capacity to enter into the lives of others" opens up new significations, encounters, relationships, one borne of trauma, shared trauma. In order to do this, we must first come to terms with what it feels like to be afraid, helpless, vulnerable. If we are "truly able to do this, it would be impossible to discount the oppression of others, except by again forgetting how we have been hurt" (Moraga, 30).

Sitting in the car that day and hearing my son forced me to confront the racism and sexism I had experienced at my institution, truths I had "hidden" in my body and "been terrorized into keeping silent" (Jones 2010, 10). I had tucked away neatly in my body the effects of police brutality against unarmed Black men on me, until my son spoke his truth. Though cognizant of the Black Lives Matter movement and the rhythm and blues and hip-hop songs that protested the brutality on Black bodies, it was my son's question, "Will they kill me too, when I grow up, Mama?" that forced me to confront my own fears and misgivings about the brutality on Black bodies, on my body. It recalled painful historical memories sedimented and residing in my bones. White-body supremacy, "how the white body is elevated above all bodies, made ostensibly supreme standard against which other bodies' humanity is measured, and beliefs of white-body supremacy are reinforced through institutions as practice, procedures, and standards, causing endless stress and trauma,"[38] had arrived at my doorstep through my son's question. I had finally arrived in America, and entered the lives of Black women, especially those with Black sons and daughters, walking the tightrope of preparing our sons to be free, while restraining and repressing them. I connected. As an artist, it has been my job to perform truth and "to unearth stories that people try to bury with shovels of complacency and time" (Mwende Katwiwa 2018), unearthing, confronting, and claiming our collective trauma. Entanglements. Diasporic intimacies.

After I shared my journey to America on my walk with my friend that begins this essay, I tell him that I had no idea, when I first arrived, that African Americans had endured so much trauma throughout their history

---

38   Resmaa Menakem.

in this United States—enslavement, lynching, sharecropping, Black codes, chain gangs, the burning down of Black Wall Street by a white mob, police brutality, and so much more. I complain to him that one of my friends once told me that I was "privileged" as an African immigrant. He responds, "White Americans do not feel threatened by you because you are not domestic. You don't have claims to this land like we do. You are a new thing. They are fascinated by you and want to know you when you first get here. Your accent is cute. So initially, you don't see them for what they truly are. But your children will let you know" (Jerry James, personal communication, June 1, 2020). Between the world and me. *My Body* let me know.

Wise Ghanaian Akan Elders say, ɔhɔhoɔ ani akɛseakɛse, ɔmfa nhunu hwee! "The visitor has big eyes; she cannot see anything!" So, when I first came to the United States, I was oblivious to its racial and cultural politics, and the untreated trauma in African Americans as I experienced it from female students at Fisk. It would take decades and my walk with other Black women, including Urban Bush Women, before my "eyes opened" to "see" and feel. My "coming to America," my work as a scholar, and my interactions with women of African descent has been characterized by connections and disconnections. Our entangled histories of separation, religion, language, gender identities, racial politics, aesthetics, and other entanglements provided platforms for how we interacted with each other. According to Wise Nigerian Igbo Elders, *Otu nzo ukwu biri ogologo njem*, "A step taken marks the end of a long journey." Each step on this American journey brought me closer to understanding the experiences of Black women. Each step allowed the white-body supremacy, which now lives and breathes in my body, to invade my body. Each step helped me appreciate and understand, more deeply, the tightropes that Black mothers tread, Black mothers whose sons and daughters have been killed by white police officers or mothers who are afraid for their children's lives. Me. Their fears, wails, moans and groans, and trauma are now mine. Shared trauma. A site of diasporic intimacy. Performance as a site for emotional justice, toward healing. *Batty Moves. Walking with My Ancestors.*

> Black mothers
> You!
> Proud daughters of Mama Africa
> Cradle of civilization
> You!
> Beautiful descendants of women who dance with skulls
> Children of the panther king
> The Panther is your mystical Ancestor

Granddaughters of Mo-re-mi
The warrior Queens of Yu-ro-ba
You are daughters of Nzin-gha M-ban-de
Warrior Queen of M-bun-du
Who fought the Portuguese slave traders for 30 years

You
Great great granddaughters of Agoji
Warrior Queens of Dahomey
Put both feet on the ground
Inhale
Don't wait to xhale
Breath
Maybe some mantras
Incense, flowers, candles, herbs
Water, the first medicine
Cleansing
Sharing stories
Singing ourselves to healing
There is a balm in Gilead
To make the wounded whole

Aaa, Ahwene pa
Precious beads
Like Mama Zora Neale Hurston advised
Hit a straight lick with a crooked stick[39]
Celebrate your overlapping inter-sectionalities
Live!
Keep your heads up
W   G
  A
    L
      K
        I
          N
With Our Ancestors
ɔnantefoɔ na odi adɔdɛ
It is the walker who eats sweet things
Let us keep walking
Tim! Tim! Tim! Tim! Tim! Tim! Tim! Tim!

---

39   Zora Neale Hurston, *Hitting a Straight Lick with a Crooked Stick* (2020).

Since *Fɛfɛ na ɛyɛ fɛ, nti na ababaawa tu mmirika a, ɔsɔ ne nufu mu, ɛnyɛ sɛ ɛbɛte atɔ*
ntira
It is because of her beauty/fashion, that is why the beautiful Black woman holds her breasts when she runs, not that they will drop off
Water Dancer[40]
Dance
Twereduampɔn Ahuntahunu Nana Kwame will trouble the waters for you
Dance
Dance
DA . . . . NCE!

References

Aduonum, Ama Oforiwaa. 2004. "*Buwumu*: Redefining Black Beauty and Emancipating the Hottentot Venus in the Work of Oforiwaa Aduonum. *Women's Studies: An Interdisciplinary Journal* 33:279–98.

———. 2011. "Memory Walking with Urban Bush Women's *Batty Moves*." *Drama Review* 55 (1): 52–69.

———. 2018. "Walking with My Ancestors: A Journey from Slave Dungeons in Ghana to America." YouTube video, https://www.youtube.com/watch?v=56WTvTyyLsY.

———. 2019. "Walking with My Ancestors: Cape Coast Castle." Produced by Coalescence Theatre Project; directed by Kim Pereira and Don Shandrow.

Aidoo, Ama Ata. [1964] 1971. *The Dilemma of a Ghost*. New York: MacMillan.

Alexander, Elizabeth. 1990. *The Venus Hottentot*. Charlottesville: University of Virginia Press.

Apraku, Kofi K. 1991. *African Emigrés in the United States of America: A Missing Link in Africa's Social and Economic Development*. New York: Praeger.

Argenti, Nicholas. 2007. *The Intestines of the State: Youth, Violence, and Belated Histories in the Cameroon Grassfields*. Chicago: University of Chicago Press.

Armah, Esther. 2020. *Emotional Justice: Towards Healing*. Webinar. Armah Emotional Justice Institute.

———. https://www.theaiej.com/emotional-justice.

———. https://www.facebook.com/emotionaljustice.

Arthur, John A. 2000. *Invisible Sojourners: African Immigrant Diaspora in the United States*. Westport, CT: Praeger.

---

40   Ta-Nehisi Coates, *The Water Dancer* (2019).

Averill, Gage. 2004. "Where Is 'One'?: Musical Encounter of the Ensemble Kind." In *Performing Ethnomusicology: Teaching and Representation in World Music Ensembles*, edited by Ted Solis, 93–111. Berkeley: University of California Press.

Ba, Mariama. 1980. *So Long a Letter*. London: Heinemann.

Baldwin, James. 1964. *Nothing Personal*. New York: Atheneum.

Bonilla, Yarimar. 2011. "The Past Is Made by Walking: Labor Activism and Historical Production in Postcolonial Guadeloupe." *Cultural Anthropology* 26 (3): 313–39.

Boym, Svetlana. 1998. "On Diasporic Intimacy: Ilya Kabakov's Installations and Immigrant Homes." *Critical Inquiry* 24 (2): 498–524.

Campbell, Carol. 1983. "Yimbo Za Kaswahili: A Socio-Ethnomusicological Study of the Swahili Poetic Form." PhD diss., University of Washington.

Campbell, Carol, and Carol M. Eastman. 1984. "Ngoma: Swahili Adult Song in Context." *Ethnomusicology* 28 (3): 467–93.

Card, Caroline. 1976. *An Introduction to the Music of Swahili Women*. Nairobi: Institute of African Studies, University of Nairobi.

Coates, Ta-Nehisi. 2015. *Between the World and Me*. New York: Spiegel and Grau.

———. 2019. *The Water Dancer*. New York: One World.

DeGruy, Joy. 2005. *Post Traumatic Slave Syndrome: Be the Healing*. New York: Uptone Press.

Dyson, Michael Eric. 2017. *Tears We Cannot Stop: A Sermon to White America*. New York: St. Martin's.

Gallinat, Anselma. 2008. "Being 'East German' or Being at Home in Eastern Germany: Identity as Experience." *Identities: Global Studies in Culture and Power* 15 (6): 665–85.

Gaunt, Kyra D. 2014. "Youtube, Twerking and You: Context Collapse and the Handheld Co-Presence of Black Girls and Miley Cyrus." *Journal of Popular Music Studies* 27 (3): 244–73.

Goldman, Emma. 1934. "Was My Life Worth Living." *Harper's Monthly* 152 (December).

Gordon, April. 1998. "The New Diaspora-African Immigration to The United States." *Journal of Third World Studies* 15 (1): 79–103.

Gottschild, Brenda Dixon. 2003. *The Black Dancing Body: A Geography from Coon to Cool*. New York: Palgrave Macmillan.

Gyekye, Kwame. 1995. *An Essay on African Philosophical Thought: The Akan Conceptual Scheme*. Philadelphia: Temple University Press.

Hall, Edward T. 1976. *Beyond Culture*. New York: Anchor Press.

Haskins, James. 1990. *Black Dance in America: A History through Its People*. New York: Thomas Y. Crowell.

Hobson, Janell. 2003. "The 'Batty' Politic: Toward an Aesthetic of the Black Female Body." *Hypatia: A Journal of Feminist Philosophy* 18 (4): 87–105.

Hobson, Janell. 2005. *Venus in the Dark: Blackness and Beauty in Popular Culture*. New York: Routledge.
Hoff, Pamela. 2020. "Tits of White Supremacy." Black Radicalism Seminar. Normal: Illinois State University.
Holsey, Bayo. 2008. *Routes of Remembrance: Refashioning the Slave Trade in Ghana*. Chicago: University of Chicago Press.
hooks, bell. 1989. *Talking Back: Thinking Feminist, Thinking Black*. Boston: South End Press.
Hurston, Zora Neale. 2020. *Hitting a Straight Lick with a Crooked Stick: Stories from the Harlem Renaissance*. New York: Amistad.
Jones, Omi Osun Joni L., Lisa L. Moore, and Sharon Bridgforth, eds. 2010. *Experiments in a Jazz Aesthetic: Art, Activism, Academia, and the Austin Project*. Austin: University of Texas Press.
Jones, Tony. 2021. "*Walking with My Ancestors* Production Trailer." YouTube video. https://www.youtube.com/watch?v=tmECNNimCJs&t=4s.
Katwiwa, Mwende. 2018. "'FreeQuency' Katwiwa: Black Life at the Intersection of Birth and Death." TED Talk. https://ted2srt.org/talks/mwende_freequency_katwiwa_black_life_at_the_intersection_of_birth_and_death.
Kisliuk, Michelle. [1997] 2008. "(Un)doing Fieldwork: Sharing Songs, Sharing Lives." In *Shadows in the. Field: New Perspectives for Fieldwork in Ethnomusicology*, 2nd ed., edited by Gregory Barz and Timothy J. Cooley, 183–205. Oxford: Oxford University Press.
Lamar, Kendrick. 2015. *To Pimp a Butterfly*. Santa Monica, CA: Aftermath.
Landsberg, Alison. 2003. "Prosthetic Memory: The Ethics and Politics of Memory in an Age of Mass Culture." In *Memory and Popular Film*, edited by Paul Grainge, 144–61. Manchester: Manchester University Press.
———. 2004. *Prosthetic Memory: The Transformation of American Remembrance in the Age of Mass Culture*. New York: Columbia University Press.
Lawal, Babatunde. 1996. *The Gelede Spectacle: Art, Gender, and Social Harmony in an African Culture*. Seattle: University of Washington Press.
Lewis, Earl. 1995. "To Turn as on a Pivot: Writing African Americans into a History of Overlapping Diasporas." *American Historical Review* 100 (3): 765–87.
Lorde, Audre. 1984. *Sister Outsider*. New York: Ten Speed Press.
Menakem, Resmaa. 2017. *My Grandmother's Hands: Racialized Trauma and the Pathway to Mending Our Hearts and Bodies*. Las Vegas: Central Recovery Press.
———. 2018. "White Supremacy as a Trauma Response." *Medium*, April 14, 2018. https://medium.com/@rmenakem/white-supremacy-as-a-trauma-response-ce631b82b975.
Moraga, Cherríe. "La Gúera." 2015. In *This Bridge Called My Back: Writings by Radical Women of Color*, edited by Cherríe L. Moraga and Gloria E. Anzaldúa, eds. 2015. 4th ed. Albany: State University of New York Press.

Mwakikagile, Godfrey. 2006. *Relations between Africans and African Americans: Misconceptions, Myths and Realities*. Grand Rapids, MI: Continental Press.
Nketia, Kwabena J. H. 1969. *Ayan: The Poetry of the Atumpan Drums of the Asantehene*. Legon, Ghana: Institute of African Studies.
Nnaemeka, Obioma. 1997. "This Women's Studies: Beyond Politics and History (Thoughts on the First WAAD Conference)." In *Sisterhood, Feminisms and Power: From Africa to the Diaspora*, edited by Obioma Nnaemeka, 351–88. Trenton, NJ: African World Press.
Noah, Trevor. 2016. *Born a Crime: Stories from a South African Childhood*. New York: Spiegel and Grau.
Nora, Pierre. 1989. "Between Memory and History: Les Lieux de Mémoire." *Representations* 26:7–24.
Osagie, Iyunolu Folayan. 2000. *The Amistad Revolt: Memory, Slavery, and the Politics of Identity in the United States and Sierra Leone*. Athens: University of Georgia Press.
p'Bitek, Okot. 1984. *Song of Lawino and Song of Ocol*. Oxford: Heinemann.
Roberts, Dorothy. 1997. *Killing the Black Body: Race, Reproduction, and the Meaning of Liberty*. New York: Pantheon Books.
Schechner, Richard. 1977. *Essays on Performance Theory, 1970–1976*. New York: Drama Book Specialists.
Schechner, Richard, and Willa Appel, eds. 1990. "Introduction." In *By Means of Performance: Intercultural Studies of Theatre and Ritual*, 1–7. Cambridge, UK: Cambridge University Press.
Shaw-Taylor, Yoku. 2007. "The Intersection of Assimilation, Race, Presentation of Self, and Transnationalism in America." In *The Other African Americans: Contemporary African and Caribbean Immigrants in the United States*, edited by Yoku Shaw-Taylor and Steven A. Tuch, 1–48. Lanham, MD: Rowman and Littlefield.
Thompson, James. 2009. *Performance Affects: Applied Theatre and the End of Effects*. Basingstoke, UK: Palgrave Macmillan.
Turner, Victor. 1990. "Are There Universals of Performance in Myth, Ritual, and Drama?" In *By Means of Performance: Intercultural Studies of Theatre and Ritual*, edited by Richard Schechner and Willa Appel, 8–18. Cambridge, UK: Cambridge University Press.
Van Hear, Nicholas. 1998. *New Diasporas: The Mass Exodus, Dispersal, and Regrouping of Migrant Communities*. Seattle: University of Washington Press.
Watznauer, Kelsey. 2019. "From Ghana in Chains: Award-Winning 'Walking with My Ancestors' Comes to Bloomington." *Pantagraph*, September 12, 2019. https://www.pantagraph.com/entertainment/arts-and-theatre/from-ghana-in-chains-award-winning-walking-with-my-ancestors-comes-to-bloomington/article_8a24a7bf-7fc5-540c-8430-82b7d7428c8f.html.

Williams, Walter L. 1980. "Ethnic Relations of African Students in the United States, with Black Americans, 1870–1900." *Journal of Negro History* 65 (3): 228–49.

Wulff, Helena. 2009. *Dancing at the Crossroads: Memory and Mobility in Ireland.* New York: Berghahn Books.

Yutkowitz, Nijole. 2020. *A Letter.*

Zhao, Yawei. 2017. "Doing Fieldwork the Chinese Way: A Returning Researcher's Insider/Outsider Status in Her Home Town." *Area* 49 (2): 185–91.

Chapter Seven

Ethnomusicological Empathy

Excavating a Black Graduate Student's Heartland

Danielle Davis

I am an ethnomusicologist from outer space. A Black one planted into the margins of Tallahassee's fertile soil. My skin is Black, hair shining a coily brown, and it locs together with a twist of my finger. When the light is right you might see my eyes glow purple.[1] But I can assure you, I am not from Mars. A white man named Nettl did not write about me.[2] Black ethnomusicologists and musicologists are erased from the canonical histories of our field; through personal study I became aware of the works of Gertrude Robinson, Eileen Southern, Samuel A. Floyd, Ashenafi Kebede, among others based in the United States whose research on African American and African diasporic musics were not assigned to be read in introductory courses. I am born in the way Ashenafi Kebede lived, in the way the rest of my Black ethnomusicological ancestors lived. And just so you're sure, know that it's our rage, isolation, and grief that birthed us.

But I invite you all into a moment of witnessing my story, a last-ditch excursion into the history of my *own* musical heartland as it lies desolate and

---

1   Although I take the position of being an ethnomusicologist from outer space, I am not suggesting that Black ethnomusicologists are not human. Rather, I am alluding to the microaggressive comments about our physical appearance such as hair type, facial structure, etc., that occur frequently in the workspace.
2   Nettl 1995.

burning.³ Here I write from the perspective of a Black ethnomusicologist-in-training from outer space. By writing myself into a tradition of Afrofuturist self-definition as articulated by Martine Syms, I wish to situate myself on a spectrum that includes Bruno Nettl's "ethnomusicologist from Mars" in Schools of Music and Mellonee Burnim's "Culture Bearer and Tradition Bearer." I take this stance to show the costs of anti-Black racism on Black students' imagination, an imagination of their scholarly futures and the possibility of building multiracial coalition. In this essay I share three stories of failed attempts at anti-racist alliance building, paired with insights from race and racism scholars such as Derald Wing Sue, Zeus Leonardo, bell hooks, and Patricia Hill Collins. These kinds of anti-Blackness cause Black graduate students to become displaced from various aspects and relationships in the beginning of our scholarly careers; in reading them, hearing them, and attending to them, you are granted but a taste of our experiences.

What does it mean for Black students to build an anti-racist coalition with non-Black students? One source of frustration is acknowledging the courage it takes to call people in and dealing with their fragility and outright denial.⁴ Their inability to stomach the hurt they caused, to confront the violence of their own anti-Blackness, is often documented in defense, which is well intentioned. Some silences resound as good deeds, such as those from a mixed-race ciswoman who when called to accountability on her public silence around BLM during racial unrest in June 2020 told me, "People feel like they are just talking to the world from some sort of pedestal without doing anything to really make a change. Have they started food banks in poor communities? Have they organized donations and written grants for nonprofits? Have they experienced homelessness? I don't need to make some posts on Facebook so my friends will know where I stand."

Maybe where you stand doesn't matter if you never had honest in-person or online relationships with your Black students. What this pandemic has taught us is that the wave of pedagogical futures exists in a hybrid of face-to-face and online interactions. I was heartbroken by the lack of response about

---

3   Syms 2014.
4   See Derald Wing Sue's *Race Talk* (2015). There he spells out the multifaceted nature of consequences of Black and other minoritized people discussing race and racism with white colleagues. He writes, "To constantly have to explain their life circumstances, to justify their perceptions and reactions, to not have their groups' histories known, and to be wary of the consequences for truth telling in the face of an unreceptive audience is exhausting and energy depleting" (98).

anti-Black racism from my former orchestra directors, teaching supervisors, and private instructors. And no, their courtesy check-in during the first two weeks of June 2020 does not count. If you know the power you have within a music community, why can't you or wouldn't you align your anti-racist thoughts throughout all social spaces? Many music educators claim to champion the teaching and "the inclusion of all musics." But what does it mean to be a music educator who denounces anti-Blackness, but only in private? To be a mixed-race music educator, who surely can pass as white, and builds ties to an overwhelmingly white music community in the South because of that fact? Do your non-Black student musicians back the boys in blue? Is that what makes it ok for to you make up an excuse like, "I created a food bank in the heart of downtown, so I need not mention the murders of people whose skin happens to be dark brown?" My life is too precious, the threats are too urgent to remain obtuse about protecting your well-meaning intentions however concealed and complicated by a mixed-raced identity. So, I pull you aside, initiating a moment of "allyship," only to be left asking: what's the use?

I wonder often about pasts that never existed. A moment in which I was able to break down the empathetic barrier between a white woman professor and myself. How would it have felt to witness a trauma scholar reckoning with the reality that her teaching reproduces trauma within her only Black student? Hoping to reveal our profession's colonial forcefield, she willed it unintentionally by shifting the course calendar to front-load *my* Black History Month with ethnographic Black pain. I thought I'd be welcome to come into her office and state how the readings are wounding my bodily psyche. I unknowingly poisoned myself into believing her sharing Ta-Nehisi Coates's *Between the World and Me* was evidence of a blossoming interracial mentorship, one grounded in anti-racist pedagogy, Black studies, and sound scholarship.[5]

My reality was that of a misinformed Black woman student with postracial fantasies, feeding my starved scholarly being with what felt like hollow seminar discussions. These learning sessions truly caught me by surprise. As Patricia Hill Collins writes, "Schools, print and broadcast media, governmental agencies, and other institutions in information business reproduces the controlling images of Black womanhood."[6] When there are no pedagogical structures to deal with being the lonely only, Black students must manage their true feelings, deploying a careful professional disguise. All the while my

---

5 Coates 2015.
6 Collins 2000, 101.

peers' newly minted awareness of, and subsequent frustration with, the realities of homeless Black girls, so eloquently portrayed by Aimee Meredith Cox, shifted uneasily in my stomach.[7] I would later give that feeling in my gut a name: fury.[8]

Naturally the anger in those moments fuels a courageous need for honest discussion between a Black woman student and her non-Black woman professor. Part of growing as a young Black woman music scholar demands "negotiations that aim to reconcile the contradictions separating our own internally defined images of self as African American women with our [my] objectification as the Other."[9] I suppose I should congratulate myself, I am earning my stripes, reconciling the dissonances in budding interracial professional relationships tried and true. There were times I went to my professor's office ready to be racially vulnerable, to share my discomfort with her in hopes that she'd recognize the seminar's toll on my weary spirit. I wanted for my words to solicit a kind of emotional harm reduction, if you will. But in that moment, I received tears, hot ones that seared her mascara and fudged her foundation.[10] Did I hurt her feelings? What did I say to set her off, I wondered anxiously, while forgetting that white women educators' tears during race talk with their Black students and colleagues can indicate a particular form of personalization that is masked as frustration or fear at how their actions are perceived as racist. Am I bearing witness to white guilt, I wonder.[11] Zeus Leonardo recognizes the dangerous precedent that is set in classrooms when white guilt is allowed room to breathe in stuffy seminar discussions when race and racism enter the conversation. And ever so quietly

---

7   Cox 2015.
8   For more on the productive nature of Black women's use of anger see hooks 1995, Lorde 2007, and Collin's chapter on self-expression.
9   Collins 2000, 99.
10 It is important I state that weaponization of tears by white and non-Black individuals are not fixed to any one conception of gender—trans, binary or nonbinary.
11 Here I draw upon Zeus Leonardo's discussion on how to move beyond white privilege in "The Color of Supremacy." His treatment of white guilt as an emotion for white students, and educators alike, in education is useful here. It's important to recognize how educators become complicit in maintaining whiteness in relation to white supremacy in classrooms: there is potential to set disastrous precedence in interracial learning environments where "many whites, [and non-Black people] subvert a structural study of racism with personalistic concerns over how they are perceived as individuals" (140).

my resolute words leave me. They fade into the ether of my cowardice. My tears bellow in their ducts. But through sheer will, I control them, and not one is allowed to spill until I am in a space of safety, far away from her. Now I feel betrayed by my own body, an internalized white supremacist guilt trip. In me was an age old Black bodily panic response to white women's tears. It leapt out in protection of me and I'm grateful for it. I consider myself one of the lucky ones to have lived to tell *my* tale.

Have you ever witnessed modern minstrelsy in academia? In real time? No burnt cork required. On hallowed stages normally reserved for conference keynote addresses. It's creative to turn a plenary lecture into a metapedagogical tool showcasing one of the most important methodologies to our field, the sacred one-on-one interview. When these moments are made public for all of us, to mull over and chew, there's opportunity to learn how easily a friendly conversation slips into the vortex of anti-Blackness, transforming into a modern-day minstrel show in plain view.[12] I knew this was true in my first fieldwork experience with other non-Black ethnomusicology students; the ease with which their work with Black musicians and sonic subjects opens the door for minstrelized performances and appropriation. It can happen when a Black Afrofuturist musical master and a white ethnomusicologist are bound together in the centering, defining of musicological whiteness.

One of the first maneuvers a non-Black researcher can make is to shamelessly flaunt their access to their famous musician friend. A storied nine minutes pass us by as an audience, spent recounting the senseless shaking of a tambourine in the studio with a funkadelian. The musician's "strange" dress is the butt of sarcastic phrasing—"I mean look at what you're wearing friend." He gestures downward with his hand to the audience's gentle laughter. Audio visuals are thrown up on the screen and when Black women's booties are bouncing in the musical scene, we notice the tension in the interviewer's non-Black body, embarrassment washes over their voice at that conjured-up, uncontextualized jezebel image.[13] Patricia Hill Collins's work on historicizing controlling images of Black women and pornographic usage in media provides an important opening to recognizing intersections of race and gender as lived realities. By understanding how these images play out in popular music culture, specifically that of the hypersexualized jezebel stereotype, we can properly contextualize popular music media featuring Black women's bodies through a lens of misogynoir without feeling shame at the presence

---

12   See Davis 2019, 65–67.
13   Collins 2000.

of Black women working as video vixens. Have you seen what a reactionary syllabus looks like, it stinks of cite Black women, #citeblackwomen, #cite-Blackwomenethnomusicologists. The premise of such teachings goes without saying, but through this medium I hear them as rusty, clanging sentiments, bells of racial dissonance that bear an empathy reeking of guilt at reclaiming one's erasure. A posturing of predisposition where instructors search in vain for softer places to land, for those who have always been privileged, to have the "necessary discussions" that lead to the same comfortably dismissive conclusions.[14] Pity the Black woman.

In conducting a public ethnomusicological interview, taking time to provide proper context would have been key to disrupting the sonic and visual media's use of Black women's bodies that invites multiracial audiences "to develop an objectivity, [a pornographic imagination] that would allow [us] to participate in her objectification."[15] Just another kind of knee-jerk treatment an iconic Afrofuturist wearing cosmologies of his creation like an S on his chest can receive. Ask him whether or not he's heard of John Cage in order to get more "philosophical," because your interlocutor's music surely is just for shits and giggles, good times, and high minds. Questions and comments such as asking a Black musician interlocutor, "Do you know who John Cage is?" does not only harken back to the white male composer canon heralded in both historical and ethnomusicological discourse and foreground a white audience. To ask such a question sets the stage for one-time privileged access, a form of invitation linking the worlds of Black and white musical composition that are "necessary in so far as whites require inroads into

---

14 See Katherine McKittrick's *Dear Science and Other Stories*, especially the notes on pages 21, 25, and 26. On page 21, she writes about citational practice regarding Black women researchers stating, "I was told to cite black women. We were told to cite black women. Sometimes the ideas of black women wear out and wear down even through these narratives provide the clues and instructions to imagine the world anew." I agree here with McKittrick that Black women's ideas "wear down" and are rebirthed "to imagine the world anew." I also agree that they deserve space on the course calendar but recognize not all acknowledgement of Black women allows their ideas to mature with the canonical supremacy of Gilles Deleuze and Félix Guattari, let alone Fanon, or DuBois. We must be honest. Mediocre and dishonorable citation practices of Black women in the field exist, and all too often display the performance in such "acts" of scholarly resistance.

15 Collins 2000, 142.

discourses on race and racism."[16] No one asked themselves: did I just witness anti-Black pedagogy? But this is how ethnomusicologists are expected to represent Black music and interact with Black students in the classroom. Could it be that no one saw this coming?

Could it be that no one wondered what the aftermath would be like for his Black students, and those in programs across the country, who would return back to their scholarly homes? And just what is communicated to interested Black undergraduates looking for an ethnomusicological program to call their own? Is this an example of decades of deracinated methodologies from which we expect our non-Black students to grow? Maybe the Black senior scholars' hearts were hardened, having been broken by society again and again.[17] So when they receive a call from the perpetrator, perhaps their words flow smooth like absolution, a consolation prize. Perhaps that's why gaslighting that would come from fellow students, those present and those not, felt so familiar? One Black student looks for support. Seeking confirmation that what she witnessed was a multitextured site of harm, resonating the same erasure as of Zora Neale Hurston's ethnomusicological undertakings but highlighting instead Alan Lomax's preservation. She sits through denials from POC adjunct faculty to white tenured music professors to upper-level music administrators in private meetings, and it all sounds the same: "That's just the way he is, I've known him for years. He planned for that event as best he could. I can assure you, he didn't intend this kind of harm." And Leonardo asserts, "The discourse on privilege comes with psychological effect of personalizing racism rather than understanding it's [sic] structural origins in interracial relations."[18] Well-meaning comments in defense of particular racist events from various individuals from the university serve two functions of maintaining whiteness, the first of which is to protect the innocence of a

---

16   Leonardo 2005, 141.
17   I say this knowing, and experiencing, indescribable love from elder Black scholars in the Society, and elsewhere, in real time. I acknowledge the tiredness that exists in the reality of being Black and an academic, especially in having attending conference after conference, seminar after seminar, anti-Black courses and job talks. What I am calling for here is a loving and potentially difficult, generational interracial conversation between Black folx about the ways we can better practice solidarity with young Black students in musicology and ethnomusicology without it being a detriment to our job security, without it recreating legacies of seclusion and secrets of survival around systemic of oppression.
18   Leonardo 2005, 140.

colleague who conducted the public interview. Critical race scholars name white innocence as a hallmark of white racialization, often employed as a dialogical maneuver to avoid accountability.[19] The second function serves as contradiction, personalizing the racist comments tucked away in the interview and placing responsibility on the sole professor without acknowledging the complicity of the professional society for deferring to white supremacist structures that privilege a white male scholar—who is not a specialist in Black music, or in the genre of the musician he is interviewing—as having been the best person to conduct an interview with a Black popular musician, while Black experts in the field sit captive in the audience. What does that sound like? Dry, non-Black laughter. No one thought about the violent pitfalls of how Black students get caught up in the campaign of white male virtue signaling and his colleagues' complicity in that act. And now she's just a lost Black graduate student, a brown-skinned alien whose ethnomusicological self has been laid to rest. Cause of death: a bludgeoning by pervasive (ethno)musicological anti-Blackness at every turn.

When I imagine empathetic futures of coalition, I dream of a solidarity free of white fragility and tears. Non-Black teachers and students must learn to hold them in, to swallow and save them for later, for their non-Black peers to share in processing and releasing their guilt. So *I* won't have to bear the brunt of their emotional labor. So *I* might taste the sweetness of being able to rest, fully trusting my non-Black peers and professors to get it right the first time. For them to hear my screams and nonverbal cries in the moment that their subtle silences and violences commit against me the very first crime. I pray we sit in agreement at the discomfort. To partake in sacred vows to move us forward without burdening Black beings who look and sound like me to do the work of correcting those who harm us in the act—not long after the fact.

I am an ethnomusicologist surviving on a lonely cold planet. I mourn my musical heartland from far out in the "Othered" outer space. I'm searching for the warmth of other scholarly suns, for a new time and place, where Black aliens like me, are wholly and honorably embraced. I cry, I sing, I laugh, I strive. I learn. And I know that I'm still the alien here, shrinking into oblivion. Morphing like all my Black peers, in planetary (ethno)departments in order to ease your anti-Black fears.

---

19   See Sue 2015, 32.

References

Burnim, Mellonee V. 1985. "Culture Bearer and Tradition Bearer: An Ethnomusicologist's Research on Gospel Music" *Ethnomusicology* 29 (3): 432–47.

Coates, Te-Nehisi. 2015. *Between the World and Me*. New York: Spiegel and Grau.

Collins, Patricia Hill. 2000. *Black Feminist Thought: Knowledge, Consciousness, and the Politics of Empowerment*. New York: Routledge Press.

Cooper, Brittney. 2018. *Eloquent Rage: A Black Feminist Discovers Her Superpower*. New York: St. Martin's Press.

Cox, Aimee Meredith. 2015. *Shapeshifters: Black Girls and the Choreography of Citizenship*. Durham, NC: Duke University Press.

Davis, Danielle. 2019. "Listening to Bi-Musical Blackness: Towards Courageous Affirmation of Black American String Players in Predominantly White Institutions." Masters' thesis, Florida State University.

hooks, bell. 1995. *Killing Rage: Ending Racism*. New York: Holt

Leonardo, Zeus. 2005. "The Color of Supremacy: Beyond the Discourse of 'White Privilege.'" *Educational Philosophy and Theory* 36 (2): 138–52.

Lorde, Audre. 2007. "The Uses of Anger: Women Responding to Racism." In *Sister Outsider: Essays and Speeches*, 124–33. New York: Random House.

McKittrick, Katherine. 2001. *Dear Science and Other Stories*. Durham, NC: Duke University Press.

Nettl, Bruno. 1995. *Heartland Excursions: Ethnomusicological Reflections on Schools of Music*. Urbana: University of Illinois Press.

Sue, Derald Wing. 2015. *Race Talk and the Conspiracy of Silence: Understanding and Facilitating Difficult Dialogues on Race*. Hoboken, NJ: Wiley Press, 98.

Syms, Martine. 2014. "The Mundane Afrofuturist Manifesto." *Third Rail*, no. 3. http://thirdrailquarterly.org/martine-syms-the-mundane-afrofuturist-manifesto/.

Chapter Eight

Ethnomusicological Becoming

Deep Listening as Erotics in the Field

Carol Muller

> When I speak of the erotic, then, I speak of it as the assertion of a lifeforce of women; of that creative energy empowered, the knowledge of which we are now reclaiming in our language, our history, our dancing, our loving, our work, our lives.
> —Audre Lorde, "Uses of the Erotic: The Erotic as Power"

> We sit next to each other, [hearing] the unfamiliar rendering of the familiar, which we call performance, and we begin to bond without an initial need for words. Words will come later, as they always do. But for now, we sit on common ground, experiencing something together, supporting each other throughout the experience by the very fact of proximity … Listening may not seem like much … but it is the firm ground for building and rebuilding society the real way: the solid way based on our shared human condition. (Pujol, Artist's Journal: The Listeners, 2018)
> —Dave Isay, *Listening Is an Act of Love*

> Village women when they write their songs write songs to free themselves from the chains that bind them.
> —Thandiswa Mazwai, "Feminist Party" on Zoom

It was Thanksgiving 2016, the weekend of the opening of the Philadelphia Sudanese Community Center in West Philly, the place where graduate students in my Field Methods seminar had been conducting research.[1] Most of the students were not in town that weekend, so I went alone for the day's events, bearing a digital still camera and MP3 recorder. While I waited for events to begin, I ventured down into the basement of the building to encounter a long brightly lit room, with an array of Sudanese cultural objects, displays of food, clothing, jewelry, and walls lined with a wide array of Sudanese art—paintings, pencil drawings, linocuts, an image of Martin Luther King Jr. with a cross and Arabic script, another of an early Sudanese woman missionary in Germany, and pencil portraits of Sudanese poets and writers. A local community ensemble of teen girl string players, one of whom was Sudanese, was warming up in the corner; a small group of teens we had worked with in a freshman seminar in 2015 was rehearsing their song and dance routine; young children played on African-made drums and then wandered around the area; hijab-covered women in a rich array of colorful toobs were preparing food. There was such warmth and openness to my obvious outsider status; for those who asked, I told them who I was and where I was from. Some thanked me for coming from my university to share the day with them, though honestly, I was just happy to be able to participate. The opening was festive, with a rich programming of Sudanese and Sudanese American cultural performances for much of the day.

After I returned home, I sat listening to, and reviewing, the photographs and sound recordings I had made earlier in the day. I suddenly became physically aware of the profound sense of pleasure, deep joy, and satisfaction I was feeling once again, doing the "work" of ethnomusicology in a place where the fieldwork project was intended for graduate student training rather than my own research. In their absence, I was once again engaging in communities, learning from, and alongside groups of people I might otherwise never have come to know living in the United States, uncovering the stories and experiences of people from the new African diasporas, especially those who practice Islam. This sensory web of pleasure, joy, and satisfaction, the pull to knowledge and understanding through field research, which emerges from sharing space and listening closely and repeatedly to the words and music of our research interlocutors, is what I am calling an erotics of fieldwork, a sensibility that has profoundly shaped my sense of self as a woman in ethnomusicology. Following Audre Lorde (2007 [1984]) I locate the erotic in a

---

1   Many thanks to the kindness and vision of Michelle Kisliuk and Sidra Lawrence for their work and inspiration over the evolution of this volume and my own thinking.

place of nonpatriarchal, female empowerment that comes from sharing one's pursuits with others, knowing the open and fearless capacity for joy, never [ab]using each other as objects, and harnessing the energy within to pursue creative work and genuine social change.

Lorde wrote as a Black lesbian woman warrior, mother, and poet, always insisting in her essay writing on the rich complexity of her identity; I am a white African-born woman scholar and mother of a racially blended family, overlapping in some but not every way with Lorde. Nevertheless, Lorde's writing on the erotic has given me a language for my evolving subjectivity as an ethnomusicologist increasingly researching women's performances. It is Lorde's idea of the erotic that explains an unfettered Lacanian jouissance—the excess and abundance of feeling—that emerges from the "work" of deep listening in close proximity to my research interlocutors. This jouissance invokes a desire for the creative and poetic, something that is pulled from the inside, that inspires and breathes life into ethnographic research, writing, and representation, and constitutes a woman-centered ethnomusicological habitus. Situating our joy inside "work" largely focused on the lives of other women, we position ourselves outside of the patriarchal surveillance of the global North defining what we study, how we process materials, and write them up on our own terms as women ethnomusicologists.

In this chapter I explore, experiment, and tussle with an evolving erotics of fieldwork as a white South African working first inside apartheid South Africa, then outside the country with musical exiles; after I moved to the United States my teaching related research has engaged African Americans, new African immigrants, and recently, I have connected back "home" with South African musicians in country and abroad. I reflect on the joy that emerges from the privilege of access to the daily, performative, and ritual practices of "others" through deep listening in an attempt to increase knowledge and understanding across difference by invoking the thinking of Audre Lorde, social choreographer Ernesto Pujol, and the words and performances of South African singer extraordinaire, King Tha/Thandiswa Mazwai. I will suggest that becoming an ethnomusicologist as a South African woman has been a process where men have largely opened doors to my research interlocutors, but once in, I have shared musical knowledge and experiences with many women singers, dancers, composers, and believers in ways that increasingly reconceptualize ethnography in new, more embodied ways.

As a result, over the last four decades the sounds of many fields of performance have disrupted my world as they have pulled at my ears and memory: they have played around and around in my body, head, and heart, transforming my hearing, my understanding of the ways of many in and from Africa, and my sense of myself as an African-born "white" woman. These webs of sound and movement have shaped my thinking, my sense of being in the world, my writing, teaching, and indeed the growing pull to make my work and life move toward the erotic and a life well lived—personally, in my family, my scholarly community, and in terms of national belonging.

All this takes place in shifting contexts of research and residence—first as a "whites only" citizen of apartheid South Africa, then as a citizen of a fully democratic nation state, then as a US green card holder, and more recently as a dual citizen of both South Africa and the United States. Shifting categories of national belonging have similarly impacted how I have thought about my work. These shifts have occurred in a discipline that has slowly moved from a patriarchal position that studied music of others far way by employing an "objective" stance, to including the feminist position that field experiences are formative of our own subjectivities, and that academic research with others carries a heavy political responsibility.

I come from a country that has taken some steps to interrogate the consequences of its colonial and apartheid past; and I live in another where there is still a measure of denial by those in power of its part in colonial history inside the nation-state, and of the work of the American military and cultural imperialism from the mid-twentieth century to the present in the world at large. This has real implications for what it means to conduct research inside and beyond the United States for American ethnomusicology. Clearly, we are living in turbulent times, both as global citizens and in the field of music studies: the present moment demands we grapple with the challenges of decolonizing our discipline, and in 2020–23 we also confront the immobility and glaring social, racial, gendered, and developing world inequalities laid bare by the COVID-19 global pandemic.

Narrating Field Research

To reflect on an evolving notion of the politics and erotics of field research, I highlight a few research projects I have undertaken and the changing ways in which I have negotiated shared spaces in each of these projects as a woman in the field, or as Lorde has termed it, a "sister outsider" (1984). I began fieldwork in South Africa as an undergraduate music student majoring in ethnomusicology in the 1980s in the era of "Grand Apartheid," when the laws of apartheid were deeply entrenched in the country—these were laws that divided and discriminated on the basis of a group's "ethnicity"—so "ethnomusicology" was a complicated field of study—though in my mind, the research required for the degree took me into spaces where I could learn something about music and culture I would never otherwise have known. In retrospect I realize that my push to do the field research paralleled the work of my father at the time.

I grew up in a home where my father's Christian faith increasingly called him toward what he called a ministry of racial reconciliation: he lived by the principles of loving god, and loving your neighbor, whoever and wherever your neighbor was. And my mother questioned every assumption my father made in his weekly sermons, while she led a women's Bible study with at least one woman who came out as gay in the context of the group. Ours was a fairly turbulent household.

My research as an ethnomusicologist was less about the certainty of faith, even if it was clearly guided by the principles of loving one's neighbor in a deeply divided apartheid society, and bachelor of music degree research requirements. Ethnomusicology meant fieldwork, and my father's ventures across racial divisions instilled in me the desire as a white girl to know how the majority of South Africa lived, and perhaps because of my mother's continuous questions about the authority of the Bible, ultimately pushed me to explore how Black women lived under religious patriarchy, and how faith and music worked under conditions of extreme economic hardship and injustice.

In apartheid South Africa, the desire to know in the mid-1980s to early 1990s carried with it extraordinarily high risk: under successive States of Emergencies in the 1980s, as a young white woman traveling into Black residential areas, I could easily have been suspected of being a government spy and/or become a target of random or intentional violence—as was the case with American Fulbright student Amy Biehl in the townships of the Western Cape.[2] In the 1980s, a white person traveling into Black South African spaces required a permit from the government—in other words "fieldwork"

---

2   Biehl was killed in what was believed to be a "senseless murder" by anti-apartheid activists in Cape Town in August 1993. Her parents came to meet their daughter's killer in the context of South Africa's Truth and Reconciliation commission, transforming their daughter's death into a moment for forgiveness and nation-building in South Africa. See article on her death at http://www.nytimes.com/1993/08/27/world/how-american-sister-died-in-a-township.html.

was essentially forbidden if one was to work with anyone across the color line. Essentially, to do the work you had to break the law. There was also always a police/security presence in the townships, though I cannot say that I ever felt safer because of them. In one State of Emergency in 1986 I traveled to a Durban township to pick up my gumboot dance research partners for a social event at my home, and my mother told me later that she thought I would never come back alive.

My first official "field research" was in about 1984, when I carried it out together with fellow student and now curator of the International Music collection at the British Library, Janet Topp Fargion. We were ethnomusicology undergraduates who asked our advisor Veit Erlmann where we could "find African music." He suggested we travel to the Eastern Cape to the Lumko Missiological Institute where Catholic priest Dave Dargie was indigenizing the Catholic mass using large marimbas and the Xhosa language, while conducting research on Xhosa traditional music.[3] Janet had a small car, so armed with a map that revealed little about Black homelands in the Eastern Cape and few signposts or clear routes, we drove to the Lumko mission station for the long Easter weekend.

I have two visceral memories of that place and its music: in the first, I recall lying in bed embraced by the solitude of the mission. We fell asleep each night and woke early the next morning to the endless repetition of the Easter liturgy from a nearby building—performed on marimbas accompanied by hundreds of singing voices. The music resonated over the open landscape, seeping into our hearts and minds, pulling us into the edges of Catholicism, Xhosa style. The song I remember most distinctly from that weekend, "Ntsikana's Bell," is a nineteenth-century hymn composed by Xhosa prophet Ntsikana Xaba that would resurface a few years later in the popular styles of marimba band AmaMpondo;[4] but more poignantly for my own research, in the jazz performances of South African pianist Abdullah Ibrahim and bass player Johnny Dyani. Recorded in the 1970s while both were in exile in Europe and the United States, "Ntsikana's Bell" combines a soulful Xhosa/Arabic rendering of the words and music of the old hymn in Eastern Cape jazz improvisation (see Muller and Benjamin 2011, 179–80 for a description of the performance). Sounding out, it registers the deep longing and desire for a return home that seemed an impossible quest for

---

3   Lumko Institute located in the former Transkei, near the town of Lady Frere. see http://lumko.org/history/ (accessed November 29, 2016).
4   For further information see http://www.music.org.za/artist.asp?id=56.

South African exiles in the mid-1970s. It would be the music I played on August 20, 2013, when I received a forwarded email from Ibrahim about the death of his ex-wife, singer Sathima Bea Benjamin, a story I will detail below.

The second moment of a kind of sensual/erotic recollection comes from Easter Saturday around lunchtime. Janet and I followed Father Dargie to the site of his core research associate: Mrs. Nofinish Dwyli, the bearer of a style of singing performed largely by Xhosa women and called *umngqokolo*—Xhosa women's overtone singing.[5] Out of the soothing warmth of the midday sun, we stepped into the cool darkness of Nofinish Dywili's hut, from the certainty of the light outside into the obscurity of her dwelling. The unfamiliar smell of the floor made of cow dung, the dampness of the mud walls and the absence of internal lighting, electrical or otherwise, produced an unease for us. All we could hear was what then seemed to be the eerie and unfamiliar sounds of umngqokolo: the deep gruff fundamental chest tone from which escaped high-pitched overtone melodic lines. I had never heard anything like it before.

It was so dark inside, shivers of the unexpected moment sent chills down my spine. Where did these sounds come from? Were these the voices of ancestral spirits possessing the musician's body? How could she create such sounds if not through possession? And then there was the challenge of the clicking without stumbling—umngqokolo—the q is a hard click, like the sound of a horse hoof galloping on solid turf. As we left a woman gave me some brass bracelets. "You should be a *sangoma*," the interpreter told me, "A traditional healer." Objectively there was nothing to fear beyond the power of my own feelings of cultural and linguistic incompetence, and my inability in this brief encounter to learn anything about this woman (though Dargie would publish on her a decade later). This was, nevertheless, the moment of my first-ever field recording: I carried out into the sunlight a cassette of Nofinish Dywili's singing, the capacity to later listen closely to and eventually become

---

5   There is a wonderful documentary filmed by Father Dave Dargie on the overtone singing of Xhosa women that we heard that morning, actually with one of the singers we heard that day. See https://www.youtube.com/watch?v=MYj-55T6Uzs retrieved November 29, 2016. This was filmed 1985-1998. It is loaded by Quang Hai Tran. A second video includes musical bow performances by a group of Xhosa women from the same district. See also this clip on Xhosa Overtone Singing at https://www.youtube.com/watch?v=MYj-55T6Uzs&list=RDMYj-55T6Uzs&start_radio=1&t=99 and here: https://www.youtube.com/watch?v=H5ufUjLQBXk&list=RDMYj-55T6Uzs&index=2

mesmerized by the deep guttural tones of her chest voice and the exquisitely formed overtone sounding of her song accompanied in some instances on the musical bow.[6] I return to the pull of women's bow music at the end of the chapter, with a brief discussion of the 2021 quarantine streaming of the performances of Nofinish Dwyili's student, the woman now known as a "national treasure," Madosini, the Xhosa musical bow player, and written about by a former student Sazi Dlamini (2008).

The following year there were two core ethnomusicological experiences: one involved an invitation to learn to gumboot dance in a Black male migrant dance team in Umlazi township,[7] and the other was hearing the music of jazz pianist Abdullah Ibrahim/Dollar Brand in the context of an undergraduate seminar on South African jazz. There was little scholarly writing on South African jazz in the country at the time,[8] so our knowledge was gathered by reading press articles about Ibrahim's 1960s conversion to Islam and 1968 pilgrimage to Mecca; we also listened to cassette copies of his music. I remember being completely mesmerized by, and drawn into, the sound of his playing—a complex layering of so much South African history and ethnicity: the harmonies of the European mission hymn, the sounds of popular township music, Islamic overtones, bow rhythms, and so much more.

At the time, Ibrahim's music was available only in the university music library, and for every track we listened to, we were held accountable by the apartheid regime—we had to fill in a form describing our listening to the government. We could listen and be transformed only in the context of the seminar and the library. We never imagined in the mid-1980s that we would

---

6   Years later, when I met the Tuvan Alash ensemble and heard their songs produced by overtone formation, there was an "I have heard this before" kind of familiarity with the otherwise "exotic" sounding of these male voices from Central Asia. QuanTraiHan is a Vietnamese ethnomusicologist who was long associated with CNRS in Paris; he filmed the overtone singing of the Xhosa musicians but has a wider interest in Central Asian overtone singing, jews harp performance, and so forth. See http://www.tranquanghai.info/p1263-tran-quang-hai-bio-updated-2011.html (accessed November 29, 2016).
7   See for example, the chapter on gumboot dance in Muller 2008.
8   David Coplan's doctoral dissertation (Indiana 1984) was the first comprehensive accounting of Black urban performance history, with some focus on South African jazz, written when I was an undergraduate. There is an abundance of South African jazz records, archives, and academic writing in the 2020s.

ever have a chance to hear Abdullah Ibrahim perform live in South Africa, or even to meet him at a performance abroad. His music was forbidden because by the mid-1980s he was banned in South Africa. But I was drawn to the strains of his music, desiring more but stopped short by the rules of a racist and oppressive regime.

In 1990 I returned to South Africa after three years of coursework at New York University to work with the female members of Ibandla lamaNazaretha, the followers of Zulu prophet Isaiah Shembe, headquartered in KwaZulu Natal. These were Nguni traditionalists who had modeled their religious community on stories of polygamy, cattle ownership, and the Ten Commandments of the Old Testament mixed together with miracle stories of Jesus in the New Testament to create their own "third testament" of the African prophet Shembe. They embraced traditional dance regalia and magnificent beadwork, for congregational worship on Saturdays, the Sabatha, and traditional dance ceremonies on Sundays. Ibandla lamaNazaretha convened an annual three-day walking pilgrimage to the holy mountain of Nhlangakaze, the site of the creation of a new sacred song and dance repertory for the community in the 1920s. I walked with Nazaretha women in January 1992. When we arrived at Nhlangakaze there was an organ powered by a car battery on the top of the mountain. It was amazing, and I remember at the time thinking how easy it would be to sensationalize this community through sophisticated cultural theorizing about exotic/erotic rituals and beliefs: female bodies, female virginity, spiritual/sexual relationships between women and their religious leaders could easily have been written about in this manner.[9] And yet, in the context of the twilight of apartheid, with very low levels of literacy in the religious and wider community, I was ambivalent about writing racial and culture difference in ways that would distance in terms of academic language. It was politically imperative to describe, explain, and situate this community in the most honest and straightforward manner possible, to make their focus on a blending of Nguni tradition, cultural memory, and biblical authority comprehensible.

In *Rituals of Fertility and the Sacrifice of Desire* (1999), I wrote about ritual performances and the faith of Shembe virgin girls and married women.

---

9   Jean Comaroff's 1985 publication, *Body of Power, Spirit of Resistance* (Chicago) is a sophisticated cultural reading of the parallel Zionist religious movements in South Africa, which had been a real academic winner—by the time I spoke to the editor at Chicago about my own work in the mid-1990s it had sold over twenty thousand copies, an unusual number for an academic monograph.

In the context of this chapter and three decades after the end of apartheid, Nazaretha practices are perhaps read more easily in erotic terms—theirs is a spiritual union with the leader Shembe—the founder who died in 1936, his successor son, Johannes Galilee, Galilee's brother, Amos, and Amos's son Vimbeni, all of whom have now passed on and inhabit the ancestral realm. While the founders were alive, many young women became part of the Shembe lineage through sexual relations with their founder: Amos was reported to have fathered over one hundred children.

Married women (called "amafortinis") regularly met together in the middle of a twenty-eight-day cycle, symbolic of the middle of a woman's menstrual cycle, when they would be (metaphorically) at their most fertile. Instead of being home with their human partners, they consummated their spiritual relationship with the ancestral Shembe, sharing with other women through prayer, song, dance, and testimony to the spiritual and miraculous force of the leader in their lives. When Shembe women sang, they followed the melodies/pathways of the words given by the founder and his son; these were the words of Shembe's experience inscribed in the hymn repertory, a repertory conceived from the ancestral realm in dreams and gifted to the community. In singing these hymns Shembe women claimed the words as their own, and they moved their bodies to the rhythms he created for those words. Female spiritual eroticism seemed to lie at the heart of Shembe women's subjectivity and religious being, even if I didn't write about their faith using an erotic interpretive strategy in the 1990s.

As to my own ethnomusicological subjectivity, my research with ibandla lamaNazaretha is now two decades behind me but my longing for return is triggered by listening to recordings of the awesome beauty of Nazarite women's spiritual singing in Paradis, the open-air temples of ibandla lamaNazaretha. My sense of being able to comfortably inhabit the now familiar sound world of Nazarite women contrasts markedly with the ongoing disorientation I initially experienced at the start of my dissertation research: the particularities of Shembe song style made me feel musically incompetent as I struggled to pick out a single melodic line. I felt like I was drowning in a lack of cultural knowledge, and I worried about how long it was taking me to grasp Shembe song style. With time I came to understand that it was the slow, deliberate, repetitive outworking of rhythm and syllable that extended the Shembe "hymn" into an infinite pool of possibility for women and girls. There was no single melodic line to be discovered among the women and girls. Rather, their voices were the "embroideries," the ornamentation, the elaboration, the wistful extension of a song into pure duration and sonic dwelling. When I hear that singing in my field recordings, I long to have the capacity to lose myself, once again, to surrender to the emotional outpouring and swirls of melodic fragments of Shembe women's sound and style.

On August 20, 2013, Sathima Bea Benjamin, a South African born singer of "mixed" racial heritage, died alone, her body naked on her bed in a Cape Town flat. Though she had spent much of her adult life in exile in Europe and then New York City, she always said she wanted to return to Cape Town for her final days. Sathima and I had shared a twenty-three-year-long research partnership and friendship that began while she was living in the Chelsea Hotel in New York City in 1989. Over the years I had listened closely to her voice, heard pieces of her story, and patched together what she couldn't remember through conversations with many others, digging in archives, and hearing her singing on record and in rare live performances. There was so much in our lives initially that should have kept us apart from each other. Though we were both from the city of Cape Town, South Africa, and both passionate about living in New York City, Sathima was born into a family from many parts of the world; she would ultimately be classified by the apartheid regime as "Cape Coloured," having "many nations in me" as her song "Nations in Me" tells it. I had been born "European" and become "white." But eventually we co-authored a book together: *Musical Echoes: South African Women Thinking in Jazz* (Duke, 2011). It was structured as a kind of call and response: Sathima's story called, and I responded with reflections on the broader significance of her story as my academic training had equipped me to do.

On August 20, 2013, Sathima Bea Benjamin's voice came to a sudden and unexpected end. The announcement came in writing, in the emotionally neutered medium of a forwarded email. No sound, no beauty, just bald information. Sathima was gone. I turned on her music, and I played the lamentations of Abdullah Ibrahim and Johnny Dyani: "Ntsikana's Bell," that powerful hymn from the Eastern Cape, the hymn I first heard in the resonating echoes of the Lumko Missiological Institute sounding out in the tones of the Catholic marimba ensemble. Reaching back into Eastern Cape history, Ntsikana was himself a Xhosa prophet in the religious lineage into which Isaiah, Galilee, Amos, and Vimbeni Shembe are situated. I heard in this 1970s recorded performance of "Ntsikana's Bell" a lamentation to Sathima's life and voice. Bea Benjamin had become "Sathima," when she was lovingly renamed by exiled bass player Johnny Dyani. "Sathima" means "the one who listens." Painfully, I realized in that moment that the voice of Sathima would only now be heard as an echo of prior performances. And I longed for the presence of her voice, to be swept away by the beauty of her sound, the tenderness and graciousness of her spirit, the subtlety of her interpretation. Even though the possibility of continued stories and conversations came to an end on that day, there is something haunting, sensual, possibly even erotic about the pull of Sathima's voice on my body and heart that stays with me even in her death. The recording produces the capacity for endless repetition, allowing us to continue to be mesmerized by her voice sounding out long after her body has passed on. Even so, with the silencing of the living voice of Sathima I am tormented by the suddenness of her end.

It was through Sathima's willingness to talk to me, to tell her story, sometimes repeating the same information but in slightly different tones and with shifting attention to details, that I came to an understanding of the capacity for new narratives of African diasporas in jazz. After several years of listening closely, I began to reflect on my own diasporic experiences as our lives and stories increasingly became intertwined living in New York City and so many other places. And it is absolutely clear that while *Musical Echoes* is Sathima's story about her own life and music, it is framed by an intertwined experience of living diasporically from her perspective and my own.

When I moved to Philadelphia to teach at the University of Pennsylvania in 1998, I harnessed that sense of moving back and forth across the Atlantic Ocean between South Africa and the American northeast by extending my teaching into a more intentional community engagement pedagogy. It started with a broad field methods project in West Philly Baptist churches, and post-911 moved into an African American Islamic community. On the cusp of the Trump presidency, my teaching began increasingly to explore the diasporic experiences of African refugees and immigrants who had arrived in Philadelphia, beginning with those from Sudan who came in the 1980s and have continued to come ever since. Much of this latter work, however, was driven by the principles of what Penn's Netter Center for Community Partnerships calls Academically Based Community Service teaching, rather than by my own research agenda. That was true until I arrived at the Sudanese American Community Center and assumed the role of ethnomusicologist as outlined at the start of the chapter. Though the Sudanese community is Muslim and from the northeastern part of the African continent, working with this community arouses deep feelings of a continental longing, an African way of being in community that one simply doesn't feel anywhere else in the city of Philadelphia.

That desire to know and to share with students I teach, the longing to connect to a feeling of Africanness from my home continent, a desire for shared joy in the music, dance, art, theater, and thinking, a celebration of South African arts evolved into a Penn study abroad class that took students to the National Arts Festival in what is now Makanda (formerly Grahamstown). Two weeks online and two weeks of intensive immersion in all the creative expression of the annual festival was less about research and more about a passion for sharing together, a longing to feel in *communitas* with my students, to open up the possibilities of bearing witness to the amazing performances of all kinds of South African artists. Finding something in common through emotional reflection and sometimes painful confrontations with a brutal local history became a critical mechanism for me to feel a sense of home away from home as an ethnomusicology professor, and to bring something of my home to my American university. In the process the class opened up to students of all strands of African heritage studying at Penn who came to know a world of Southern African art making that was troubling, amazing, beautiful, provocative, and a gift that keeps on giving.

A key piece of the National Arts Festival was the Standard Bank Festival of (South African) Jazz, a festival where I first encountered musicians I had taught in the mid-1990s at UKZN, alongside a new generation of university-educated improvisers and composers, many of whom I have now reconnected with through the innovative presenting by South African born, American educated Seton Hawkins, head of jazz education for Lincoln Center Jazz in New York City, who also managed Sathima Bea Benjamin before she returned to South Africa. It is hard to explain the deep sense of connection, of sonic intimacy, of the desire to listen, know and to share the rich acoustical complexity of language, history, and experience that is South African jazz when it travels across the Atlantic Ocean. Through community engagement teaching we have showcased, filmed, recorded, and created podcasts out of the brief encounters with South African jazz in New York City and Philadelphia.

In the 2020s the "field" is no longer bound to a single place: South African musicians are traveling; their music is being downloaded and listened to literally all over the world. Mixed in with the sound of African language, the memories of African traditional and ritual music making, the longing to find a place for the music in the global marketplace, are some of the resonances and freedoms of (American) jazz history one hears echoed in South African jazz, but they no longer sound American. These are the ideas, innovative gestures, and improvisations deeply rooted in a southern African nesting of sounded experience; the pathways to investigating the fragments and traces of a precolonial African past boldly inserted into the aesthetic processes of contemporary African jazz sounding-out. Even with the stark immobility of human movement thrust on all by the COVID-19 pandemic, South African musicians have continued to collaborate, to record, and to live stream.

Living in the global North, with the silencing of so much by the ravages of an out-of-control COVID-19 pandemic in 2021, I had the chance to listen in to so much South African jazz on Youtube, Zoom, Facebook and Instagram Live, to buy tickets to local South African platforms now with a global reach. While we had been humanly immobilized our ears had been fed the warm and rich tones of South African–made jazz. And it is this experience of the 2020s that pulls me ever more deeply into a place of deep listening, of longing, desire, and ultimately of consummate joy. The field is at once locally produced and sounded, but now with ears listening in from a thousand plateaus scattered around the contemporary world, at any hour of the day, depending on where you are located in that moment of musical performance.

It was in such a place and moment that I listened in to the exquisite rendering of the mouth-resonated performances of Madosini's musical bow, Madosini the student of Nofinishi, Madosini who was brought to Cape Town by the group AmaMpondo, the marimba players inspired by the work of the Catholic liturgy led by Father Dave Dargie at the Lumko mission. My journey in the field has come full circle, back to the deep and ancient sounds of Xhosa women singing, though this time there is no darkness, only white walls and the scattering of spring blossoms in the room where Madosini is filmed for live streaming to anyone anywhere who purchases a ticket.

Drawing Things Together

I never thought I would be able to write a piece about erotics and fieldwork—the usual understanding of intimacy, and sexual relationships between couples (scholar and research assistant, scholar and performer) wasn't a piece of my experience. I suspect that is because in 1980s South Africa a white woman was quite obviously untouchable across racial lines. The consequences of allowing desire to roam in sensual or sexual ways may have meant crossing over into absolutely forbidden and dangerous territory, which if discovered by the police or security forces could have meant death or imprisonment. This was apartheid South Africa, after all. The voices of the women singing, however, had greater freedom to meander, to explore, and to possess the listener across racial categories. And it was that liberty to spread its acoustical tentacles that enabled a kind of seeping into the body, mind, and soul of the ethnomusicologist.

Though I would regularly feel deep anxiety and had moments of profound fear traveling into the unmapped territories of Black South Africa under apartheid, the passion to know, and the pressing need to understand what was at the other end, lured me in, over and over again. In this chapter I have played around with the possibilities of a subjectivity shaped by a kind of eroticism, a desire, a passion for knowledge and human understanding evoked through hearing musical difference in contexts of personal risk, and in a shifting political context both in South Africa and the United States. At its core this erotics of knowledge acquisition is formed out of negotiating the feelings of initial distance but growing proximity that characterize being in "the field," the continual tug between familiarity and difference as a way of coming to know oneself in relation to another, sometimes enabling the other to be on equal footing, sometimes submitting completely to the other's wisdom, knowledge, and sounds as a new but integral piece of the ethnomusicological self.

Hearing the music and the stories pulls us into shared space and ultimately into community; we allow the words and music to wash over us repeatedly, to flood our bodies and memories. Repeated listening and immersive research into the place, meanings, and value of music making in a community shapes our hearing over time, enabling a recognition of the sounds of others as something that has become a part of who we are as individual ethnomusicologists, drawing us closer to those we have heard, layering memories of field experiences we carry with us, back into our lives as citizen-intellectuals inside the boundaries of the nation-state and well beyond, particularly as we write the research and teach.

My longing and desire to know leaves me ensnared, entwined in the layers of emotion, beauty, suffering, and personhood conveyed through the voices of women in song, voices I may never have known had it not been for the necessity of field research, deep listening to song and story, to the pull of the ear by these voices, and the need to know more and more. The ethnomusicological imperative is itself one of social marginality: venturing out, called by the sounds of difference and familiarity, inscribing knowledge, producing some understanding, and validating endless pools of sonic beauty, and acoustical power, often in faraway or dangerous places in a racialized, often religiously intolerant, world characterized by racial, economic, and gendered inequality. And perhaps our work now is to engage more deliberately the place and positions of our interlocutors in the societies we share: immigrants, refugees, Muslims, minorities, children, and women; seeking ways to promote greater understanding and interfaith dialogue out of the rich resources of musical knowledge and performance embedded in these communities. Nevertheless, there is a clear imperative to examine our histories, our relationships of power and domination, of imperialism and subservience, inside the nation-state and well beyond. In this, perhaps, the limits of the erotic in ethnomusicology are exposed—the place where the cracking foundations of the "common ground" and "proximity" we claim forces us to know and reckon with our pasts, not to presume entry into a foreign community but rather to envision more equitable modes of research, partnership, and representation for our discipline to retains its relevance in the twenty-first century. For as South African lesbian, womanist, rebel, Afropunk singer King Tha/Thandiswa Mazwai so eloquently reminds us, when village women write their songs, they do so in order to free themselves from the chains that bind them.

References

Dargie, Dave. 2011. "The Redoubtable Nofinishi Dywili, Uhadi Master and Xhosa Song Leader." *South African Music Studies* 31 (30–31).

Dlamini, Sazi. 2004. "The Role of the Umrhubhe Bow as Transmitter of Cultural Knowledge among the amaXhosa: An Interview with Latozi 'Madosini' Mpahleni," *Journal of the Musical Arts in Africa* 1 (1): 138–60.

Ibrahim, Abdullah, and Johnny Dyani. 1979. "Ntsikana's Bell." *Echoes from Africa.* Germany: Enja 3047 ST.

Isay, David. 2007. *Listening Is an Act of Love. A Celebration of American Life from the StoryCorps Project.* New York: Penguin Books.

Lorde, Audre. 2007 [1984]. "Uses of the Erotic: The Erotic as Power." In *Sister Outsider: Essays and Speeches by Audre Lorde.* Freedom, CA: Crossing Press, 53–57.

Mazwai, Thandiswa. 2020. "Celebrating First Anniversary of Women and Gender Studies at Nelson Mandela University." YouTube video, streamed October 2, 2020. https://www.youtube.com/watch?v=kNm5li0769s&list=UUhgJhLchQSrZMYyV06zy9pw.

Muller, Carol. 1999. *Rituals of Fertility and the Sacrifice of Desire: Nazarite Women's Performance in South Africa.* Chicago: University of Chicago Press.

Muller, Carol, and Sathima Bea Benjamin. 2011. *Musical Echoes: South African Women Thinking in Jazz.* Durham, NC: Duke University Press.

Pujol, Ernesto. 2018. "Artist's Journal: The Listeners." *Theater* 48 (3): 101–11.

Chapter Nine

Mirror Dancing in Congo

Reflections on Fieldwork as Blanche Neige

Lesley N. Braun

As the drummer hits the cymbal, the dancer pivots on her front foot with her arm raised above her head, marking *le passage*, the passage beat. She turns to intently face the crowd while vigorously rotating her hips in a movement originating from the knees. Shrugging her shoulders rhythmically upwards, head cocked to the side, she holds her arms to her rib cage, locating the center of movement. She is stoic; her facial expression is fixed but not emotionless. The drummer embellishes each subsequent movement in the choreographic sequence, carefully keeping watch, predicting her next move. I watch her too, from the side wings of the stage where I wait with the other dancers for her solo to finish. The audience explodes with cheers when she leaps into the air at the moment when the music reaches an ecstatic crescendo, her hands clapping shut above her body as if to catch something visible only to her. This concert, not unlike other concerts across the sprawling city of Kinshasa, is incomplete without the presence of stage dancers, or danseuses. And it is in this expressive milieu that women are the most visible performers in the city, and where their bravado is felt.

I am also a danseuse in the band. Though like the others, I was given the stage name Blanche Neige,[1] I feel more like a clown and an other. I am a far cry from the celebrated image of femininity in Kinshasa, the capital of the

---

1   Snow White

Democratic Republic of Congo, as I am bony and do not move with the same elegance and mastery as the others. Nevertheless, the band invites me to rehearse and perform with them several times a week. I muddle through *entrainement* (training), doing my best to learn the routines. My main preoccupation is not so much to pass as a professional dancer as it is to spend time with the dancers, build relationships with them, and to better understand this mode of work that these young women have chosen to devote themselves to. Every ethnographer strives for cultural intimacy, and I approached this through the sensuousness of dance, reflected back to me in and through my own participation.

Filip De Boeck, an urban anthropologist of Congo writes, "The manner of production of space and time in the city is thus inextricably connected with the production of the body. Body and society reflect and are mirrored in each other" (2004, 238). The mirror topos also reveals different perspectives on gendered and sexualized forms of power in different contexts. For dance scholars Sally Ann Ness and Carrie Noland, "A dancer's body appears as something very much like a living monument to a given technical 'discourse'" (Ness and Noland 2008, 22). To be sure, dance is not merely a mirror reflecting society; it also has the potential to call into question and reshape norms and values. The dancing body is inscribed with norms and values that are performed, but it is also engaged with ways in which selfhood is created and expressed through pleasure.

Part of a larger research project beginning in 2009 in which I spent several years working with concert dancers, this essay is a reflection on different dance milieus in Kinshasa and the women who actively take part. Specifically, I consider several ways in which dance is refracted in the city, as well as how it relates to some of the broader concerns about how femininity is constructed. Figuring into my own reflections as a dancer and ethnographer, the presence and absence of mirrors in the different contexts where dance takes place reveals arrangements of gazing, both by spectators and individual performers. This essay is a reflection on a set of encounters that occurred during my fieldwork in Kinshasa that highlight the spaces in which dance, desire, gaze, pleasure, and sexuality are intertwined. In the first encounter, I will describe my concert dancing activities, followed by a discussion of the importance of dance videos in the apprehension and mastery of dance. Here, I also make connections between social norms, morality, and dancing. Finally, I discuss the role that mirrors play in Kinshasa's nightclubs and the imagination they inspire, as well as the interiority they reveal.

Concert Music in Kinshasa

The legendary Congolese rumba music scene has been extensively explored and written about over the years in no small part because this musical expression maintains a rich history not only within the African continent but also worldwide.[2] Sounds from Cuban rumba arriving through Greek trading networks to the Belgian Congo in the 1930s mingled with ethnic music from across this vast region, coalescing into what is now referred to as "Congolese rumba." The borrowing between genres have been ongoing and the spheres of sacred and profane musical genres continue to overlap considerably. Currently, Pentecostal churches appropriate Congolese rumba's concert format to suit their own liturgical interests. The concert spectacle has long been the means of revenue relied upon by orchestras, particularly because selling albums to fans with limited disposable income is not a realistic prospect.[3] Rumba bands, called orchestras, are composed of dozens of performers, creating a vertiginous hierarchy of members who play for audiences both locally and abroad—some of the most famous bands regularly pack large musical venues across Europe and North America. Similar to the revenue strategies that other bands internationally adopt, the concert is the primary means through which money can be earned. It follows that a dynamic performance is needed to attract an audience.

While the men in this musical milieu have been chronicled, little has been written about the participating women, partly because they were largely absent as musicians and singers.[4] Despite this omission in academic texts, since the birth of this musical genre, which emerged in the colonial city of Léopoldville (now Kinshasa), women have nevertheless been shaping this genre of music in their own way. Since the 1980s young women have been integrated in the concert model—most bands now employ both male and female dancers to generate energy that animates the audience (Braun 2014). Troupes of dancing women on stage create a hyperpresence of sensuality and eroticism. Men for their part are also sometimes hired as dancers—their

---

2   There is a rich body of literature discussing Congolese rumba music. See: Lonoh 1969; Steward 2000; Gondola 1993; White 2008; Tsambu 2004; Trapido 2017.
3   For an elaborated discussion about the music industry in Congo see White 2008.
4   There are exceptions among popular music singers, but overwhelmingly, singing is dominated by men.

dancing is equally erotic following the same choreography as that of their female counterparts, though on stage, men and women dance separately.[5] Costumed in provocative attire—spandex outfits from China—concert danseuses in their vital manner entertain the audience by providing sensuous visual accompaniment during the first half of a song. During the longer instrumental sections, when the song tempo changes, dancers exhibit their mastery of movement set to the syncopated drum rhythm and looping guitars riffs. Many songs are often accompanied by a specific choreography and, with some luck, can become a hit, sparking an associated dance craze. Dance steps showcased in music videos and at concerts spread among Kinshasa's denizens, who then perform these same steps in nightclubs, at weddings, funeral parties, and other social events. At concerts, depending on how crowded the event is and how much space is allotted to the dance floor, attendees will perform the steps to the movements called out in the song. These are opportunities for people to demonstrate their own knowledge of this popular archive of vernacular dance. Popular concert dancers are powerful cultural agents, performing choreography that resonates internationally, especially now with sites like YouTube and Facebook that offer live streaming services. Performances are also filmed and aired weekly on television, becoming mediated spaces in which young people copy and learn the choreography.

Despite Congolese music's international notoriety and the space it occupies in quotidian life, people are nonetheless ambivalent about it, especially with the entrenchment of Pentecostalism all over the country. While danseuses are arbiters of dance aesthetics, they are nonetheless confronted with social critique, relating to people's perceptions about the morality of concert dancing. As I have explored elsewhere (Braun 2019), part of the ambiguity associated with concert dance resides in some of the choreographic blending of genres, as well as in the transfer of movement practices from village contexts to the concert stage. The indexical meaning of the movement found within concert choreography has thereby been transformed into a narrower notion of the erotic that is qualitatively and ideologically different from what these movements represent in a rural village context.

Congolese dance is also being written into contemporary fiction, most notably by Jean Bofane, a Congolese author who offers several snapshots of popular dance in his novel *Congo Inc*: "With powerful basses and guitars that sounded like piercing claws, with his hip gyrations and lecherous

---

5   For a discussion about "sexual eccentricity" in Kinshasa's popular cultural landscape especially with regards to men, see Hendriks 2017.

body language, Werrason, the King of the Forest, incited them all to plunge deeper into their own depravity" (Bofane 2014, 74). The language he uses to describe dance in Kinshasa is laden with dark overtones that suggest a moral degeneration, and it is unclear whether these are the author's views or if he is intentionally channeling earlier colonial attitudes about obscene dance that are currently being taken up by contemporary Pentecostal discourse.[6] The manner in which Bofane describes women's dancing as an aggressive display of unbridled sexuality invites some speculation about his own views on what he perhaps sees as an intimidating feminine energy. Consider the following passage: "Spilling over from the dance floor, men and women surrendered themselves to violent movements of the pelvis, thrust forward in a rhythm that pulsed like the blood flow of someone in a manic frenzy" (120). Achille Mbembe similarly describes Congolese popular dance in his article "Variations on the Beautiful in the Congolese World of Sounds," analyzing the aesthetic dimensions of popular Congolese music with a particular consideration to the forces that simultaneously evoke pleasure, joy, and pain. Framing the dancing as hysterical, frenzied, and cacophonous, Mbembe journeys into what he perceives as dark and depraved to make the point that joy and pain are intertwined, at least in the sensorial experience. For him, economic despair and histories of violent conflict are embodied and performed as hypersexual displays verging on the grotesque. Ecstasy is achieved through what he refers to as the "ugly," which is reminiscent of how Nietzsche and later George Bataille understand ecstatic abandonment:

> At the same time, jubilation is an expression of the mixture of sensual delight and cruelty so characteristic of the regime of the ugly and the abject. There is always a grotesque and brutal power to be found in jubilation. What Nietzsche called "the duplicity of the mad" comes to life in the outburst of frenetic activity that is dance and the spaces of transfiguration that are the spectacle (Mbembe 2005, 91).

This ecstatic quality in the dance is precisely what concerns religious groups in Kinshasa, prompting them to follow the specter of earlier colonial decrees by deriding the world of "profane dance" as immoral and anti-Christian. While Bofane and Mbembe provocatively address the qualities they understand to be integral to Congolese popular dance music, namely that the performative expressions reflect the political and economic violence inflicted

---

6   For more about the historical factors that have shaped attitudes about popular dance see Braun 2019.

and experienced throughout the region, they do not consider the dancer's own erotic subjectivity. These descriptions of dance are certainly compelling, yet I argue that they also obscure people's own understanding of what they are expressing when they dance. The politics of pleasure in Kinshasa's dance scene have been bound up in literary discussions of the grotesque, consequently casting somewhat of a dark shadow on dance celebration. There indeed is a sense of giving oneself to the feeling of the music, but there is also a recognition of one's subjectivity in the dance—and feeling oneself mastering movement. Further, part of the pleasure also lies in making oneself visible to others and in the conviviality of the experience.

Blanche Neige Learns to Dance

As a girl growing up in Montreal in the 1990s, I was introduced to vernacular forms of dance, as this Canadian city is home to a range of immigrant communities, many of which come from francophone African and Caribbean countries. School friends who were self-identified members of the African diaspora brought me to nightclubs and introduced me to shops that sold VHS tapes of concerts filmed in Congo, footage that would become my initial introduction to the world of Congolese popular concert dance. I stood in front of my television, mimicking the danseuses' movements from the recorded concert, later attempting them in front of my bedroom mirror. Learning a new system of movement takes time because it's not merely about mastering the steps but also about the subtle modulations, the way in which the head moves, or doesn't move. It's also about nonmovement and, as I learned, stillness can be pure intensity. When I danced with friends, timidly showing them what I had learned, through movement and gesture I felt that, despite my otherness, which was largely visible through my whiteness, that I was a welcomed guest. Later, when I discovered the field of dance ethnology, I would understand dance as a method for doing anthropology—building both rapport and understanding with people can entail learning and sharing the same modalities communicated through dance.[7]

---

[7] Dance anthropology gained momentum in the 1970s, especially as it intersected with feminist theory. Movement practices became an entry point into broader discussions of gender and sexuality. For more on this see Kaeppler 1971, Royce 1977, Hannah 1985, Cowan 1990, Kisliuk 2001.

Throughout the region, the Lingala word *mundele* is used for white people; it is a complicated term, with historical underpinnings linked to the colonial presence, though less connected to race than it is to conceptions of otherness. Here, I do not wish to override the racial politics in the city—indeed it is a fraught subject embedded in a longer colonial history—but I hope to introduce a little complexity by offering the following anecdotes. Several of my acquaintances working for NGOs in Kinshasa and who self-identified as Black recounted stories in which they sometimes were referred to as *mundele* by passersby on the street when they got out of their SUVs. United Nations Indian peacekeepers in the eastern part of the country are also called *mundele* and *muzungu* (Swahili). Further, the increasing Chinese presence in the city has added yet another layer—on several occasions I was called *chinois* while moving through the city on foot or in public transportation. Conversely, several Chinese shopkeepers I was friendly with told me that they were sometimes referred to as *mundele* by people while they did their shopping at the market. The idea of who is "other" and "foreign," though historically tied to race, perhaps assumes new qualities, pointing to the ways in which race is not always the sole indicator of otherness and privilege.

Through a series of serendipitous encounters, during my first research trip to Kinshasa in 2009 I had the privilege of being invited to dance with a small local band called VIP: Chic en Couleurs. I was aware that the band regarded my presence as having a promotional value, not because I was a necessarily good dancer, but rather because I was white. As the bandleader put it, "We are now a firmly cosmopolitan band because your presence." This perceived "cosmopolitaness" was important to the identity of the band, especially because their name refers to colors being "chic." At rehearsal, Jerry, the choreographer and only male dancer of the trio, sternly informed me that if I was going to hang out with them, I also needed to learn the choreography and "work," as he put it. My weekly lessons began, and I slowly learned the movement sequences with Jerry counting out the steps. We did this in the bandleader's concrete-laden courtyard where the band holds rehearsals. Most rehearsals began with warm-ups wherein dancers stand on the balls of their feet and lean against the wall, rolling their hips in figure eight formations. As there were no mirrors in this courtyard, one of the most challenging aspects in the learning process was not being able to see myself move. Instead, I had to rely on the choreographer and other dancers to demonstrate what I was doing wrong. This was a frustrating process because I was never certain of my form and whether I was in sync with the others. Perhaps, my over reliance on mirrors had atrophied my own potential for kinesthetic empathy (Reynolds and Reason 2012), and it took considerable time for me to be able to discern whether I was grasping the steps as well as if I were able to see myself. This was compounded by the fact that we often trained in the absence of music, and therefore the choreographer had to mimic the sounds of the battery with his own verbal cues.

Determined to see a reflection of myself so that I might better make corrections, I introduced my handheld video camera during a rehearsal. This created a situation in which the other dancers clamored around me to watch the playback, and soon filming and watching the video footage was integrated into the regular rehearsal routine. Though the camera became a mirror for my own scrutiny in relation to the other dancers' movements, for the others it was less of a pedagogical tool to critique our own form as it was a moment to enjoy seeing oneself execute movement.[8]

On the night of my first performance, we opened the show with a *mutuashi* dance, a Luba dance from the Kasai region of Congo that had been popularized in the 1980s as part of concert dance by a famous dancer-turned-singer named Tschala Mwana.[9] Though no one in our band identified as being from the Luba ethnic group, and the audience was not necessarily composed of Luba people, it was explained to me that *mutuashi* is often featured as an introductory segment of the show. As the choreographer told me, "It's a crowd pleaser." The drummer signaled our entry, and we shuffled onto stage single-file, rolling our waists. Once the second half of the choreography began, when the tempo of the music changes to a faster pace, I noticed that none of the other dancers were executing the steps on the beat we learned. Panicked, I looked at them for cues, but it was obvious that I was out of step. After the song, I asked Jerry, "What's happening?! Why are the danseuses not keeping with the rhythm we learned?" To which he responded, "What are you talking about? Why are *you* off, we practiced this many times." Perplexed, I physically demonstrated the sequence and said, "Well, on the

---

8   It should be mentioned that in 2009 and 2012, camera phones were inaccessible to most people in Kinshasa. As of this writing, the city is awash with affordable smart phones imported from China, allowing more people to film themselves.

9   Popular concert choreographers appropriate dance from multifarious sources, such as funeral parties where folklore dancers perform. Once these movement sequences are integrated into the concert choreography, the original meaning becomes separated from the context, thereby becoming a new dance altogether. This has consequently contributed to the ambivalent attitudes toward women's dance.

two count we're supposed to lift one leg up, but this is happening before two, and on the eight count we were intended to turn, but this happens a later beat. This is even what I filmed on camera." Jerry looked at me mystified and asked me why I insisted on counting. "Why are you counting it all out? We just counted for practice, but this is the real thing. You need to listen to the music, to the passage beat. That is what you follow."

Jerry was less concerned with whether or not each dancer's form precisely matched each other than with whether they moved on the same beat and if they expressed *sentiment*, or feeling. Dancers, while maybe at first glance seeming to be performing the same movements, are not actually moving in perfect unison. Within the choreography there was space for each of us to embellish movements to suit our own bodies. The dancers with fuller hips didn't need to work as hard in their gyrations and could therefore play with the ease of movement in a way that those dancers with more slender physiques could not. Inserting one's own stylistic embellishment is also a way of expressing musicality, which is a sign of masterful dancing. The solo section of the song is marked by a tempo change in the song structure, whereby the soloists break free from the group choreography to dance alone on stage. There is a heighted individualism that shines through these solos, in which the dancer has an opportunity to make a name for herself as an individual star, or *vedette*.

Growing more familiar with local body language and gesture, I began to incorporate what I observed from quotidian life into my own solos. For instance, while taking taxis in Kinshasa, one must be privy to the various hand signals used to communicate with drivers. Since taxis operate on designated fixed routes, drivers and customers use hand signals to indicate locations. For instance, a finger making a twirling circular motion indicates that the driver's destination is Rond Point Victoire, one of the city's central locations marked by a large roundabout. It took me considerable time to learn the dozens of different hand signals, which change depending on where you are positioned in the city. I admired the grace with which people extend their arms to make the signals to the extent that I began to mimic these in my own onstage dance solos. Audience members were delighted and thrilled to recognize the hand signals. In this embodiment of cultural code, I was able to reflect a common experience of the city, and the audience became witness to my own experience in the city. This is perhaps reminiscent of Michael Herzfeld's notion of "cultural intimacy" (2005), wherein microperformances of gesture can be powerful means of communicating one's cultural competency as well as co-constructing a shared space of intimacy. In this way, mastering a gesture performed on an everyday basis, or harmonizing physical movements with those of others, can transform one's appearance, potentially inviting insider knowledge.

As the months went by, I became a more proficient dancer and was invited to appear on television with the bandleader to participate in what he called "promotion." As we all got dressed in our stage outfits, I noticed I was not given any tights, unlike the other dancers who had their legs covered. When I inquired with some of the organizers, I was told that my white skin would look lovely on camera. It should also be mentioned that Congolese women do not show their thighs in public as it is considered a highly erotic part of the body. Concert dance often features women in shorts, which has caused controversy in the past with state censorship.

The televised performance itself was brief—we danced a small section of the choreography, which was then followed by a short interview and a photo shoot. In the promotional photos taken at the studio, the bandleader assumed an intimate position, draping his arm around me and lightly touching my exposed knee, suggesting that I was perhaps more than simply a dancer in the band. Later, during the interview, the reporter inquired whether or not I was married. Though I was single, I thought that responding that I was engaged to be married would prevent possible solicitation. My response made the bandleader squirm in his seat and laugh nervously. The reporter posed a follow-up question about what my fiancée thought of my dancing in Congo and whether I thought it is appropriate for an engaged or married woman to dance with a band. I in turn asked the reporter if dancing in a band is only acceptable for single women, to which he chuckled and responded that in Congo things were undeniably different than in Europe or North America.

Upon leaving the television station, the bandleader asked me if I thought the interview had gone well. "I think it went smoothly," I responded. Grinning and looking down at his feet a little meekly he said, "But it would have been nice if you had said you were single." I asked him if he thought such an answer would have boosted the band's popularity. The bandleader responded with one word: "Voilà."

A few days later, the interview was aired on national television, which resulted in a heightened visibility not only for the band but for me as well. I received several journalists at my door requesting interviews, which left me feeling vulnerable to new solicitation but perhaps also to social stigma. In Kinshasa, the notion of female virtue is clearly linked to the idea of visibility, and women who perform as professional concert dancers are referred to as "exposed." While this visibility was something I had not intended to cultivate, this kind of recognition is precisely what young dancers hope for, as it fosters an expanded social network, which itself represents opportunity.[10] The promise of international touring provides the possibility of increasing one's prestige but also of meeting men who might provide financial support (Braun 2019). Within this context, concert dancers are women who are widely considered to be "exposed" to the public and are consequently stridently seen by the general public as opportunistic.

While my outsider status, most clearly visible in my whiteness, afforded me more liberties that one could otherwise expect as a Congolese woman, my visibility as dancer nevertheless left me feeling self-conscious. Female friends of mine, one of whom is a medical doctor, were ashamed during social situations when it was revealed that I was not only studying concert dance but also dancing with a band myself. They thought that if people knew, it would provoke suspicion about my personal morality. My friend Martiny implored me to quit:

> Why do you have to perform? Isn't interviewing dancers good enough? A nice woman like you, getting your doctorate degree, and you're dancing with these nonserious women?! At least keep it to yourself and don't talk about it with the people I introduce you to. Some of them are good Christians, and it will confuse them and make them uncomfortable knowing that you are doing this. Plus, they'll think you're sleeping around. Is that the kind of reputation you want?

She then muttered, "Maybe this is why you aren't married." I responded by asking if she thought if I was a "serious" woman, to which she snapped: "Of course! This is why I dislike what you are doing." Martiny clearly wished to see me position myself as socially superior to Kinshasa's performers, or at least to differentiate myself from them. Dancers, with very few exceptions, come from very poor families with limited means, which means they enjoy little to no formal education. The general perception is that young women performing for bands sexually loose women who have nothing to lose by being instrumentalized by the male-dominated band hierarchy. My friend was thus telling me how I appeared to people. Martiny and I would have many discussions about the implications of my dancing and what it meant

---

10   Leon Tsambu Bulu's research among concert dancers highlights that while dancers are paid very little for their work, social mobility is nevertheless possible (2004).

in general to be a danseuse, which yielded a collaborative process of understanding the observations and interviews I had collected.

Mediated Mirroring

Dance is an integral part of sociality in Kinshasa, bringing people together during wakes, in churches, at parties, and in nightclubs. Further, dance is a driver of "ambiance" and people who are imbued with dancing ability liven up social events and are considered valued guests. Young men and women are taught from an early age how to dance, and, not unlike my own initial experience in learning, in an urban setting they learn with visuals from Congolese popular bands aired on television. Television has allowed popular concert dance to circulate more widely across different social spaces. People feel it is important to stay "in the know" about the latest dance crazes, and watching television is an important part in learning to dance. Popular concert bands, generally internationally famous ones, broadcast their weekly public rehearsals on television every week. Avid fans tune in weekly to catch the latest choreography performed by dancers in Kinshasa's most popular bands. Men and women, old and young, will stand in front of their televisions, mimicking the dancers' movements in efforts to master them.

Committing steps to memory requires considerable time and energy, but the return on effort comes later, when the same choreographies are then performed at parties. Kinshasa's concert dancers are a vital element of the contemporary experience and are celebrated by people all over the country who strive to attain a level of dance competency. Further, knowledge of the latest trends in popular culture, and specifically knowledge of songs and dance, is an important part of being Kinois. I watched a mother teach her four-year-old daughter the choreography to the wildly popular song of the moment entitled "Vimba" by the well-known group Zaiko Langa Langa. When the little girl failed to execute the shoulder movement correctly, her mother scolded her in a light-hearted manner: "Not like that, like this [demonstrating the movement]." In the absence of real mirrors, her mother became a personal mirror, reflecting back how the movements should look. Scenes like this illustrated the importance for young women to be good dancers. On several occasions, I overheard friends deriding each other, "You are no good, you get a 6/10, watch me as I do *loketo* [hip gesticulation] you'll never get a boyfriend if you don't learn."

The private space of the home is a milieu where young women can experiment with new ways of dancing without being subjected to the public's gaze. I often witnessed people's living rooms transform into ludic spaces where young women perform silly dance moves for each other. In one house I visited, there was a thin full-length mirror in the corner of the salon that, when music was played, was carried to the center of the room and positioned against the television. This television, which sometimes served as a medium through which we learned choreography, would be covered by the mirror while we danced so that we could look at ourselves. Perhaps the act of covering the television with our real-time reflections can be interpreted as a gesture to reclaim dance, one that is disseminated through mass culture. We all took turns dancing in front of the mirror propped up against the television, playfully nudging each other out of the way to see more of our own reflections. Here, the gaze was being controlled, being directed back at ourselves. These convivial moments we shared were pleasurable *because* of the intimacy we produced by dancing together. Family members become audiences, sometimes praising, other times light-heartedly criticizing this dancing. In this way, family members—in particular female family members—become a kind of regulatory board, reinforcing dance aesthetics and reflecting back what "good" dancing looks like. It is common for siblings to teach younger family members how to dance—young children are positively encouraged to dance, and when a child shows a particular talent for or interest in dance, they are praised and become the family's pride during formal family events such as weddings, where people can show off their dance abilities.

Mirror Dancing

Upon entering most nightclubs in Kinshasa, regardless of neighbourhood, the first thing to catch one's eye will invariably be the mirrors, which in Lingala are called *tala tala*. In the darkness illuminated by strobe lights and neon décor, the mirrors lining the walls almost disorient. The effect they create is transportive and spatial, making the club seem larger than it really is. Since one is met with their own reflection everywhere, it becomes difficult to resist the temptation of consulting one's appearance. Of course, mirrors are not an uncommon nightclub ornamentation around the world, but it is perhaps how people interact with them that makes the Congolese context more unique.

Beyond mere ornament, nightclub mirrors allow for men and women to see themselves dance. When a popular song is played, the entire club will make their way toward the mirrors, jockeying for a position to ensure good visibility. One evening, I watched a group of club-goers take over the entire dance floor to perform a choreography made popular by Congolese hit songs. The dance steps that are executed in these nightlife spaces have come to represent popular culture in this megalopolis and have become part of a popular embodied archive. Men and women danced individually, in rows facing the ceiling wall of mirrors, performing not merely one sequence within the choreography but often the entirety of the song's accompanying dance. For the duration of the song, dancers gazed at their individual reflections, performing for themselves, as if seduced by their own image. These were no furtive glances, but rather transfixed gazing. In those moments there was no self-consciousness, rendering the dancers' individual performance simultaneously private and public. Once the song ended, people walked away from the mirrors with an insouciance, to resume socializing and dancing at their own tables.

In writing about mirrors in the context of Gabon, Joseph Tonda pays particular attention to women locally referred to as *tuées-tuées*, or young prostitutes who solicit in Libreville's nightclubs (2007). These women are notorious for dancing in nightclubs with their own reflections, something that Tonda argues is symptomatic of the city's unraveling social fabric. Embedded within consumer culture, he interprets the bodies of the *tuées-tuées* through an economic register, linking women's dancing with the intention of extracting money from men. For Tonda, mirror dancers become narcissists, consuming their own image, driven by their own consumerism (2007, 89). He also touches on the supernatural quality of the mirror in Gabon, and the links it has to witchcraft, and by his association, to prostitutes. The doubling of images through mirrors points to the ontological relationship between the visible and invisible worlds where several selves can exist simultaneously, which is also echoed in the very word for mirror, *tala tala*. The association between mirrors and the spiritual realm is also present in Kinshasa, especially given that the iconic figure of Mami Wata, a mystical erotic siren who seduces men, is often depicted in popular paintings holding a hand mirror.[11] The notion that a person can exist simultaneously

---

11   There is a rich body of work about Mami Wata representations in Kinshasa. Mami Wata is often depicted as light-skinned with long flowing black hair, which is itself suggestive of "otherness" in the city. Mami Wata interacts with

here and elsewhere, as African cosmological systems of witchcraft suggest, has a potential to be extended to the experience of feeling both here and elsewhere when dancing.[12] In a similar vein, Foucault contends that one is made aware of invisible parts of the body, those that can potentially travel through fantasmic projection (Foucault 2009, 15). "After all, is not the dancer's body a body dilated according to a space that is simultaneously inside and outside of it?" (17). The self is doubled, or even multiplied, existing as a spectacle for both the self and the other in realms that are visible and felt invisibly.

One might begin to read these mirror dances as an extension of ontological views on the role that doubling plays in the supernatural; however, this might be an overinterpretation. I do not intend to eschew Tonda's argument about the process of individualization through mirror gazing, nor the potency of the mirror itself in discussions about the supernatural. Perhaps, in refracting his argument against the same nightclub mirror, we might acknowledge that mirror dancing facilitates a public experimentation with selfhood, a selfhood that is often inspired by the movements made popular by professional concert dancers. Though the corporeality as captured in the mirror also has the partial effect of making one's own body the object of the other's gaze—as in the case of women attempting to seduce men—it also opens up a space where pleasure is felt in simply seeing oneself. In the same manner that concert dancers are not in the position to see themselves until their weekly show is aired on television, the opportunity to see one's own dancing reflection, an exercise in proprioception, becomes a propitious occasion. Rather than being interpreted as symptomatic of social decay, or even late capitalism, the pleasure derived from mirror dance represents positive creative reflection, regeneration, and transformation.

After a night out, I consulted Martiny about the mirror dancing I witnessed. Without hesitation she incisively retorted, "What is there to say? Who doesn't like to dance in front of the mirror? Don't you? It just feels good. It's especially fun at a club because of all of the *ambiance* around you. It makes me happy to see all the club lights and people reflected in the mirror." She drew my attention to the cinematic quality of watching oneself dance in a nightclub in front of a mirror and also reminded me that many people don't have full length mirrors at home. However, mirror dancing

---

influences from India, the Middle East, and most recently China. For more on this, see Jewsiewicki 2003; Braun 2016.

12 For an extended theoretical discussion about the dynamic aspects of corporeality, see Mark Franko's 2018 collection of essays.

can be understood beyond mere novelty. When the conditions are right, in momentary rapture offered through mirror dance, a language of introspection becomes available. There is something undeniably reaffirming in the deep absorption of the dance, seeing one's own performance reflected back in the mirror, especially for young women who are confronted with messages, often conflicting messages, concerning how to manage and perform their femininity and eroticism in public. The temporality of mirror dancing—the quality it has to take people out of time and space—becomes a vehicle not only for imagining the good life but also for seeing it reflected back. In *Of Other Spaces*, Foucault discusses the potency of the mirror in envisioning another reality:

> The mirror is, after all, a utopia, since it is a placeless place. In the mirror, I see myself there where I am not, in an unreal, virtual space that opens up behind the surface; I am over there, there where I am not, a sort of shadow that gives my own visibility to myself, that enables me to see myself there where I am absent: such is the utopia of the mirror. [...] Starting from this gaze that is, as it were, directed toward me, from the ground of this virtual space that is on the other side of the glass, I come back toward myself; I begin again to direct my eyes toward myself and to reconstitute myself there where I am (1984, 25).

Mirror dance also offers people an opportunity to perform and witness their mastery of a particular dance reflective of their membership in the city's larger sphere of popular culture. There is an undeniable pleasure in seeing one's body in mirrors. Contrary to what some theorists contend about it being a reflection of corrupt, individualistic consumerist culture, mirror dance offers people a chance to watch themselves travel beyond the physical limits of the self, and to understand in a new way. Mirror dance also becomes an imaginary temporal space to fantasize and communicate one's own sensuality, in the presence of an indirect audience, or an imagined audience.

Coda

This essay has focused on only three modes of dance reflected in and through various vectors of performance in the city. As is true for many cultural contexts, dance is crucial to sociability, creating moments and spaces of shared intimacy and pleasure. Celebrated dancers, showcased on television and packing concert stages around the world, are also paradoxically stigmatized. Knowing specific dances, especially those made popular by Kinshasa's concert dancers, is a way of demonstrating and performing one's cultural knowledge, which in turn allows for a wider participation in popular culture. This is no less true for ethnographers who strive to bridge horizons and gain entry into people's lives by spending time learning new movement practices with people. In learning to dance with a concert band, I relied on the choreographer and dancers for guidance and correction, especially in the absence of mirrors. I thus learned relationally, mirroring movement, with validation coming from the people I was learning from.

My involvement with a concert band pushed me into a new visibility, one that invited questions and concerns from my local friends and colleagues, revealing that the position of the female concert dancer is fraught with controversy in Kinshasa, reflecting some of the social mores relating to female visibility. Further, some of my friends told me that my participation as a concert dancer would reflect poorly on them. Dancers often become a source of prestige for bandleaders, and the danseuse's position within the band is linked to her sexuality, not only in how her body might suggest this through dance but also in terms of what she represents as a band member. Dressed in provocative attire and performing in front of audiences led me to feel what so many people had told me before about concert dancers. "Elles sont exposées," or they are *exposed*. This visibility is what invites moral critique; however, it also forms part of the pleasure associated with performing.

Young women implicitly learn about the boundaries and limits of expressing one's sexuality, and yet the space of the mirrored nightclub is where these boundaries can be negotiated through self-reflection. Watching oneself exercise control and mastery over one's body in a mirror is a source of pleasure. It contributes to a feeling of connection to the expressions being produced in Kinshasa and ultimately projected abroad. As dance scholar Mark Franko puts it, "The dancer's medium is the self as object of knowledge performed by the self as subject of knowledge" (2019, 184). The recognition of one's own reflection during these moments of dancing with the mirror holds a generative potential of projecting oneself into an elsewhere while being grounded in a present that is constructed with others. Rather than interpreting the eroticism in mirror dance as a moment alienation from the self, or one of violent excess, as some theorists have attempted to show, I hope to have shown the ways in which pleasure is derived and experienced. A pleasure in dancing with oneself, with others, with the other, and with reflections of all three.

References

Bofane, Jean In Koli. 2014. *Congo Inc: Bismarck's Testament*. Translated by Marjolijn de Jager 2018. Bloomington: Indiana University Press.
Braun, Lesley Nicole. 2014. "Trading Virtue for Virtuosity: The Artistry of Kinshasa's Concert Danseuses." *African Arts* 47, no. 4:48–57.
———. 2015. "Cyber Siren: What Mami Wata Reveals about Popular Culture and the Chinese Presence in Kinshasa." *Canadian Journal of African Studies* 45 (2): 301–18.
———. 2019. "Dancing Ambiguities in the Democratic Republic of Congo." *Critical African Studies* 11 (1): 103–20.
de Boeck, Filip, and Marie-Françoise Plissart. 2004. *Kinshasa: Tales of the Invisible City*. Ghent: Ludion.
Foucault, Michel. 1986. "Of Other Spaces." *Diacritics* 16:22–27.
Franko, Mark. 2019. *Choreographing Discourse: A Mark Franko Reader*. Abingdon: Routledge.
Gondola, Ch. Didier. 1993. "Musique moderne et identités citadines en ville africaine: Le cas du Congo-Zaire." *Afrique contemporaine* 168:155–68.
———. 1997. "Popular Music, Urban Society, and Changing Gender Relations in Kinshasa, Zaire." In *Gendered Encounters*, edited by Maria Luise Grosz-Ngaté and Omari H. Kokole, 65–83. New York: Routledge.
Hannah, Judith Lynn. 1979. *To Dance Is Human: A Theory of Nonverbal Communication*. Chicago: University of Chicago Press.
Hendriks, Thomas. 2017. "Queer(ing) Popular Culture: Homo-Erotic Provocations from Kinshasa." *Journal of African Cultural Studies* 31 (1): 71–88.
Herzfeld, Michael. 2005. *Cultural Intimacy: Social Poetics in the Nation-State*. 2nd ed. New York: Routledge.
Jewsiewicki, Bogumil. 2003. *Mami Wata: La peinture populaire au Congo*. Paris: Gallimard.
Kaeppler, Adrienne. 1971. "Tongan Dance: A Study in Cultural Change." *Ethnomusicology* 14 (2): 266–77.
Kisliuk, Michelle. 2001. *Seize the Dance!: Baaka Musical Life and the Ethnography of Performance*. Oxford: Oxford University Press.
Lepecki, André, ed. 2012. *Dance: Documents of Contemporary Art*. Cambridge, MA: MIT Press.
Lonoh, M. B. 1969. *Essai de counentaire sur la musique congolaise moderne*. Kinshasa: S.E.I./ A.N.C. in collaboration with the Zairean Ministry of Arts and Culture.
Mbembe, Achille. 2005. "Variations on the Beautiful in the Congolese World of Sounds." *Politique Africaine* 4:69–91.
Noland, Carrie, and Sally Ann Ness, eds. 2008. *Migrations of Gesture*. Minneapolis: University of Minnesota Press.

Reynolds, Dee, and Matthew Reason, eds. 2012. *Kinesthetic Empathy in Creative and Cultural Practices*. Chicago: University of Chicago Press.
Royce, A. Peterson. 2002 (1977). *The Anthropology of Dance*. Bloomington: University of Indiana Press.
Steward, Gary. 2000. *Rumba on the River: A History of the Music of the Two Congos*. New York: Verso.
Tonda, Joseph. 2007. "Entre communautarisme et individualisme: La 'tuée tuée,' une figure-miroir de la *déparentélisation* au Gabon." *Sociologie et sociétés* 39 (2): 79–99.
Trapido, Joseph. 2017. *Breaking Rocks: Music, Ideology and Economic Collapse, from Paris to Kinshasa*. London: Berghahn.
Tsambu, Leon Bulu. 2004. "Enfants et jeunes dans le métier de la danse au sein des groupes musicaux modernes à Kinshasa." In *Children and Youth in the Labour Process in Africa*, edited by Osita Agbu Dakar, 197–223. Oxford: Council for the Development of Social Science Research in Africa.
White, Bob. 2008. *Rumba Rules: The Politics of Dance Music in Mobutu's Zaire*. Durham, NC: Duke University Press.

Chapter Ten

ethnography and its double(s)

theorizing the personal with Jews in Ghana

Michelle Kisliuk

Theorizing the personal.
  Summoning intersubjective awareness.
  Not to mine it or use it. Not to appropriate it or reduce it. But to creatively, feelingfully, critically position what is relevantly personal and interpersonal. It might seem at first that theorizing and the personal are at odds, and that intersubjectivity is unknowable. There is a legacy—an affliction—that asserts these binaries. But once we understand how the personal infuses everything we know whether or not we show it or even recognize it, and once we allow for embodied, empirical ethnographic scholarship to also be intermodal, contrapuntal, and co-present—to become creative nonfiction, performance art, and collective creation—the false dichotomies evaporate. What is unapologetically human then exposes and expels the stifling pedant in our midst. Released, we can stride ahead baring our gaps and mistakes. Embracing our stumbles and bumbles, we can delve into vulnerable and open questions—tumbling into the unplanned lessons we most urgently need.[1]

---

1 Parts of this essay were prepared for conference papers and presentations. These include for the Performance Studies International conference in New York City, 2007, a paper titled "From Intangible to Material in Jewish Africa: A 5-Year-Old Stand-in Gets Immersed in 'Heritage'" as part of the panel "Intangible Heritage in Transit: Mediation, Mobility, Modernity." Another early version was for the UC Berkeley Music colloquium in 2011,

the conceptual setting

ethnography and its double(s)

In *The Theater and Its Double* (1938), the genius madman Antonin Artaud articulated a socioaesthetic vision of performance that challenged the complacent bourgeois theater of those perilous times. Here, in our own perilous times, I extend Artaud's "double" to encompass performance, ethnography, and academia more broadly. More specifically, I propose that we identify an avant-garde approach to ethnographic research and writing; some may call it radical but really it's just human. It leads to poetically grounded description/evocation and interactive reiteration of musicking, dancing, and social and spiritual practices.² This approach can be (and has been) vital for generating empathic intercultural bonds for healing across smoldering neocolonial and

---

titled "Theorizing the Personal in Ethnographic Research and Writing: Jews in Ghana—Challenges and Chances," also presented for the University of Virginia Jewish Studies program. Some of this material was prepared for an invited keynote address titled "Theorizing the Personal" at the conference "Performance, Creativity, Collaboration," at the New Zealand Musicological Society Annual Meeting, Wellington, New Zealand, November 2011. More recently I presented a revised version of that material at the 2016 Society for Ethnomusicology Annual Meeting in Washington, DC, as part of the panel "Emergent African Jewish Communities: Reconfiguring Local Selves within a Global Politics." I also did a brief interview for Afropop Worldwide in 2007 as part of a longer program on "Jewish Communities of Sub-Saharan Africa." I am grateful for those opportunities and the feedback they generated, which helped shape the material into what I offer here.

2   This point is related to discussions in ethnography since the 1980s such as Steven Tyler's essay "Post-Modern Ethnography: From Document of the Occult to Occult Document" and Barbara Kirshenblatt-Gimblett's ("Confusing Pleasures") in which she critically discusses points where an aesthetic of the avant-garde meets ethnography. My argument here is intended to move beyond an aesthetic of the historical avant-garde into an avant-garde politics that intersects with ethnography but is in a constant dynamic dialogue across social/creative institutions more broadly. I have written elsewhere about an idea of ethnography as speculative nonfiction (Kisliuk 2019). Also, as this manuscript goes to press, a new essay on a related theme by Sean Williams is about to be published that addresses poetry writing as "transgressive ethnography" (2022).

other divides. Ethnographic intercultural exchange, like metaphor, offers us a perceptual clearing as we expand and enter new domains. Intangible vulnerabilities that render all parties open to being changed are required. But without vulnerability we get instead a regressive mirror image—a deadening double—of what would have been a vital process.

To understand the dynamics of this double is to learn to distinguish the endeavors and enactments that dismantle oppressive forces from those that uphold oppressions. And the trickiest part is that the two contrary realms of scholarly (and artistic) production often exist in the same spaces as "near enemies"—in universities, departments, classes, academic societies, performances, articles, or talks—they can share trappings, routines, or surroundings and therefore may seem akin, but they aren't.[3] For clarity let's call these the *pernicious* versus the *propitious* sides of a double. So, you might picture a circle, sort of a yin/yang circle but in this case without the fruitful dialectical dynamic between the two sides. Here one side asserts a stifling binary while the other side contains within it a flourishing dialectic. So, the pernicious and propitious sides of this circle can live alongside each other even within the same project or person. And beware that a propitious position can shift into a pernicious one (and vice versa) over time or circumstance.[4] The first task is to become sensitive to the pernicious dynamics, ideas, and language that perpetuate patriarchies and supremacies so that we can more effectively repel, circumvent, resist, and counter them. And one way to get at this is by introspectively honing *critical practice positioning* whereby, with care, we examine and weave our subjectivity and intersubjectivity into our analytical and creative processes.[5]

---

3   Psychologist Brené Brown (2021) discusses the Buddhist concept of near enemies, which parallels my pernicious/propitious concept here. Brown is a popular advocate for vulnerability.

4   Queer positioning and other-otherwise ways of being tend to be within the propitious side of this double insofar as they reject binaries and offer perspectives that challenge conventions regarding what one may think, enact, or become. See Barz and Cheng (2020). See also Cheng, 2016.

5   Adding the word "practice" to the formulation "critical practice positioning" was voiced presciently by Jessica Bisset Perea during a UCLA PEER Lab group discussion and conference that I attended, hosted virtually by Nina Eidsheim (with Ellen Waterman) in June 2021.

what does vulnerability have to do with critical positioning?

> Practice until you see yourself in the cruelest person on Earth, in the child starving, in the political prisoner. Continue until you recognize yourself in everyone in the supermarket, on the street corner, in a concentration camp, on a leaf, in a dewdrop. Meditate until you see yourself in a speck of dust in a distant galaxy. See and listen with the whole of your being.
>
> —Thich Nhat Hanh ~ *Teachings on Love* (2002)

A critical practice position is not arrived at by peppering unexamined bits of "reflexivity" into ethnography. Such fashionable (bourgeois?) tokenism actually equips the pernicious double by veiling, impersonating, and defanging critical practice, turning it into a near enemy. Models of effective positionality have been developing in various ways especially from the 1970s to the present in ethnographies of performance: for example, Berliner (1982), Browning (1995), Babiracki (2008), Hagedorn (2001), Wong (2004), Hahn (2007), Kapchan (2017), Barz and Cheng (2020), Daughtry (2021), Crosby and Flanders (2021), Lawrence (2017), Aduonum (2022) and other contributors to this volume. Recently Dylan Robinson has forcefully advocated for *critical affective writing* grounded in indigenous "listening that is strategically flexible, agile, and responsive to intersectional layering of positionality" (Robinson 2020, 38). This advance is extended by a new generation of artist-scholars committed to anticolonial, abolitionist, feminist, queer, and otherwise subaltern overlapping and ever-evolving positions. This emerging generation understands that our situated frames of reference—our experiences, perceptions, and inevitable but malleable biases and ongoing interactions—fundamentally configure and reconfigure the work that we do.[6]

The efficacy of our voices can vary both within and outside of institutions. When we press on, boundaries and hierarchies between scholarship and creative practice, between theory and everyday life inevitably rise to the

---

6 A foundational example of what I address here from the field of anthropology is Renato Rosaldo's important essay, "Grief and a Headhunter's Rage" (published in various forms including in 1993 and developed in subsequent work). Two examples of research and writing from the next generation are Lee Bidgood's 2017 *Czech Bluegrass: Notes from the Heart of Europe* and Maria Guarino's 2018 *Listen with the Ear of the Heart: Music and Monastery Life at Weston Priory*.

surface, poised to evaporate. Crucially, a positioned critical approach offers an analytical precision that is unavailable when such positioning is absent. As the reservoir of examples of embodied critical positioning grows, the more the avoidance of such positioning becomes obvious by comparison. I am not saying that every scholarly project or creative act must explicitly incorporate the author/researcher/performer's life; sometimes indirect approaches are most appropriate. But if insight is the goal, vulnerable grounding is required at some stage of preparation, and that preparation will show through in the work that emerges. The lack of such positioning can no longer be successfully hidden behind a cloak of distancing conventions or generalizing language; an author's lens and crafting hand is now evident whether or not it is acknowledged in the work.

In this chapter I challenge myself, hoping to take you along with me, to plunge yet further into understanding the ways in which *who* we are at a given moment—*how* we might therefore experience an instance of research and writing (and teaching and performing)—by necessity sheds light on *what* our work is discursively about. Swimming within this inquiry I seek to clarify more specifically how our own lives illuminate, whether by likeness or by contrast, any ethnoscape we aspire to understand. Contrary to the mistake of self-indulgence, a thoughtful, openhearted self-situating can reliably take us to the trenchant issues within our research in ways that we may not have anticipated. By identifying contexts and creating settings for welcoming what is relevantly personal into critical discussion, we blur and eventually dismantle that fast-held body/mind dualism, opening instead into a multifaceted dialectic (or rather a rhizomatic multilectic) among the personal, interpersonal, political, spiritual, aesthetic, somatic, intellectual, and more.[7] We can move to think about this double as doubled twice again into six elements: first is a basic double as I've outlined, splitting a circle in two. But then splitting each original side again in two. This is important because the pernicious side of the larger double holds within itself a binary (like the Cartesian body/mind binary) while the other side holds a dynamic dialectic (more accurately conceived of as a multilectic).

Like in Artaud's 1930s Europe, now in the United States "the neo-Nazi agenda has metastasized into the mainstream Republican agenda" (Ratner

---

7   This *binary* versus *multilectic* dynamic I hope will be evident in the examples that follow. This dynamic is evident in subjective/objective binary thinking that I address in Kisliuk 2002 with the help of some charts. See also footnote 91 in this chapter.

2021). Therefore this conceptual grounding—an ability to distinguish the propitious from its double—is all the more urgent. These times cry out for us to rustle up as many countersupremacist, counterauthoritarian, and propitiously empathic interventions as we can.

my grandpa's eyes

When I was a kid, I noticed my grandpa's eyes when he looked at me. I had seen this look sometimes from elder strangers too; a deep kindness and understanding, tinged with sorrow. I will give this look a temporary name: deep eyes. Any grandparent tends to regard a grandchild with love and warmth, and we exchange similar looks in close relationships or momentary connections throughout our lives. But the deep-eyed look I want to draw attention to is more capacious. Those eyes invite us to trust because they tenderly grasp that life exists alongside inevitable loss. When I caught that look, I sensed that they were perceiving me within a larger existential scheme. We shared something resonant. Something silently, momentarily exultant about being alive. Though I could not fully comprehend it, those looks nourished me with the countermessage that even though I was just a kid surrounded by much superficial cultural detritus, I too had a place within something infinitely profound. I hoped that I might one day be like them, know too what they knew. I now understand that look as both emitting and inviting *empathy*.[8] This phenomenon does not only apply to children and old people, but in those pairings interhuman communication seems to exist in its most crystalized moments of ephemeral recognition, of capacious love.

Empathy has gotten extra attention lately; a reaction to the *antipathy* that has surfaced in this deadly national and global political climate.[9] The glut of attention, though, can distort and reduce something as elemental as empathy.

---

8   As I enter my own sixth decade, I find that individual children respond differently when I think I am offering this look. Some reciprocate (though I do not pretend to be offering the same quality of gaze or to be conveying the depth that someone like my grandpa did). Maybe those children are actively looking for that connection like I was. Other children either do not seem to notice or reject the reciprocity altogether.

9   The virulent absence of empathy (which is the definition of an oppressive position) is killing Black and other people vulnerable to hatred, demonization, and marginalization. And as I draft this in 2021, the quintessentially horrific example of the murder of George Floyd in 2020 looms large.

Despite this threat, ethnographers as boundary-crossers need to commit to cultivating better empathic skills so as to most effectively engage— especially where heightened, complex human differences surface.[10] I am not suggesting an impossible imperative to internalize all suffering. Nor should we abide evils. Yet it is important to remember that people with whom it is hardest to empathize—especially the powerful ones—are often impelled, however destructively, by fear. Most important is to invest ourselves as fully as we can in the actual spheres within which we live.[11] That level of empathy is a fertilizer that has not yet seeped to the core of what we usually define as the practice of ethnography—and this is still the case despite long-standing, often feminist-leaning efforts such as Abu-Lughod's *Writing Women's Worlds* (2008) and Ruth Behar's *The Vulnerable Observer* (1996). Enduring assumptions about "professional" remove in ethnographic work persist in part because the roots of ethnography emerged alongside exploitive colonial ventures—and therefore also alongside corresponding academic pretensions to authority and distance that still hold strong. After a period of self-searching (e.g., Clifford and Marcus 1986 and what followed), ethnographic fields, and the emerging critically positioned ethnographers of performance such as those I listed previously have been moving ever more effectively toward what is actively anticolonial.[12] To circle back, I have framed this ideological push and pull as the pernicious/propitious double, hoping that by doing so we can, moment to moment, more effectively articulate and shape ourselves within these dynamics. Empathy, then, maps onto the propitious side of the double.

---

10 As implied by Thich Nhat Hahn above, radical empathy extends past humans to all living beings (and even beyond to a speck of dust or to the cosmos). Indigenous knowledges from around the world maintain this. See for example Viveiros de Castro as cited in in Kisliuk 2019. Also, Kimmerer 2013.

11 Dahlia Lithwick, personal communication September 22, 2022. See also Lithwick 2021.

12 Even if the core impulses of the most influential ethnographers were antiracist, they were inevitably still actors within the dominant oppressive system (e.g., Malinowski, and see Foucault). As noted, institutions like the Western academy, because of the largely oppressive ideologies from which they emerged, are structured in a way that marginalizes what they detect as vulnerable or intimate in their midst. Left unopposed, the marginalizing forces predictably push to categorize as feminine and to racialize—and thereby disempower, demote, and silence—the propitious melding of scholarship with the empathically personal.

My maternal grandpa was born Zalme Szeer in a small town in Poland in 1898.[13] After his bar mitzvah, his family sent him to Germany to avoid conscription into the Polish army, where there was harsh discrimination against Jews. This exile made him officially stateless (now we would call it undocumented). He met my grandmother in Munich, where they married and had two children. But persecution after the first World War sent them fleeing to my grandmother's birth city of Vienna, Austria, known then as the "city of song," where my mother was born. She described days in her early childhood as having been full of singing; songs like "Wien Wien nur du allein" and "Muss i'Denn."[14] We sang these with my grandparents when I was a child, but I could not intuit the layers of wistfulness and heartbreak this singing evoked.[15] In 1938 when the Nazis arrived, the songs my mother heard wafting up from the street—where from the apartment window she saw Jews being beaten—called for Jewish blood to flow.[16] She witnessed from that same window Hitler's hideous welcome parade into Vienna. Under airfire the family escaped to Brussels Belgium, where my mother became "Irène" in an attempt to hide her origins. But fascism pursued them again when the Nazis invaded Belgium. They were forced into hiding, moving from place to place until Liberation Day. In addition to the murder of dear aunts and cousins, they had suffered the devastating loss of my mother's sister Herta, age nineteen, who was deceptively lured away, kidnapped, then deported and murdered at Auschwitz in 1942. I think that somehow, over time, my grandpa's acute pain from having lost his "bestest kind" (best child) to genocidal hatred steeped within him over the years, coming through to me (and surely to others) in his deep eyed look of loving empathy.

How much empathy is inborn with personality, and how much is acquired through life experience? Could empathy also be epigenetic like trauma? My mother said that as a younger man her father was comparatively harsh.[17]

---

13   Stawiszyn, Kalisz.
14   Written in 1912 by Rudolf Sieczynski. The actual title is "Wein, du Stadt meiner Träume."
15   Please see this link for audio of my grandparents singing with us in 1969: YouTube video, https://www.youtube.com/watch?v=OGmDrXRA4AM.
16   Smithsonian interview with Ingrid Kisliuk 1992, at (https://collections.ushmm.org/search/catalog/irn509145. In Charlottesville, Virginia, in August 2017, I found myself living in a terrifying time warp that felt again like the rise of fascism.
17   From Ingrid Kisliuk's memoir, *Unveiled Shadows: The Witness of a Child*, 1998:102–5: "[M]y father's propensity for self-examination and feeling

Why did empathy come out in him as an old man, after trauma, but did not arise that way in my grandmother? Before the war my grandmother joyfully sang her Viennese/German songs in harmony with her daughters and sisters, knowing she was Jewish but also considering herself fully Viennese. Ferociously betrayed then by her beloved home—by her neighbors—her message to my sister and me became: never trust a *goy* because they will turn around and "shteel" (steal) you, just as they stole our aunt. We loved our Granny. She was a sharp wit. She made us strudel and loved small animals. But she was a fundamentally shattered person with a stinging sense of humor and apparently insufficient bandwidth for sustained empathy.[18] Or maybe empathy is in the eye of the beholder, and this is only how I see it. Maybe empathic looks could even be deceiving. But my grandpa's cute accent,[19] his soft gravelly voice (encumbered by the emphysema that would eventually kill him) always on the verge of a chuckle or a moan; the relaxed warm touch of his calloused hands as he lifted me onto his lap near the "chicken cemetery" that he called his little round belly; all of this verified what was in his eyes.[20]

Now I hesitate: Maybe this whole phenomenon of deep eyes and empathy is better unspoken—to be known simply by those who already feel it.

---

became evident to me only in my adulthood. Although very loving, he was, during my childhood, at times a severe and occasionally an unreasonable disciplinarian" (45). Ingrid Kisliuk died of COVID-19 in April 2020.

18   Though my grandparents both loved and took care of each other very sweetly.
19   It was a Yiddish accent from his youth, but we never really understood this because Eastern European Jewishness was associated with the worst victimization of European Jews and implied lower social classes in the Germanic context. So, my grandpa's Yiddish background was reflexively suppressed by my mother's Austrian side. This class-inflected theme of suppression of tradition and identity in the face of oppression will surface again below with Jews in Ghana.
20   BaAka forest people from Centrafrique (Central African Republic), with whom I have focused my most in-depth ethnographic research, also have something to teach about empathy. They know how to sidestep foolish but also deadly pretentions to hierarchy that blur fundamentally shared humanity. When they are among themselves, they readily level such hierarchies. And BaAka elders tend to have that deep-eyed look more than most people I've known. But it is also common among seasoned traditional artists and craftspeople, musicians and healers wherever they may be. People who are blind can also emit this quality through other aspects of their bearing.

from risk and discomfort to vulnerability and growth

Challenging ourselves to move into the unspoken and therefore potentially unknowable evokes an important kind of discomfort; there is a key difference between discomfort that is a physical or a psychic warning signal—something hurts so you should avoid it or remedy it—versus the *necessary* discomfort that accompanies impending growth. Sometimes we can only know in retrospect which kind of discomfort we've been feeling (we might feel both types at once). And unfortunately, recognizing and naming the discomfort of a growth process does not provide a pass to then skip that discomfort the next time it comes around. I am going through the discomfort of an unknowable challenge right now as I prepare this essay. Also, understanding that we might provoke rebuke from the ranks of the pernicious double for having crossed boundaries and taken necessary risks will not shield us from such a rebuke if it comes, or from "epistemic violence" that might be foisted upon us as backlash (Robinson 2020, 16). We need to trust that we are capable to the challenge, can withstand the discomfort, can delve into honing an endeavor—especially when it is still nebulous, in formative stages, and therefore likely to stir the greatest anxiety and spark skepticism (both our own and others'). The possibility is always there that we may be making a mistake, not doing justice to precious people, practices, or ideas. But if we don't give up, we usually arrive after twists and turns to where we need to be.

All of this is what it takes to be in a field research situation, and to write (or perform or make films) about it and teach it: to be some kind of bold beginner over and over—even when one's research site is at home. J. Martin Daughtry defines the ethnographic field site as "a palimpsestic ecosystem of interconnection and difference within which the discrete experiences of individuals and groups matter" (2021, 4). We approach such a site ready to breathe in and move beyond ourselves. But with care; because our choices will surely affect others who may be both structurally and circumstantially more vulnerable than we are (and as noted we surely are also vulnerable). Yet it would be the greater betrayal if, out of fear of doing harm or being hurt, we were to decide not to use our oft-cited privilege as researcher/scholars to make connections and forge new mutual understandings. To retreat from striving for an embodied knowing of what may initially be poorly grasped people or practices would amount to running away from the possibility of mutual empathy and growth. To forsake Thich Nhat Hanh's challenge to practice an empathy that guards against our human tendency to dehumanize difference is also to retreat from vulnerability. That kind of retreat is what, broadly speaking, leads to genocide.

Crucially for ethnographers, there is a give and take: one can risk betting that vulnerability borne and worn on one's sleeve functions as a softening agent, most of all for those who do not yet know us; vulnerability invites goodwill from gentle people. Offering real vulnerability and the humility that goes with it, expressly in a neocolonial or other context of power disparity, can guard against the harm or mistrust that otherwise arises when we risk crossing cultural, racial, class, age, religious, educational, gendered, or other boundaries.[21] Maybe if we think of the self-questioning—the critical practice positioning—that goes along with literal or metaphorical border crossings as a low-hanging medicinal fruit effective for disrupting supremacies, it can help respond to the call to disassemble the pernicious double.

empathy and praxis

If we extend the idea of empathy and vulnerability to a logical next step for performance research and teaching, we arrive at practice—or more clearly *praxis* broadly conceived. The buzz in recent years in neuroscience linking mirror neurons to the arts upholds a conviction that embodied doing—musicking and dancing for example—leads physiologically to both empathy and vulnerability.[22] Indeed, "Mirror neurons respond both when perceiving an action and while executing an action. They provide a direct internal experience of another person's actions or emotions and may be the neurological basis of empathy. The multimodal nature of mirror neurons reflects the multisensory environment that we live in" (MacGillivray 2009,17).[23]

---

21 A softening with empathy does not necessarily guarantee that unforeseen harm, rebuff, or hurt won't still happen.

22 For example, MacGillivray (2009), Iacoboni (2009). The socioesthetic and political flip side of this is that mirror neurons can also play a role in mindless militaristic entrainment and in mob behavior.

23 There are three overlapping components of empathy currently understood by those who research this (Denworth 2020,61): The first is emotional empathy—the ability to respond to the emotional signals of others. This component is a biological response that is consistent with mirror neurons. We share this capacity with many other animals, and it is a necessary building block for social functioning. Next is cognitive empathy—the capacity not just to respond as reflex but to understand another's feelings. This we may also share with other sophisticated animal species. It is a building block of friendship

The centrality of the mirror neuron phenomenon is a counterargument to those who slap a blanket label of "appropriation" onto any musicking and performance that, amid contested positions of privilege, cross apparent ethnic, racial, or class boundaries. These concerns reflect in part a healthy and new (but in fact late in coming) awareness by the privileged not to impose control, to exploit, or claim ownership in a supremacist context. But excessive caution or fear of chastisement in response to facile or pernicious invocations of "appropriation" (or from a willful ignorance about how constitutive cultural processes actually work—which is interactively) can also end up precluding the vulnerability that is needed to extinguish those supremacies. By physically learning something, as a beginner or as an in-depth learner, you are submitting to that practice in a way that by default makes you vulnerable. This is true on a spectrum from what happens between, say, two or more people during contact improv modern dance, to an intercultural immersion in a musicking, dance, ritual, or otherwise embodied practice. With some commitment, this kind of praxis allows you to understand with your entire being aspects of what it feels like to be part of a particular way of experiencing the world. And it shows your collaborators and teachers that you are open to exchanging, to mutual growth and discovery, to becoming.

But if you please: I am no better at summoning empathy or vulnerability than most people. I have to make myself work at it and I fall short as often as not. My goal is not to model empathy or even vulnerability but to think together about processes, about understanding how these intimacies can find their most powerful place in our work, our lives, and in our thinking as we refine how to radically position ourselves. What is most important is that an unflinching critical grounding of the personal in our practices of research will reliably steer us to pressing social and ethical concerns of the moment—to making and imagining new connections, relationships, and practices. Coming up now, I illustrate.

---

and community. Finally, there is empathic concern, or compassion, a quality that is likely necessary for interpersonal and intergroup survival, but which also seems to be perpetually precarious, something we humans have to always keep working at to relearn and re-teach. Some cultures and subcultures teach it better than others; BaAka in the Central African Republic tend to have this honed pretty well and they keep it sharp through singing and dancing together.

a case study; a different doubling

with Jews in Ghana

What I have been leading up to—trying to get at—is to foreground a second type of doubling that emerges from only the propitious half of that original pernicious/propitious circle that I began with. This other sort of doubling is the multilectic; a heartening echo and generative mirror image of the life we're engaged with that comes into view *after* we have disentangled it from that first binary double and ejected the pernicious side. Imagine the yin-yang-like circle from before, flinging off the pernicious half and reconfiguring itself as a new circle, the whole of which has become a dynamic multilectic. This dynamic materializes when we narrate and theorize, live and re-live field research stories that run along the fault lines of risk and disclosure. In other words, we can simultaneously track our felt experiences and personal struggles so as to, with humility, understand ourselves while we try to understand the people/place(s) in our ethnographic focus. It's like a semiotic polyrhythm, the hemiola that allows for a third and much more dynamic reality to emerge from two formerly distinct trajectories (Harkness 2022). That empathic double—that paralleling—undergirds the rest of this essay. And unlike the first Cartesian double that is ever constrained by binaries, this double is a fertile traveling companion.

From the beginning of my own scholarly/creative path, I set out on a trajectory within which I could meld professional research and writing with embodied creative practice, and therefore also meld that work with the rest of my life, however it might emerge. I have chronicled within my research narratives in Centrafrique a partnership with Justin—whom I met when he was a villager from Bagandou. He grew up near—and has ancestral clan alliances with—BaAka forest people, and he speaks their language. That partnership took us from language learning to forest trudging, music and dance learning, intimate relationship and marriage, birth, death, serious illnesses, political upheaval, family dislocation and rupture, while I maneuvered to position that reality within the world of a US university.[24] My life chronicle, with Justin in a significant chunk of it, has run alongside and informed what I have learned as an ethnographer. And I am grateful.

The following research narrative took place in the midst of this trajectory, which by the time I am drafting this piece is already fifteen years ago. I have

---

24 See Kisliuk and Mongosso 2003, and Kisliuk 2019.

written elsewhere about what came before and after this time.[25] I choose the Ghana case study example for this essay, a research moment I have not written about until now, because our brief visit with Jews in Ghana was especially illustrative of the doubles I have delineated above. And because writing about this visit at this current historical moment—also a transitional moment in my own life—inevitably bears upon our upended world of the 2020s and beyond as conflicts and reconfigurations of race, ethnicity, religion, and identity are churning in the warming tides.[26] And, as I hope will become clear, this episode led me to see mutually illuminating parallels between this moment in my own life and the issues emerging within this community.[27]

touching down: materializing identities

Come with me, please, to summer 2007.[28] We have been traveling for forty-eight hours (including a sleepless layover in the smoke-filled Frankfurt airport).[29] I'm sweaty already. My heart beats faster as we touch down in Accra. Despite all my previous experience, I still get nervous flying into certain African airports after dark. Not that it's always bad, but it occasionally has been, and my five-year-old sits next to me—this is his introduction to Africa, to part of his identity. *Internal dialogue: What am I doing bringing my little child into the unknown, what will he face that I can't control? I don't even know where we are sleeping tonight. What kind of mother does this? Oh, stop worrying, I scold myself, you know Africa. It's fine if you relax.* My Centrafrican husband, Justin, is himself wary of this foreign (for him) region, so it's up to me to pave the way. I'm not the young adventurous American student I was

---

25 See for example Kisliuk 1998 (2000), and Kisliuk 2019.
26 My dear parents died within ten days of each other during the COVID quarantine of April 2020, and my son Max moves away to college as I draft this. And sadly, for reasons noted elsewhere, by necessity Justin and I no longer live together.
27 This field research was supported by a University of Virginia Sesquicentennial Fellowship for spring 2007.
28 Many thanks to colleagues, especially Ama Oforiwaa Aduonum, Jeffrey Summit, Janice Levi, and Nathan Devir for helpful comments and corrections on drafts of the following text.
29 These were the cheap tickets. Grant funds did not pay for family tickets even though my family was essential to my research.

twenty-five years earlier, which was the last time I'd set foot in the country of Ghana. Without apparent warning I am now a middle-aged professor mom. Can I meld these two personae, the young student so free and flexible and fun (as filtered through memory) with the coded-white professor mom? This is the reality that I need to make fit, like a pair of jeans long in the drawer.

We are waiting at the luggage belt, wondering if whatever we checked in at Newark will come out again here because we have a *huge* load of luggage; obligatory gifts for Justin's family and friends for later when we make our way to Centrafrique.[30] First we must haul it across Ghana (then Togo), which seems impossible.[31] I feel this luggage weighing like an albatross, like the commitment I made to have a family split between two continents and between vastly different worlds.[32] If we had been arriving instead at the airport in Bangui—less developed and certainly less safe after dark, we'd at least have a crowd of friends and relatives waiting. In Accra all we have is an email arrangement for a taximan with a sign.[33]

I turn to see my sleepy kid holding hands with a baggage worker. When I get Max's attention he looks up to the stranger's face and lets go.

"He has the same hand as Daddy's."

"There are lots of African men in Africa honey," I smile back at the bemused man. It is nice to be in an Anglophone country for a change.

As we approach customs, a burly agent's face lifts into a smile.

"Ah, black and white together. That's good. You are welcome (*akwaaba*)," he adds, using the traditionally hospitable phrase promoted by the country's tourist industry. As we heave our luggage down the walkway, I wonder

---

30 Justin had decided to pack the parts of a chain saw to take home to CAR. Unsurprisingly it was confiscated somewhere between Newark, Dakar, Lagos, and Accra.

31 Francophone countries and Anglophone countries have separate networks of flights—another vestige of colonialism. So, the only way on a budget to travel from Accra to Bangui (and then back again to catch our roundtrip flight home) was via Togo, overland.

32 The return trip from Centrafrique, back through Ghana, involved far less baggage. But getting past the Ghana customs agents with Justin's pungent packages of smoked caterpillars from Centrafrique to take to the United State was another episode. Easier though, than when we were held up for hours at the overland border crossing in Togo because they were checking to make sure we were not child-trafficking Max.

33 Already dire, the political and economic circumstances in Centrafrique have gotten far worse since 2007.

whether "black and white together," with Max as evidence, signals an implicit declaration conveying something like "we are antiracists." Here in this country with its specific history, might we be read as anti-colonial? We each of us get our own kind of scrutiny through difficult, colonially generated assumptions about who we are—those assumptions exacerbated by modern global inequalities. I wonder if we merit a visually superficial pass (not that I think we don't pay our own small dues every day—for example that massive luggage). But right now, the goal is to make our way to a community of Ghanaian Jews.

So please take my hand and let's jump ahead, over the mud puddle (rainy season is just beginning). A bus from Accra; then overnight in Kumasi.[34] We finally climb into a *trotro* minivan, hot and packed so that kneecaps push against each other. Busted seat springs goose us at every bump in the road and Max lies in an almost comatose sleep halfway on the lap of the stranger next to me. This van will take us to a town that is spelled—probably erroneously by British mapmakers—as though it should be pronounced Sefwi Wiawso but it is really pronounced *seffi rio-so*—an agent at the airport had curtly corrected me.[35] No, this is not like Centrafrique for me, though I have studied and taught basic Ewe music from the opposite side of Ghana for decades and traveled there a few times. In this Western Region I'm a newcomer. When I learned about this small community of African Jews, I pictured myself visiting them because they are Ghanaians, and therefore more familiar to me as compared to, for example, what it might mean to go as a newcomer to Zimbabwe or Nigeria where there are other Jewish groups

---

34   In a weak moment I decided we needed to stay in a fancy hotel in Kumasi to recharge. There, my fears about Max's safety became real very fast when my boy, playing around at the swimming pool with no shallow end, slipped off the ladder and sank like a log. I jumped in, getting under him to push him back to the surface, swallowing a lot of questionable pool water. I was quite ill for the rest of that expensive overnight.

35   The Sefwi people are considered broadly as a subset of the larger Akan ethnic group living predominantly in western Ghana. But Janice Levi clarifies, "The 'Sefwi' spell themselves as Sehwi […] And, per local historians/orators were incorporated into the Akan ethnic group upon their migration to the area [from Ivory Coast], hence becoming a subset of [Akan]. This also explains why […] Twi speakers can't understand Sehwi, while Sehwi can understand Twi […] with Sefwi really being a mix of Anyi and Twi" (Levi, personal communication via email, December 2021).

with different histories and compelling musicalities.[36] By visiting this community in Sefwi Wiawso I was hoping to fuse my long research focus in Africa with my experience and identity as a Jewish American and daughter/granddaughter of Holocaust survivors. As established above, I have strived to critically position my research in any context, but an intersection with Jewish Ghanaians might offer something uniquely fruitful and synergistic.[37]

I also thought this visit might be a way to counter essentialist assumptions especially in the West in recent decades that, if one is coded as white, one should study and teach only about one's "own culture." The colonial hypocrisy embedded in this idea is evident when one considers how many not-European musicologists (such as white Americans) study and teach European musics without being questioned about whether or not it is "their" culture. The pattern of white scholars extracting and representing Black cultures as part of the colonial (and modernist) legacy has justifiably sparked overall skepticism and critique of anyone speaking about anything that isn't "theirs." But deeper issues arise when we interrogate, as I try to do here, what we really mean by "ours" or "theirs." This research context, I thought, could open up particular anti-essentialist questions about how culture is constructed or labeled as one's own (or not one's own)—who is perceived as a bona fide Jew, what things are perceived to be African (and by whom) and how are they valued—and what are the politics and implications in such constructions. The complexity of Jewish identities in relation to race and ethnicity had, moreover, long been a compelling topic for me. These were seeded in my own family history as shared above, and enhanced by studies with my graduate mentor Barbara Kirshenblatt-Gimblett, who taught me that the

---

36   Sociologist Bruce Haynes explains that in the wake of the airlifts of tens of thousands of Ethiopian Jews to Israel in the 1980s, with "this new attention, other self-identified African Jews, such as the Lemba of southern Africa, the Abayudaya of Uganda, the Igbo of Nigeria, and even the Tutsi of Rwanda, began seeking recognition as Jews, although with varying success." (Haynes 2018, 7). See also Miles 2019.

37   One of the eye-opening aspects of this research in Ghana for me has been that I have begun to question the transparency and apparent simplicity of some of the narratives associated with this and other sites of African Jewishness (see Parfitt 2013 and Entine 2007). I am not referring to questions of "authenticity," but rather to the complex cultural and identity politics that I now expect to be pervasive in the context of any of these groups (including mainstream American Jewish groups), as people construct themselves and present themselves to others.

Jewish example can be especially helpful for understanding cultural processes because the multiplex manifestations of Jewishness, juxtaposed beside each other, throw into question static narratives of cultural, religious, and "racial," identities or essentialized differences.[38] Or as Devir puts it, Jewishness "is not a static signifier, but a spark that lights up dissimilar, contested meanings" (2017, 51).

Bruce Haynes, in the introduction to his study of Black Jews in the United States, points to a particular historical formation of an idea of Jewishness in America as linked to whiteness: "The period between 1870 and 1920 was when 2 million eastern European Jews immigrated to the U.S., and modern racial classifications were solidifying."[39] Haynes continues to note that "[b]oth East/West and black/white binaries shaped the racial morphing of Ashkenazi Jews throughout the nineteenth and twentieth centuries until their newly imagined whiteness *became inextricable from their Jewishness*" (Haynes 2018, 25, emphasis mine).[40] Our visit now to Sefwi Wiawso, perhaps especially because it is located outside of an American context, could offer a way of reframing questions at the intersection between Black and Jewish identities "that pushes us to reconsider the relationship between race and ethnicity" (Haynes 2018, 2).

After fourteen hours of travel since the capital, we pull into the dusty transit area in Sefwi Wiawso: "Mami, where you going?" a taxi driver shouts to me through the van window. *Good question*, I think, as he vies with vendors selling boiled corn, buns, or little plastic bags of drinking water.[41] We

---

38 See for example Kirshenblatt-Gimblett and Karp 2008. See also Koskoff 2002.

39 This is the same period, and these are the same forces that had pushed my grandpa to flee from Poland to Germany and then to Austria—and after the Holocaust, via Argentina, to the United States.

40 Haynes points out that "Jews had fled the *pogroms* and persecution of eastern Europe and hoped to remake themselves in America. At the same time, over one million blacks were fleeing the inequities and mob violence of the rural Jim Crow South to remake themselves in the industrial North and Midwest. Yet Jews—who had been viewed as racially distinct in Europe—were able to reframe themselves as ethnics, and therefore whites, within an emerging black-white binary that determined all civic, social, political, educational, residential, labor, and cultural boundaries and opportunities" (Haynes 2018, 1). For another narrative of the history of Jews being viewed as Black, see Parfitt 2013 and 2020.

41 The ubiquity of disposable plastics in Ghana is to the point where bits of it are embedded in the hardpacked earth in almost every populated area. The

pile out into the bustling market, stretching our cramped legs as we inhale this verdant hillside town. My directions instruct us to take a taxi to the neighborhood of New Adiembra located within a reconfigured former colonial townscape. This area, I'll discover later, contrasts with a hidden-away section of town, Old Adiembra. And it takes me a few weeks to detect the divide between the two. The latter exists within a more traditional Sefwi lifestyle that contrast with newer identities. As I will learn, attitudes in New Adiembra toward those who live in Old Adiembra are shaped by the history of colonial-era Christian missionization since the early 1800s. These were at first mostly Catholics, Methodists, Anglicans, Presbyterians, and Lutherans, but more recently Pentecostal and other evangelical movements spread across Ghana and much of sub-Saharan Africa (and the Caribbean). A common motif in this historical constellation celebrates aspects of the Old Testament in popular and religious culture. And with the exception of African ceremonial political pageantry, it also pervasively demonizes efficacious and still widespread traditional health practices, cosmologies, and lifestyles viewed by Christians as antimodern and sometimes as an existential threat—as anti-God.[42] This theme will emerge in more detail as I become increasingly aware

---

government has recently been contemplating a plastics ban but plastic seems already as embedded in the economic infrastructure as it is in the soil.

42 Devir outlines and surveys scholarly literature about some of the nuances of these perspectives, particularly between African Christian movements that have separated from their missionizing sources and those that have not, the relationship between Old Testament and Pentecostal self-understandings, and the integration of traditional spiritual practices within independent Christian churches (see Devir 2017, 35–38). This constellation of elements also exists in heightened microcosm in places like Haiti and Jamaica (see for example the work of Butler 2019 and McAlister 2004). I have been aware of the emphasis on the Old Testament in the region ever since my first visit to West Africa in 1982, when one of my young Togolese (Ewe) friends in the family I lived with insisted I call him Moshe (instead of Moise—which is Moses in French). He later became a Seventh Day Adventist while also abhorring the traditional African spiritual practices. Devir notes that Ewe (and Ga) origin stories also refer to Jewish (or rather Israelite) roots much as do Sefwi (2017, 101). He adds that the Ewe origin narrative generally does not go beyond "a liaison with the chosen people as a strategic method of finding a place marker in the history book of the colonial mindset" (2017, 102). This parallels similar processes and emphases with Black American Christianity.

of how much I need to learn to comprehend the dynamics of this place. And as I get oriented, the questions simultaneously multiply and come into focus.

As we arrive in New Adiembra it is Friday, midday, just before Shabbat. Piling out of the taxi with all that luggage, we are welcomed informally to the family compound of Joseph Armah, an interim community leader of this regional group of Sefwi Jews (about seventy families, I'm told) called House of Israel (or Tefereth [beauty of] Yisrael). I had read about this community in sparse posts on the internet, mostly from American Jews with various affiliations and agendas. Among these sources I inevitably found references to this and other African Jewish community's "hauntingly beautiful" melodies.[43] "Haunting"—an exotifying descriptor that seems to pop up regularly since the 1980s when Americans first became aware of the Ethiopian Jews (Falasha, Beta Israel). Practices in the Sefwi area led some commenters to accord Sefwi Jews a potential "lost tribe" status: these include male circumcision (common in many African cultures), a kosher-like way of butchering animals, and a traditional Saturday rest day.[44] The narrative I later pieced together regarding the origins of the community is this: Waves of unsuccessful efforts at Christian conversions were followed by a late colonial-era wave in the 1950s (Devir 2017, 70). This was sparked by missionaries attracted to the area by an economic boom, and they converted many Sefwi, including the long-sitting paramount chief and other influential leaders.[45] Then in the

---

43 See also Miles (2019) and Salamon (2001) regarding stereotype about Ethiopian Jewish culture.

44 Haynes notes that "the story of the biblical exodus of the Jews from Egypt (Exodus 12:38) serves as an archetype of nationhood in the Western imagination. Over the centuries, such varied groups as the Celts, Sami, Finns, Inuit, Maya, Berbers, Igbo, Zulu, and Native Americans have traced their origins to one of the lost tribes." Haynes continues, pointing out that every aspect of the ten tribes of Israel story "is fraught with existential controversy and with epistemological conundrums" (Haynes cites Lyman 2001) (Haynes 2018, 18–19). Devir, citing Parfitt, also discusses the lost tribe trope in relation to "Judaizing" communities (2017:17–18). Citing Kirsch, Devir notes the connection between how Christian/colonial powers commonly ascribed to any indigenous people a lost tribe status, and how therefore "a major figurative element of the biblical library was transcribed into the colonial one" (18).

45 Chief Nana Kwadwo Aduhene Okogyeabour II was Paramount Chief of Sefwi Wiawso from 1953 to 1996 and his promotion of Christianity influenced the region for decades. Levi adds that the Sefwi "House of Israel maintains that when a village chief converted to another faith, the entire community

mid-1970s a local Sefwi visionary named Aaron (Toakyirafa), emphasizing the Old Testament, made an impassioned case to the Sefwi people that they were really Jews.[46] Other Sefwi were also impassioned by the idea, it felt right to them, and in 1977 they decided to begin learning all they could about mainstream Judaism.[47]

There is also a wider Akan and more broadly Ghanaian pattern to consider here of borrowing deities and rituals from other culture groups, especially in times of crisis. Pobee and Mends note that it was historically common in traditional Ghana to import neighboring regional gods—and also aspects of Islam—that "were not indigenous to Akan society but were

---

would follow suit. Ultimately, to maintain a minority faith practice was an act of passive resistance against leadership and colonial intrusions" (Levi 2016, 98). Devir notes, however, that House of Israel founder Aaron was not ever a Christian, and that prior to his awakening he had apparently "dabbled in both Islam and animism" (2017, 72). See also Summit 2003a for parallel history in Uganda.

46 Interview with Alex Armah, June 2007. That the Sefwi people themselves at one time immigrated to this region, as they told me, most recently from Ivory Coast in the early 1700s, further complicates assumptions about Sefwi indigeneity. The 2016 documentary film *Doing Jewish: A Story from Ghana* offers a clarifying version of this narrative of Sefwi connections to a lost tribe past (about twelve minutes into the film) and also features Alex Armah and footage of the community in their practice. Devir more recently offers a detailed account of the oral history of the emergence of the House of Israel community (2017, 72–84).

47 In a 2012 article, historian Janice Levi, who visited the community in 2010, adds further details: "Toakyirafa proselytized the religion in surrounding villages and persuaded a handful to join through his oral testimony and faith observances, which echoed known pre-colonial 'traditionalist' rites. Although the terms Judaism, Jew, and Jewish were not evidenced in other known oral histories, the belief that he maintained the religion of the ancestors was enough to cement the belief that the Sefwi ethnic group were in fact descendants of Jews. At first, this now proclaimed Jewish community was not well received but over time and with the passing of the freedom of religion law in Ghana, the House of Israel was free to exercise their faith with less fear of a backlash (Levi 2012). Furthermore, with the advances in technology, the House of Israel was able to connect with Jews worldwide and through their interactions and exchanges become more aware of how their indigenous practices mirrored those of the Jewish faith" (Levi 2016, 95).

adopted during crises such as wars, epidemics and personal crises attributed to witchcraft" (1977, 2).[48] This circles back to a theme common to cultural practice: to look beyond familiar ways in a search for new tools, especially at times when critical change is at hand. Noted earlier, the emancipatory and creative potential of such reaching into liminal territory is mirrored in ethnographic and in music/dance/ritual research and praxis—and underlies my own journey with my family to this place at this time.[49] So, as people seeking new interconnections and contexts that fertilize growing and changing realities, my family from the outset had this in common with Sefwi Jews.

We continue up the walkway, past the family kiosk that sells soap, onions, eggs, and sundries to the neighbors. We step through the gate that keeps in the sheep and the miniature goats—Max will soon be playing with these goats as an emotional break for him from the overwhelmingly unfamiliar surroundings. Sitting on the concrete stoop as we enter is a Canadian study-abroad student introduced as Benjamin. He is visiting from Accra for the Shabbat weekend—a common type of North American visitor here, we'll find out. Joseph and his sons discreetly prepare a room for us—surely displacing someone in the family.[50] I have only a dim picture of who is who in this community, aware of four current leader figures: Joseph Armah, who welcomes us now, and his neighbor Alex—who happens to have the same surname[51] and who turns out to be the most advanced local rabbi in train-

---

48 See also Friedson, 2008, for an in-depth example of southeastern Ghanaian Ewe people borrowing gods and rhythms from Northern Ghana in the practice of Brekete. See also forthcoming work by Elyan Hill on Tchamba practices in Togo. Other examples from Ghana include Agorsah (2014, 103) in which Fante Koromantse people borrow witch-capturing practices from northern Ghana.

49 See the work of Richard Schechner and Victor and Edith Turner on liminality and creative processes.

50 We pay him fairly for our lodging. His sister Marta, a schoolteacher, prepares our lunches.

51 The name Armah (or Arma) may be an important clue for tracing the origins of this community. Levi (2021) cites Haïdara (1999) explaining that in Mali, in order to conceal their Jewish identities, "the Jews adopted 'pater familias' with new surnames: the Cota and Abana taking on Wakorey, and the Kuhin adopting Arma. For the House of Israel, many carry the last name of Armah, which may be an alternative spelling of the 'Arma' detailed in Haïdara's work; thus, corroborating the oral history of the House of Israel, which declares a

ing (he was denied visas to Israel and to America to study, so the year after our visit he was sponsored by Americans to study in the Abayudaya Jewish community of Uganda).[52] Then there was Kofi, the long-time congregational president who owns a dry goods shop in town right next to Joseph's photo portrait studio. But when we passed by this store Kofi seemed to avoid interaction with us. Another, older fellow named David was also mentioned on those internet documents but now too seems to be on the outs with just about everybody. I learned later that David (Ahenkorah) had been the community leader since 1993 (Devir 2017, 75). This is all intriguing while adding to my puzzlement as I try to grasp what is going on here.

Some clarification emerges when we discover that in fact the congregation is in the midst of a drawn out leadership conflict now coming to a head in court after a long delay, they told me, waiting for the regional Akan queen mother to be present to pass her judgment.[53] We attend an interim municipal hearing in which representatives of the majority of the House of Israel membership stand collectively facing just three on the opposing side. This split offers a microcosm of the liminal space this small Jewish community occupies both symbolically and literally: between local and global Jewish identities, between New Adiembra and Old Adiembra, between local and global economies, between conflicting colonial histories of the region that intersect with world religions (especially Christianity), and between competing laws and moral/behavioral codes.

---

    past in Mali (p. 22–24). [...T]hese links could potentially provide evidence that validates the migration of Jews from Iberia through the Sahara and into the interior of West Africa and ultimately to Ghana." (Levi, 2016, 99) Earlier work by Meyerowitz (1952) on the contention that Akan, or the founders of the Akan states, were Libyan Berbers from a remote oasis in the Tibetsi region of the Sahara might also corroborate this line of inquiry. Levi adds a caveat in a footnote, however, that "the adoption of the surname 'Arma' is intriguing but may also be influenced by Moriscos who fought in the Timbuktu region and were known as arma or 'sharpshooters.' See Michel Abitbol. 1979" (Levi 2016, 99n19).

52 Alex officially converted to Judaism while there. Then in 2012, again in Uganda, he was certified in rabbinics at an introductory level (Devir 2017, 90).

53 For more on Akan and Sefwi law in light of the precolonial, colonial, and postcolonial nation-state, see for example Pobee and Mends 1977, and Bono 2000.

During our first few days, our host Joseph Armah was called to the police station because of us. We did not know that as foreign visitors this far into the countryside we were supposed to have registered with the local police. Joseph told us afterward that he got around the requirement by saying we were visiting members of their "church." It seems at this time the police and many of the neighbors were unaware that this Jewish community existed; because of a local history of antisemitism, they had been careful to keep a low profile in town. But Justin had unwittingly been wearing the fatigues he'd bought in a Virginia Army/Navy store, which drew the attention of the local police—who Joseph said were surprisingly curious to understand his Judaism.

As we settled in, I learned more, bit by bit, about the pending court case—obviously a sensitive topic and I was new here, so I hesitated to ask pointed questions. The case involved tension over the community's international internet sales of decorated challah covers and kente-cloth prayer shawls, and about who should control the profits. This business started in 2002, facilitated by Harriet Bograd, an American from Kulanu, a small organization based in New York that supports "isolated, emerging, and returning" communities of Jews around the world.[54] Locally, the stakes were high, because this internet commerce translates into significant income; opportunities have been scarce to earn money in Sefwi Wiawso. Kulanu had sponsored one member of the community, Ben Baidoo, to study elaborate machine embroidery in Kumasi. And now Ben was doing all the labor to make these items to sell internationally. Yet the proceeds went into one, now frozen, community coffer.[55] After some more indirect inquiry I learn that the rejected former spiritual leader, David, along with the congregation's president, had been accused of having used communal funds for their own benefit. The bank account had been frozen by the court, so the cash was no longer flowing. One day, Ben showed us his little workshop on a hillside high above the busy

---

54   Before we traveled to Ghana, on the advice of my longtime ethnomusicologist colleague Rabbi Jeffrey Summit, who worked in Uganda with the Abayudaya, I had reached out to Harriet Bograd of Kulanu. She kindly gave me names and contacts in Sefwi Wiawso. I also spoke with her while preparing this essay and she generously updated me about some of what had since transpired in the community. Harriet died in September 2022.

55   http://www.kulanuboutique.com/challah-covers/.

town market, quietly telling us how he was suffering: although he was working, because of the court case he was not getting paid.[56]

What especially sparks my interest, though, is a hushed and tense rumor that while siphoning community funds and equipment, the accused former leader David had been consorting with mystical dwarves (*mmoetia*, pronounced memo-eh-tee-ah). In Akan lore, mmoetia resemble humans but are only two feet tall and cannot be tracked because their feet point backward. Rarely observed or heard, mmoetia are rumored to have high pitched voices, and they snatch their initiates away to visit their world. With prayer and sacrifice they grant their follower's wishes for financial prosperity and protection but can also bring misfortune to those who have done wrong (Bannerman-Richter 1982, 1987). In short, they are associated with witchcraft. People whispered to me that the dwarves shoot mystical arrows at the enemies of their followers—who are usually traditional healer/diviners chosen by the mmoetia to enter into their mystical world.[57]

Then emerged a related and even more divisive rumor: David had allowed into the congregation a "fetish priest" (the English term for traditional spiritual healer/diviner as translated through a colonial lens). This man, they said, was using the congregation's prayer book to perform divinatory readings for clients seeking his council.[58] While I found this creative cultural/spiritual amalgamation fascinating, the inclusion of this person within the congregation so alarmed the majority in the community that they had structurally separated leader David and the small group of his sympathizers. While

---

56   Ben Baidoo, still a young man, died in 2019.
57   Similar mystical dwarves appear also in some African-Caribbean cultures with Akan roots. Magical elves, gnomes, or dwarves are also a global folkloric phenomenon, with particular and sometimes far-reaching social-symbolic manifestations. But mmoetia are rarely mentioned in any formal scholarship I have seen about Akan religion. A fascinating aspect to me of the mmoetia is their high-pitched, screechy voices and mode of interactive communication with humans (from *The Practice of Witchcraft in Ghana* by Gabriel Bannerman-Richter, chapter 6: "Mmoetia the Witch-Fighting Fairies," 60–67). These qualities bear a striking resemblance to the spirit entities called Boyobé for BaAka (Centrafrican forest people, see Kisliuk 2000, 157). These interconnections point toward deep indigenous knowledges and to the sonic components of that knowledge, and I hope to continue research about those connections.
58   This divination practice may be similar to ways in which the Koran has been used historically by Akan practitioners, according to Pobee and Mends 1977 (p. 3).

waiting for the court case to be resolved, they had agreed to allot each faction a different time slot in the synagogue building.[59] Joseph and others I spoke to dodged my direct questions about any of this, while taking care that I and my family would not cross paths with David or his faction. I could not very well go against the preferences of my gracious host and insist on finding David to interview him, much as I would have liked to.[60] The prevailing view of most of the community was that they did not want the congregation to be associated with African mystical practices assumed to be witchcraft. Biblical laws prohibiting various forms of witchcraft and divination can be found in the books of Exodus, Leviticus, and Deuteronomy, but in fact divination and related mystical practices have long been part of Judaic folk and esoteric religion (Dan 2006)—a compelling topic related to this context but beyond my scope here.

Elsewhere in Africa I have seen a similar rejection of traditional praxis (see for example Kisliuk 2000).[61] Such rejection consistently involves the uninformed melding, through a Christian lens, of witchcraft practices into a much broader attitude toward African spirituality; subsuming deep, aesthetically and philosophically rich cultural life into the category of witchcraft. The result is the distortion of all efficacious African spiritual/social/expressive practices, which might range on the negative side from charlatanism

---

59   It seems the dispute was never fully settled. A new bank account was opened later so that the sale of the cloth items could support the building of a new guesthouse to take the burden of the many visitors off of Joseph Armah and his family (personal communication with Kulanu president Harried Bograd in August 2021).

60   Devir (2017), whose field research in Sefwi Wiaswo took place several years after our visit, notes that former leader David Ahenkorah was definitively voted out of the House of Israel community in 2008. Devir goes on to recount a phone conversation he had in which David says he subsequently joined the Black Hebrews while noting the divisive effect that, in David's view, white Jewish visitors had had on the House of Israel community. Perceptions of racial and ethnic affiliation, and related perceptions of colonial and anti-colonial positions, become even more complicated with this development. Devir reminds himself and his readers that in Ghana, as elsewhere, "there are multiple ways of enmeshing oneself in the spirit of the Hebrew Scriptures, without ever taking on the yoke of normative Judaism" (2017, 56).

61   In the case of BaAka in the southern forest of the Central African Republic, as well as for popular musicians in Bangui (CAR's capital). Kisliuk 1998 (2000), and Kisliuk 2006.

to sorcery, superstition to magic, but also encompasses guiding myths and folk narratives and traditional medicinal and healing practices. Included on this sometimes intertwined spectrum is private devotion such as the use of ancestral altars (often astoundingly artistically elaborate in Ghana, Togo, Benin, and Nigeria), divination consultations with master diviners, or more public trance ceremonies in religious subcultures that are part of profound cosmological webs for comprehending life and death.[62] In this region of West Africa (and its Caribbean offshoots), trance ceremonies that activate and embody guiding cosmologies rely heavily on symbolically saturated and technically elaborate music and dance traditions. So the indiscriminate—and racist—fusion of the category of witchcraft with these broad and important practices amounts to the destructive vilification of core African culture.[63] In Centrafrique and elsewhere I have seen this kind of pernicious vilification engender new variants of sorcery, superstition, and charlatanism refracted through Christianity in a defeating process of self-demonizing that further effaces what is propitious, meaningful, and life-giving.[64] Therefore I came to Sefwi Wiawso with an understanding that the careful deliverance of traditional knowledges from this kind of neocolonial vilification is required to underpin African futures. [65] I had also thought that my Jewish background had made me extra sensitive to such harm. So, it especially pained me now to see African praxis again vilified, but this time not in the face of Christian missionization but in the name of Judaism.

Before this, I had assumed that in any Jewish context people would know what it means to defend one's ethnic identity or religious practices against

---

62 See for example work of Margaret Thompson Drewal (1992), and Steven Friedson (2008), and Olupona and Abiodun, eds. (2016).

63 James Burns, focusing on Ewe experience in Eastern Ghana, identifies three groups of actors within the social complex that denigrates traditional practices: Christians, mediators, and culturalists, and he also points to the related denigration of traditional practices by the upwardly mobile who prefer to associate themselves with global capitalists, which in Ghana means Western Christians. Burns notes that since the late 1950s "'culture' becomes the province of the marginalized" and that mediators, here corresponding to Sefwi Jews, can blend roles and may swing one way or the other (Burns 2009, 6–7).

64 For example, see Dijk 2001. For detailed examples from Eweland in Ghana, see Burns 2009 and Meyer 1999. Similar dynamics of vilification are also prevalent in the Caribbean, including Jamaica and Haiti (see for example Butler 2019 and McAlister 2004).

65 See also, for example, work by Michael Atwood Mason.

oppressive or assimilative forces. To me, that is one of the things Jews are especially good at. When my mother was hiding from Nazis in a Catholic school in Brussels, she could not bring herself to prostrate herself in front of the cross during Easter because, she said, she knew who she was—and this knowing was about being a Jewish person, not about being a pious or religious person. During mass she would secretly turn around and rub from her chest the invisible gesture of the sign of the cross. This refusal of a gesture became a dangerous giveaway to observing eyes, and she left that school before she could be caught and denounced to the Nazis (Ingrid Kisliuk 1992). But news to me here: the majority of the House of Israel would not defend or want to be remotely associated with the supernaturally inflected aspects of African culture—that is, whatever could not be rendered innocuous or elided with a Jewish narrative. And the many Jewish visitors from North America likely did not even perceive African mystical practices. Those visitors were scanning for what would be familiar to them as Jews. So the complicated relationship that most of this community seemed to have with traditional African spiritual praxis, while troubling to me, began to make sense; the choice to embrace Judaism by members of this community was in part a way to exit neocolonial Christianity while simultaneously sidestepping traditional practices vilified by Christians.[66] They could claim (or reclaim) a Jewish identity in the wake of colonialism as an alternative rootedness; not Christian or even ultimately European, and also not vilifiable as witchcraft.[67]

---

66   The history of adjudicating witchcraft in Africa, including pre-colonial, colonial, and postcolonial contexts, is fascinating and complex. See for example Gray's dissertation on the legal history of witchcraft in colonial Ghana (2000).

67   Devir corroborates my impression here regarding Sefwi Jews' choice as being about rootedness (2017, 85). Devir characterizes this move, in fact common in a swath of spiritual practices and beliefs across Ghana (and surely beyond), as "finding one's past in the story of another Other" (2017, 115). Parfitt (2013) and Devir (2017) have since also posited related conclusions as I did regarding Sewfi and other African Jews; Devir writes that initially House of Israel founder "Aaron and his followers insisted that European's imposition of an alien way of thought—Christianity—also masked the truth about the Sefwi as a special people chosen by god" (2017, 75). Summit notes a similar trajectory with the Abayudaya of Uganda (2003a).

my ethnographic doubling

The identities of those in this community are complex, emergent, and fraught, and the same is true for my own family. Part of why I was excited to bring young Max to this place was because so far in America his experiences had taught him that Africans are not Jewish, and that his two "halves" are somehow mutually exclusive.[68] Max's dad was raised as a Catholic (via a now-defunct Italian mission in Bagandou village, Central African Republic), and Justin throughout his life has tried many other religions (from Islam to Baha'i, to Jehova's Witnesses and Mormonism). For Max in America, as Haynes explains, "black Jews (those recognized within rabbinic Judaism) carry the burden of continually asserting their legitimacy; without a counternarrative of their own, they struggle to fit within a Western narrative of Jewishness that precludes their very existence" (Haynes 2018, 25. See also Parfitt, 2020). I thought this visit might offer Max a counternarrative: here in Ghana the kids in the Armah family take Max under their wing, get him bathed, teach him to fetch water and to play soccer in flip flops. Among my research goals, I hoped to complicate (and eventually integrate) Max's reality, to burst pernicious binaries by immersing him, however briefly, in an African Jewish context while he also attended Hebrew class with Ghanaian children who knew more Hebrew than he did.[69]

---

68   For related discussions about this popular and historically constructed perception in the United States of Blackness and whiteness as related to Jewishness, see Brodkin 1998, and Levi 2012.

69   After this we would bring Max to his dad's country, Centrafrique, where English is not common, where we would be the only Jews, yet he would be among his relatives showering him with affection. That portion of our travel warrants an essay of its own, but I offer this moment: one afternoon in Justin's natal village, Max and I joined an open-air meeting of elders gathered behind the town hall—a tall and rickety wooden vestige of the colonial presence. They were seated in a circle drinking palm wine and corn whiskey, discussing current affairs. I introduced Max, saying that his middle name is Mungwadi (from *mungo a di*, meaning "god is present" in Bagandou, where *mungo* is the supreme being). Hearing his name, they began singing Ngando dance-songs about mungo, passing Max around to bounce on their laps. Though Max does not remember this moment anymore, I have to believe it matters that it happened—it reverberates in people who do remember it, he'll continue to be told about it, and it affirmed his roots in that place.

Figure 10.1. Joseph Armah's children impeccably singing the "Aleph Bet" song to the melody by Debbie Friedman. Max (right) knows just a little, trying his best to fake it. Sefwi Wiawso (New Adiembra) Ghana, 2007. The little girl pictured here is Rahel, Joseph Armah's daughter, at age six. She is featured in cameos several years later in the Zilkha documentary film *Doing Jewish: A Story from Ghana*. Photo by author.

layering

After leaving Sefwi Wiawso and on the way to Centrafrique, we'd be stopping in Eweland, eastern Ghana (Volta region). There, Max experienced music and dance familiar to him from attending my university classes and concerts throughout his childhood. I'm parlaying Max here as a kind of identity stand-in; as mothers will know, young Max's whole being was viscerally fused with mine, and his experiences ricocheted to my own gut. Though as noted I did hope that our visit to the Sefwi Jewish community would reinforce for Max that one can be both Jewish and African—doing all that we did in this short trip also allowed each of us to connect with and to question a number of things at once about who we are, who we were, and who we might be becoming.[70]

I never planned for my visit with the Sefwi Jewish community to be a long-term or deeply informed study. Given the complexity of the scene, and the copious related expert scholarship in Akan/West African studies, in Jewish studies, and now in proliferating research about African/Black Jews, such a task, though worthy, was not my goal. Nevertheless, it has taken me years, and really through completing this essay, to be able to substantively sort out what I did learn by going to Sefwi Wiawso. The voice of an academic superego told me that I should not even visit, much less write a published piece involving this place and these people unless it were to be fully informed by extensive ethnographic study. But by now I know that I can, and in fact should write about it from my own grounded perspective, however partially informed it is; because the questions I am raising here are not what a conventional ethnographic study would likely address.[71] With this project I am pushing back on a pernicious curtailing of an exploration focused on the synergistic meeting between what was going on in this community at this moment, my own family history and immediate reality, and urgent issues in this third decade of the twenty-first century. It turns out that a monthlong visit fifteen years ago suited exactly this purpose. And that critical practice positioning is what allows for this focus—it is what leads to insights about the personally interactive, intersubjective, contingent formations of race,

---

70 One of the most fascinating and perplexing aspects of Jewishness for me, as at once an ethnic, cultural, and religious category, is that it is not possible to be a secular convert; traditionally, the only way to become Jewish if not born to a Jewish mother is to convert in a religious domain. Yet there is still a presumed cultural affinity between secular Jews (those born and/or raised as Jews but not religious) and converts who hail from other ethnicities/religions. The intermingling of secular Jews with Jewish converts can therefore be revealing of how both are constructed. My presence in Sefwi Wiawso offers one example of this.

71 The ballooning references and notes section that has emerged from writing this essay signals the scope required for a comprehensive academic/ethnographic study. The closest I have seen to my foray with Jews of Sefwi Wiaswo are Janice Levi's recent graduate research and initial publications, and Gabrielle Zilkha's film (which is a first-person documentary and though it offers many insights, does not claim to be a scholarly project). I also just recently learned, via Janis Levi, of the work of Nathan P. Devir (2017), and I have integrated citation of that work late in my revision process.

culture, and identity. It allows me to more fully model a perspective I raised decades ago (Kisliuk 1996, 1998): that while ethnography is partly about certain places and people in focus, it is equally about and shaped by the lens that is offering that experience of a place and a people. So, the entire relevant background—the life—of the person who brings that lens to bear on the moment is what unites an ethnography through a unique path of inquiry.

Our host Joseph Armah also had expectations about what visitors staying this long should normally be doing. As our stay wore on, Joseph approached me and asked pointedly, though politely, what was my program. He and his family had been generously accommodating us to their own undoubted discomfort and though I was compensating them, I felt guilty. But I did not have a good answer for him; I could not say without offense or confusion that I wanted to know more about David and the dwarves, or, on the opposite end of the spectrum, that I wanted to let my research focus gradually emerge over time. I had expressed that I wanted Max to see that Africans can also be Jews, but I did not imply that this was the only reason for the visit. I had ostensibly come to learn about the community's music, but this too was a murky topic—the musical life of this community was thus far not particularly interesting (more on this below). At this juncture there were many intersecting streams of interest all of which were still confusing. But I did say, in answer to his question about my program, that I wanted to visit Old Adiembra, which is why, finally, at the last minute they brought me there, as I describe below.

praxis and embodiment: movement, rhythm, ritual

In the synagogue in Sefwi Wiawso, a combination of ritual gestures and everyday actions mark affiliations with varied pasts, coming together at this geocultural place and moment. Our stay here raised for me many questions about the micro-enactments of identity and participation that stood out among the practices of members of this community, especially during their Shabbat morning service. I claim no authority as an arbiter of what is or is not "Jewish" (or what qualifies as "doing Jewish" as the 2016 film contends). In fact, many of the members of this congregation in Ghana are certainly more ritually observant than I have been in my life—they follow (or did in 2007) largely the equivalent of an American Conservative Shabbat service, some of it in Hebrew. They owned a small Torah scroll from which Alex would read every Saturday.[72] In any case, what constitutes being observant is open to debate, and such debates have been at the core of much Jewish life.[73] Interpretations of appropriate ritual action, language, and conception vary greatly, changing with setting and circumstance. But here some elements stood out, for example people usually do not talk about going to synagogue (or temple, as I was taught to say growing up in Boston). Rather they say they are going to "church"—Tefereth Israel in Sefwi Wiawso was incorporated as a church because the category "synagogue" did not officially exist in Ghana at the time.[74] Also, I was told quietly, that incorporating as a church offered some cover against suspicion and discrimination from the Christian majority, which had apparently been quite harsh in decades past (Zilkha 2016) and continues today. Even Alex, then the community's rabbi-in-training, would make slips of the tongue, sometimes saying "preaching the Gospel" when he meant teaching Torah—a hard one for me as an American to reconcile with being Jewish—but here the meaning is more generic; the associations do not translate the same way.

To ground this research as critical embodied practice means locating how it felt to sing the songs and clap along, to speak familiar prayers and join

---

72 According to Devir, this scroll, along with prayer books, was gifted to the community by Daniel Braden, an American Jew of Ghanaian origin who visited the community in the mid-1990s and sparked subsequent, usually brief, visits by many Jewish Americans (Devir 2017,78; Braiden 1998).

73 Haynes boils down scholarly consensus to this definition: "A Jew is someone who both considers himself or herself to be Jewish and is considered to be Jewish by relevant others" (2018, 10). But this begs the question as to which "others" are "relevant" in a given context, and who decides (*halachic* [Jewish law] and *minhagic* [Jewish custom] would argue varied criteria and authority that differ from Haynes's definition). Haynes also note that claims "to an unbroken ancestral history bolster the notion that the Jewish people constitute a biological group. The search for the genetic history of the Jewish people or an identifiable set of Jewish genetic markers is testament to how we continue to reproduce these notions. Scholars are only now beginning to reevaluate common understandings of Jewish identity and to recognize that, like the ancient Israelites, modern-day Jews are 'a mixed multitude'—that is, descended from multiple tribal and ethnic origins rather than a common ethnic or racial stock (Biale 2006)" (Haynes 2018, 19). See also extensive work by Parfitt.

74 According to Zilkha's documentary film, Alex incorporated the synagogue officially as a business in 2016.

in familiar gestures along with initially unfamiliar people in an unfamiliar setting; and to live day-to-day in this sensory place getting to know people and learn about their complex lives. The constant juxtaposition of familiar Jewish things in an African/Ghanaian/Sefwi context—and conversely familiar African things in an unfamiliar Jewish context—hit me with a barrage of cognitively dissonant startles. Some of the gestures, rhythms, and songs used on Shabbat are rooted in Sefwi, and some are adapted from various Christian practices; some songs incorporate Akan musical elements like the common three-strike syncopated ostinato which is not originally related to Christianity but has been melded iconically into Akan Gospel and church music. Other elements, like the melodies sung to the most common Shabbat morning prayers, are imported Jewish practices from abroad, introduced to this community by visitors over the past forty years—the span during which they gradually became self-identified as Jews. Some of these elements were very familiar to me, but at first were surprising to see here. These included *davening* (from the Yiddish *davenen*, meaning "to pray") rocking movements done here by both men and women while reading silent prayers. While speaking aloud the prayer "kadosh, kadosh, kadosh" (holy, holy, holy—the Kedushah prayer), the congregants rose to the balls of their feet three times as they repeated the word. Additionally, after the Torah reading, they followed the custom of lifting and turning the scroll so that the congregation could see the text that was just read and pointing to the open text while speaking a prayer of acknowledgment. These gestures I'd seen only in more traditional settings than the one I grew up in. Also in Sefwi, as elsewhere around the world, the closed and dressed Torah is paraded through the congregation while the congregants sing joyfully. As the Torah goes by, members of the congregation touch the clothed scroll with a prayer book or shawl, then lightly kiss the book or shawl. This I did not grow up with in a Reform synagogue, but it has since become part of most Torah reading rituals I have become used to in the United States. The most familiar element was the recitation of the *shema*, the iconic Jewish prayer (the first half of which is "Hear o Israel, Adonai is our god, Adonai is one"). They sang those words, in Hebrew, to the global melody so familiar to me and millions of others (composed by an Austrian Jew named Solomon Sultzer in the nineteenth century).[75]

---

75 This site has some interesting perspectives and includes a link to an example of the melody: http://teruah-jewishmusic.blogspot.com/2007/03/

During our visit in Sefwi Wiawso, an American rabbinical student named Michael arrived, sponsored by Kulanu to offer much-appreciated Hebrew classes. One day, while the young people were cleaning up after class in the synagogue building, Michael played a CD of songs from the Abayudaya Jews of Uganda (Grammy-nominated in 2004 and produced by ethnomusicologist Jeffrey Summit). The children sang along happily with the now-familiar tunes. During Shabbat services Joseph Armah wore an embroidered skullcap also from the Abayudaya, while offering his Torah commentary in the local Sefwi language (as distinguished from Twi, an Akan lingua franca and one of the common languages of Christian worship). He strode down the center aisle as he spoke in Sefwi, his prayer shawl (tallit) sliding off one shoulder. He lifted it back to his shoulder, a nonchalant gesture familiar to Jews worldover—but also mirroring the gesture that an Akan man makes as he pulls back onto one shoulder his heavy kente robes, perhaps after offering a libation or honoring an elder.[76]

After the Shabbat services and the evening meal, Joseph invited me, Max, and Justin to join with his wife at that time, Gladys, to participate in Havdalah, the sunset ritual to end the sabbath. Their mood was solemn and gave the impression that this was an important ritual for them. This seemed not only essential to their observance, but it included the recitation, directed by Joseph to his wife, of a prayer in English about a woman of valor who is at the center of a Jewish home (Proverbs 13:10).[77] Several years later historian Janice Levi attended a Havdalah ritual with other leaders in Sefwi Wiawso and described a very similar ritual (also depicted in the 2016 Zilkha film).[78]

---

shema-was-composed-really.html. See also: http://www.chazzanut.com/articles/sulzer.html.

76 In Zilkha's film there is footage of a Havdalah ceremony led by Alex Armah. After the blessing over the wine (or in this case probably Coca-Cola), an assistant takes the glass and lets the children, and everyone in the circle in attendance, take a sip from the glass. The drink is offered and accepted only with the right hand—a West African custom. This moment evokes for me as much a Havdalah ceremony as a traditional Ghanaian pouring of libations to ancestors. And it seems perfectly reasonable that these elements be melded here, but it also seems important to acknowledge the melding itself.

77 In traditional rabbinic Jewish households, this prayer is often recited by a husband to his wife at the Friday night meal. The version of this practice in Sefwi Wiawso I would guess was introduced at some point by a visitor.

78 "As the sky darkened and three stars became visible on a Saturday evening in Sefwi Wiawso, Ghana, two kippot wearing boys alerted their father that it was

Alex and Joseph told me that the community prefers to do things their own way—though what constitutes their own way is contested—Alex having become a controversial leader more recently, increasingly pursuing learning beyond his community. Newly composed songs by some of the members rarely, though sometimes, make it into the ritual practice.[79] Instead, at the time of my visit, songs in Twi comprised much of the music for this worship community, coming from the familiar pasts of various congregants (mostly Anglican, Pentecostal, or Methodist), but deleting references to Jesus or Christ. Participants draw on their pasts and reshape them into their morphing identities. This kind of process happens everywhere, of course. And Jewish music across time and diaspora is often cited as a tradition that liberally integrates elements of the surrounding sacred or secular musical repertoire (see Summit 2003a). When I was a teenager, I derided my Reform synagogue in Boston for not having more engaging singing and participation; with its organ and stiff choir, it resembled the high Protestant practices of northeastern cities, or, even less appealing to me especially because it precluded participation, it aspired to operatic-style tenor vocalizations by the cantor—seeming to align with the aesthetics of the upwardly mobile, dominant culture of the United States. That kind of assimilation did appeal somewhat to my mother—perhaps the epigenetic effect of my grandparents' traumatic experiences in Austria—a way of

---

time to begin the Havdalah service, signifying the end of Shabbat. In a private guest room, a table was adorned with a white embroidered cloth, two candles placed into silver candlesticks, a bottle of Coca-Cola to be used as the special libation (as wine cannot easily be acquired), and a bundle of Queen of the Night—a local plant that served as a fragrant spice. This closing ritual symbolized the end of a holy day of rest and worship, a practice that has arguably been long observed in the Sefwi Wiawso district. For the 'House of Israel'—a self-asserting Jewish community in the Western Region of Ghana—this ritual tethers the community to the global faith of Judaism along with a past heritage, which was arguably interrupted by various forces, including colonialism and the influence of Christianity. In the oral narrative of the House of Israel, it is this practice that is referenced most often. This ritual performed by their ancestors creates a link to the past but also authenticates their claim to a Hebraic heritage in the present. It serves as a physical relic, a residual memory of a past faith indicative of their indigenous beliefs" (Levi 2016, 93).

79   Joseph Nippah, Alex Armah's older brother, composed most of the new songs with Sefwi lyrics. He told me though, that it was difficult to merge them into the weekly service.

burying their Yiddish links and roots. This in some way parallels the burying of traditional African ways by the Sefwi Jews.[80]

Here in Sefwi Wiawso there was a comparatively lively and participatory musicality, especially those songs adapted from the Ghanaian Pentecostal gospel genre that incorporates polymetric clapping. But compared to recordings of music of African Jews elsewhere (specifically the Abayudaya, Lemba, or Ibo), this community did not stand out musically. Elsewhere in Africa, especially in rural places, I was used to hearing within the daily soundscape drumming and singing, along with popular dance music.[81] By contrast, during my stay in New Adiembra I felt relatively musically deprived. All I heard beyond the synagogue was recorded Ghanaian gospel wafting ubiquitously through the air, and some lackluster amplified funeral hymns accompanied by simple drums—a kind of common generic church music. This may be the result of the particular missionary history in this area; as noted earlier, a Sefwi chief (Nana Kwadwo Aduhene II) converted to Catholicism in the 1950s and ruled Sefwi Wiawso until the late 1990s, admonishing his people to abandon their customs (Boni 2000, Zilkha 2016). But my hosts said that if I were to go to Old Adiembra, there I would hear traditional Sefwi songs. When I asked if someone might accompany me there, however, they were oddly evasive, just as they had been with my questions about their former leader David and the diviner involved with the mmoetia.

Old Adiembra is not far from Joseph's place. So, Justin and I walked there ourselves one day in half an hour. But from the dirt road where we stood when we arrived, only the backs of the mudbrick dwellings were visible, and from there we could not see any people out in the open. We did not feel comfortable just strolling in uninvited; I needed a local liaison to introduce me. So finally, the afternoon before we were to leave Sefwi to continue our travels, Ben the tailor and his cousin Abigail offered to take me. Abigail was an energetic young woman whom I'd already noticed because she was especially active during Shabbat services, singing and reciting Hebrew prayers, and her father was a founding member of this Jewish community.[82] I was

---

80 And also parallels the attempt to dominate BaAka forest people by the missionized in Central Africa (see Kisliuk 2000).

81 It could well be that only a month in Sefwi Wiawso was simply not long enough for me, as a newcomer, to get a fuller sense of the musicality of the place.

82 Abigail had been offered a scholarship from Kulanu to study in the United States but was denied a visa. So now she was preparing to attend the local

perplexed when they deliberately hired a taxi with darkened windows and asked me to sit, hidden from view, in the backseat. Later I understood that they were concerned that their neighbors would see them taking me to Old Adiembra and might suspect them of being involved with the "fetish" people.[83] But Ben and Abigail also brought a bottle of gin along as a gift for the elders whom they knew would use it to pour libations to ancestors. They both seemed excited about the visit. Stepping out of the taxi, we slipped into the neighborhood by zigzagging through back pathways among the mud-brick homes. We arrived in the compound of the village chief, who, I was intrigued to learn, was Ben and Abigail's elder uncle. The whole neighborhood gathered around, and we spent a few hours exchanging ideas. Some elder folks sweetly sang a few songs, but they explained that they would have needed more time to prepare to show me a more extensive music and dance event.[84] The chief answered my translated questions about the history of this place, about their perspective on Christian missionaries and British colonists, and about the Sefwi Jews.[85] Ben and Abigail ended up happily leaving with what they said was new and interesting knowledge about their Sefwi traditions.[86] Odd perhaps that I, yet another Jewish American visitor, was the one who provided them with an occasion to go to Old Adiembra and interact

---

teacher's college instead.

83   Joseph Armah's sister Marta is a schoolteacher and is also Jewish. While visiting her school I learned that at work she was not open about being Jewish; when I asked her why for an English class, her colleague used Christian Bible quotes as examples on the blackboard, she admonished me to hush up my question for fear that she would be exposed as Jewish. She said she was not sure what the reaction of her colleagues might be to learning that she is Jewish, but she did not want to risk it.

84   There were young children there too, but the only working-age person in attendance was a drunk man. This was a weekday, but I do not know if working-age people from Old Adiembra would commute into town or had simply left the village altogether. I tend to think it is the latter.

85   Pobee and Mends point out that it "is difficult to draw neat distinctions between Christianity and European culture for the two were presented as two fronts of the same phenomenon" (1977, 5).

86   Ben Baidoo stayed up late that last night with me trying to translate it all, but it was not possible to work in haste with the necessary care. Some of the information in the film *Doing Jewish: A Story from Ghana* shows some informative interviews with some regional chiefs and elders, but not those from Old Adiembra.

with the elders. But because this interview had been delayed for so long, I did not have time left to get the proper translation of the chief's elaborate answers. Maybe this information was all too deep and complex as compared to my level of involvement in this community anyway, and therefore perhaps appropriate that the details of the conversation remained inaccessible to me.[87] And maybe what did come through is most important here anyway; in the gentle songs and the receptive neighbors, even in this brief meeting there was a palpable feeling of mutual warmhearted respect and appreciation. The chief, and the elderly ladies who sang, had the deep-eyed look.

What, then, connotes as African or Jewish? For whom, where? What feels Sefwi or Ewe or Centrafrican or American? And for whom, where? Specifically, when and under what performative and interactive circumstances does something feel categorically *not* Jewish or *not* African? Gestures and terms, melodies and rhythms as I sang along, might connote iconically to me as African, but in Sefwi Wiawso they are neutral as to whether they are Jewish. Because of my own cultural history, though, if something seems Christian to me (like calling the synagogue a church), those things could not be reconfigured as Jewish. While for the Sefwi Jewish community, some things that denote Africanness, such as divination or mystical dwarves are for them (as previously defined by the Christians and perhaps also by foreign Jews) most definitely not Jewish things, even while the same people are relaxed and inclusive of other elements that signal to me as Christian or African, including rhythms, harmonies, and language.[88] The result is a web of micro-aesthetic expressions that, from the standpoint of each person and negotiated within groups, contain a multilectic microcosm, a constant dynamic rebalancing between stability and innovation, between what is known and what is emergent, what is incorporated or rejected; and the propitious side of the double-within-the-double we began with.[89] At the

---

87   I still have the video recording of this visit and may soon still ask someone to help me translate from Sefwi.

88   The realm of ceremonial political pomp, such as drumming, dancing, and ritual surrounding the chiefs and kings, occupies a fascinating liminal ground in the Akan context, and in the dynamic tension between Christian and traditional (ancestor-related) practices.

89   Elsewhere I have called this the fixed/mixed dialectic (Kisliuk 2002, and Kisliuk and Gross 2004). I am aware this has some resemblances to European philosophy such as Husserl and Heidegger and later Walter Benjamin, Bourdieu, and Raymond Williams—and of course to Buddhism and other Asian philosophies and indeed to pan-African ontologies (see for example M.

same time, the particular choices each of us makes in this setting have micro-implications within a pernicious/propitious double—a complex that can shift depending on the lens of agency and power as determined within both microsocial and macropolitical contexts.

At the end of the Shabbat service, Max sat at the back of the synagogue with the other young children. As the closing song rang out—this one in the Sefwi language—Max put his arm around the shoulder of Joseph's young daughter Rahel, and they swayed.

conclusion

The Jews of Sefwi Wiawso are poised precariously between the local majority Christians and the world of the marginalized traditionalists represented in Old Adiembra. But I wonder what might be the price of the doubly liminal position taken by this community to choose a minority Jewish identity that rejects the ancestral practices and spirit-laden side of their own African roots. What is at stake—politically, aesthetically, economically, and otherwise—in this kind of position and what level of understanding and self-searching does it call for in a setting that is so fraught and uneasy? Since the time of my visit, there have been ongoing crises in leadership, and some people who had been active no longer participate—or are flat-out "not Jewish anymore."[90] That is a stance that most American Jews, no matter how secular, rarely consider an option.[91]

And what, if anything, was "mine" here? The Jewish or the African or neither? In some ways I felt just as ambivalent about the Jewish practice here as

---

Drewal and H. Drewal). But at least in the West, these philosophical abstractions have been constrained by the academic pernicious double, and therefore most often not applied concretely and in an embodied way to our understanding of the dynamics of creative/aesthetic and intellectual praxis.

90 As per a personal communication with the president of Kulanu (Harriet Bograd, August 2021), the leadership of Teffereth Israel has been in ongoing flux, and conflicts about use of funds and other issues by various leaders have continued to beset the community. Alex, meanwhile, has become the leader of another congregation closer to Accra.

91 Even "Jews for Jesus" seem to see themselves as Jews on some level even though their belief in Jesus as the Messiah would obviate their claim to be Jewish according to accepted Jewish belief and practice. I thank Jeffrey Summit (personal communication 2022) for suggesting the above wording.

I might have felt visiting an unfamiliar Jewish community anywhere in the world. At other moments I felt wondrously connected. I also (ambivalently) felt that, after decades researching and teaching African-rooted performance and living in African contexts and joining together in family, African culture is in a way part of me, and in some specific ways that many Sefwi Jews apparently rejected. In yet other ways, though, I was totally unfamiliar with the particularities of Sefwi culture and history. What is familiarity? When does a practice or a people meld with who you feel you are, and in ways that others might acknowledge that you are? What might be the overlap, if any, between the Jewishness of my European grandparents (which also is not the same as my own Jewishness, nor was theirs that of their parents) and the Jewishness of Joseph, Alex, and others in this community? By the end of the visit, I wondered if anything at all was mine here besides my own family (also in flux) and the new friendships and interconnections I was making because of this visit. Coming back now to the threat of a pernicious binary I outlined earlier, if one should only study/research/participate/share in what is "mine" and not presume to ever understand or meld with anything "other," the question becomes how small should the bubble of "mine" be in that scenario, how large the bubble of "other"?[92] Moreover, when "mine" is confined to a binary racial or religious category, while it serves as an important place to strategically root identity and community, it also, as we know by now, can readily become something essentialist, something pernicious.[93] In the end, the only thing that seemed inarguably mine here was a point of view that was now both expanded and further grounded, and which yielded more questions than answers. These questions were shared and collectively generated in sparks of rhizomatic, intersubjective, sometimes just momentary brushing

---

[92] There are longstanding and evolving discussions about insider/outsider research. For example, Lila Abu-Lughod and related and subsequent work in anthropology about "halfie" research (Abu-Lughod 1990). See also Alcoff, "The Problem of Speaking for Others" (1992) and Subedi 2006. Other examples closer to the area topic in this essay are Summit (2013) and Devir (2017) and Zilkha (2016). Also see Ama Oforiwaa Aduonum's essay in this volume.

[93] This argument about performance and identity overlaps with the perennial issue in aesthetics that addresses the rhetorics of authenticity and which famously misses the centrally constitutive and power-laden elements of those rhetorics. For examples of helpful theoretical approaches to this related argument see Schechner's "Restoration of Behavior" (1985) and Taruskin's "Pastness of the Present and the Presence of the Past" (1995).

encounters with other people—moments incubating and then expanding in myriad directions.

I invoke James Clifford's phrase "ethnographic self-fashioning" in a multilectical way here: personalized, grounded, microdescriptive performance-focused inquiry is both constitutive *and* investigative; the constitutive and the empirical are by necessity in dialectical relation to one another, they need each other. Some might take this dynamic as obvious, but circling back to where this essay began, our use of language and our conventional assumptions rooted in institutions constantly undermine the embodied living of that multilectical reality, often just appearing to be propitious while actually being a pernicious dummy of itself. Researching, and then finally writing this essay has allowed me to understand better not only what was/is going on in Sefwi Wiawso but also what was/is going on in my own life and in the world right now—and this, when I remember to keep it close, can help make me a more aware, informed, and empathetic teacher, artist, activist, person. Since the "reflexive turn" in ethnography in the 1980s, and then its pernicious backlash, many ethnographers still assume that they must choose—by some dichotomous misunderstanding— *between* "reflexivity" or "objectivity." But as I've argued and I hope demonstrated, we need both at once, always in dynamic nonbinary relation to each other: to move further into a critical practice positioning in research and writing, it is key to draw parallels that are specific, detailed, and sometimes interwoven—though not necessarily one-to-one parallels; to set one's own circumstances critically alongside the circumstances of people within a research community. Each informs and sheds light on the other, creating new visions, imagining new possibilities.

Our visit to Sefwi Wiawso did not solve anything immediate about my own life or about what my family was going through at the time and still grapples with these many years later.[94] Rather, being there with Justin and Max, meeting and interacting with the Jews of Sefwi Wiawso, offered in microcosm the chance to bring into full expression and nuance the complexity of the situation of our lives. It was an example of that complexity within a heightened period and circumstance. And this is true even if Max, now twenty, doesn't remember much of it and mixes up things that happened in Ghana with things he experienced after that in Centrafrique. One

---

94   To expand on that would take me to lengths beyond what this essay can bear, but I offer that at this very moment of completion Justin is required to self-deport back to Bangui. We may not have the chance to ever see him again. We have all come to terms with this and are relatively at peace with that reality.

day in Sefwi Wiawso Max was sick in bed with a fever and Joseph brought him a fragrant, juicy orange, handing it to him with loving concern. Max remembers this gesture of empathy, this kindness and caring, even if he forgets which country he was in or whether or not the people there were Jewish. A little later in his childhood, though, Max started to call himself the "only Jewish crocodile"—his dad's clan totem is a crocodile.[95]

What the visit did do was help us see with more clarity our changing selves at that moment and into the future, and to empathize with those who were changing around us. Understanding, via interactive and generative critical practice positioning, how and why people adopt in a given moment the embodied gestures of identity—and make decisions to move beyond what is familiar in so doing—can make us aware of the harmful constrictions of essentialist, reductive narratives while reinforcing the reasons to celebrate our complex and ever-evolving, intersecting rootedness. This approach offers a path that leads to humanization instead of dehumanization in our lives and the lives of people among whom we work and wonder. We can refuse a distinction between lived, intersubjective concerns and research concerns. We can give ourselves permission to rigorously engage the personal as part of collective becoming.

References

Abitbol, Michel. 1979. "Tombouctou et les Arma: De la conquête marocaine du Soudan nigérien en 1591 à l'hégémonie de l'empire Peulh du Macina en 1833." Paris: G.-P. Maisonneuve et Larose [cited in Levi 2016].
Abu-Lughod, Lila. 2008. *Writing Women's Worlds: Bedouin Stories*. Los Angeles: University of California Press.
Agorsah, Kofi. 2014. "Spiritual Vibrations of Historic Kormantse and the Search for African Diaspora Identity in Freedom." In *Materialities of Ritual in the Black Atlantic*, edited by Akinwumi Ogundiran and Paula Saunders, 87–107. Bloomington: Indiana University Press.
Alcoff, Linda. 1991–92. "The Problem of Speaking for Others." *Cultural Critique* 20 (Winter): 5–32.
Babiracki, Carol. 2008. "What's the Difference? Reflections on Gender and Research in Village India." In Barz and Cooley, *Shadows in the Field*, 167–82.

---

95 At the time of this writing Max has a viral TikTok presence that involves caustic comic commentary on the politics of things Black/African and Jewish.

Bannerman-Richter, Gabriel. 1982. "Mmoetia the Witch-Fighting Fairies." In *The Practice of Witchcraft in Ghana*, 60–74. Winona, MN: Apollo Books.

———. 1987. *Mmoetia: The Mysterious Little People*. Elk Grove, CA: Gabari.

Barz, Gregory, and William Cheng, eds. 2020. *Queering the Field: Sounding out Ethnomusicology*. New York: Oxford University Press.

Barz, Gregory, and Timothy J. Cooley, eds. 2008. *Shadows in the Field: New Perspectives on Fieldwork in Ethnomusicology*. 2nd edition. New York: Oxford University Press.

Behar, Ruth. 1996. *The Vulnerable Observer: Anthropology That Breaks Your Heart*. Boston: Beacon Press.

Berliner, Paul. 1982. *The Soul of Mbira*. Chicago: University of Chicago Press.

Bidgood, Lee. 2017. *Czech Bluegrass: Notes from the Heart of Europe*. University of Illinois Press.

Boni, Stefano. 2000. "Contents and Contexts: The Rhetoric of Oral Traditions in the Ɔman of Sefwi Wiawso, Ghana." *Africa: Journal of the International African Institute* 70 (4): 568–94.

Braden, Daniel. 1998. "The Ghanaian Village That Wants to Be Jewish." In *Jews in Places You Never Thought Of*, edited by Karen Primack, 264–70. New York: Kulanu.

Brodkin, Karen. 1998. *How Jews Became White Folks and What That Says about Race in America*. New Brunswick: Rutgers University Press.

Brown, Brené. 2021. *Atlas of the Heart: Mapping Meaningful Connection and the Language of Human Experience*. New York: Penguin Random House.

Browning, Barbara. 1995. *Samba: Resistance in Motion*. Bloomington: Indiana University Press.

Burns, James. 2009. *Female Voices from an Ewe Dance-Drumming Community in Ghana: Our Music Has Become a Divine Spirit*. London: SOAS.

Butler, Melvin. 2019. *Island Gospel: Pentecostal Music and Identity in Jamaica and the United States*. Urbana: University of Illinois Press.

Cheng, William. 2016. *Just Vibrations: The Purpose of Sounding Good*. Ann Arbor: University of Michigan Press.

Clifford, James, and George E. Marcus. 1986. *Writing Culture: The Poetics and Politics of Ethnography*. Santa Fe: School of American Research.

Crosby, Jill Flanders, and J. T. Torres. 2001. *Situated Narratives and Sacred Dance: Performing the Entangled Histories of Cuba and West Africa*. Gainesville: University of Florida Press.

Dan, Joseph. 2006. *Kabbalah: A Very Short Introduction*. New York: Oxford University Press.

Daughtry, J. Martin. 2011. "Listening Beyond Sound and Life: Reflections on Imagined Music." In *The Oxford Handbook of the Phenomenology of Music Cultures*, ed. Harris Berger, Friedland Riedel, and David VanderHamm. New York: Oxford University Press.

Denworth, Lydia. 2020. *Friendship: The Evolution, Biology, and Extraordinary Power of Life's Fundamental Bond*. New York: Norton.
Devir, Nathan P. 2017. *New Children of Israel: Emerging Jewish Communities in an Era of Globalization*. Salt Lake City: University of Utah Press.
Dijk, R. A. van. 2001. "Contesting Silence: The Ban on Drumming and the Musical Politics of Pentecostalism in Ghana." *Ghana Studies* 4:31–64.
Drewal, Henry John. 1988. "Performing the Other: Mami Wata Worship in West Africa." *TDR: A Journal of Performance Studies* T118:160–85.
Drewal, Margaret Thompson. 1992. *Yoruba Ritual: Performers, Play, Agency*. Bloomington: Indiana University Press.
Entine, Jon. 2007. *Abraham's Children: Race, Identity, and the DNA of the Chosen People*. New York: Grand Central Publishing.
Friedson, Steven. 2008. *Remains of Ritual: Northern Gods in a Southern Land*. Chicago: University of Chicago Press.
Gray, Natasha. 2000. "The Legal History of Witchcraft in Colonial Ghana: Akyem Abuakwa, 1913–1943." PhD diss., Columbia University.
Guarino, Maria. 2018. *Listen with the Ear of the Heart: Music and Monastery Life at Weston Priory*. Rochester, NY: University of Rochester Press.
Hahn, Tomie. 2007. *Sensational Knowledge: Embodying Japanese Dance*. Middletown, CT: Wesleyan University Press.
Haïdara, Ismael Diadié. 1999. *Les juifs à Tombouctou: Recueil des sources écrites relatives au commerce juif á Tombouctou au XIXe siècle*. Bamako: Editions Donniya [cited in Levi 2016].
Harkness, Nicholas. 2022. "The Semiotic Hemiola." Paper presented at the virtual symposium "Naming, Understanding, and Playing with Metaphors in Music," UCLA PEER Lab. April 29, 2022.
Haynes, Bruce D. 2018. *The Soul of Judaism: Jews of African Descent in America*. New York: NYU Press.
Iacoboni, Marco. 2009. "Imitation, Empathy, and Mirror Neurons." *Annual Review of Psychology*, 653–70. University of California, San Diego. https://cogsci.ucsd.edu/~pineda/COGS171/readings/Iacoboni.pdf.
Kapchan, Deborah. 2017. "Listening Acts: Witnessing the Pain and Praise of Others." In *Theorizing Sound Writing*, edited by Deborah Kapchan, 277–93. Middletown, CT: Wesleyan University Press.
Kimmerer, Robin Wall. 2013. *Braiding Sweetgrass: Indigenous Wisdom, Scientific Knowledge and the Teachings of Plants*. Canada: Milkweed Editions.
Kirshenblatt-Gimblett, Barbara. 1998. "Confusing Pleasures." In *Destination Culture: Tourism, Museums, Heritage*, 203–48. Berkeley: University of California Press.
Kirshenblatt-Gimblett, Barbara, and Jonathan Karp, eds. 2008. *The Art of Being Jewish in Modern Times*. Philadelphia: University of Pennsylvania Press.

Kisliuk, Ingrid. 1992. Oral history interview with Smithsonian United States Holocaust Memorial Museum. https://collections.ushmm.org/search/catalog/irn509145.

———. 1998. *Unveiled Shadows: The Witness of a Child*. Newton, MA: Nanomir Press.

———. 2008. *From Trauma to Trepidation: Memories Transmitted by Hidden Children to the Second Generation*. Newton MA: Nanomir Press.

Kisliuk, Michelle. 2000. *Seize the Dance!: BaAka Musical Life and the Ethnography of Performance*. New York: Oxford University Press.

———. 2002. "The Poetics and Politics of Practice: Experience, Embodiment, and the Engagement of Scholarship." In *Teaching Performance Studies: Theories, Practices, Pedagogies*, edited by Nathan Stuckey and Cynthia Wimmer, 99–120. Carbondale: Southern Illinois University Press.

———. 2007. Interview, "Afropop Worldwide." https://afropop.org/audio-programs/jewish-communities-of-sub-saharan-africa.

———. 2008. "(Un)Doing Fieldwork: Sharing Songs, Sharing Lives," in Barz and Cooley, *Shadows in the Field*, 183–205.

———. 2019. "BaAka Singing in a State of Emergency: Storytelling and Listening as Medium and Message." In *Cultural Sustainabilities: Music, Media, Language, Advocacy*, edited by Timothy J. Cooley, 220–28. Urbana: University of Illinois Press.

Kisliuk, Michelle, with Kelly Gross. 2004. "What's the 'It' That We Learn to Perform? Teaching BaAka Music and Dance." In *Performing Ethnomusicology: Teaching and Representation in World Music Ensembles*, edited by Ted Solis, 230–49. Berkeley: University of California Press.

Kisliuk, Michelle, with Justin Serge Mongosso. 2003. "Representing a Real Man: Music, Identity, and Upheaval in Centrafrique." In *Emergences: Journal for the Study of Media and Composite Cultures* 13 (1): 34–46.

Koskoff, Ellen. 2000. *Music in Lubavitcher Life*. Bloomington: University of Illinois Press.

Lawrence, Sidra. 2017. "Performing Desire: Race, Sex, and the Ethnographic Encounter." *Ethnomusicology* 61 (3): 468–85.

Levi, Janice R. 2012. "The House of Israel: Judaism in Ghana." In *African Zion: Studies in Black Judaism*, edited by Edith Bruder and Tudor Parfitt, 117–37. Newcastle upon Tyne: Cambridge Scholars.

———. 2016. "Making Visible the Invisible: Evoking Memory and Constructing Identity in Sefwi Wiawso, Ghana." In *In the Shadow of Moses: New Jewish Movements in Africa and the Diaspora*, edited by Daniel Lis, William F. S. Miles, and Tudor Parfitt, 93–112. Los Angeles: Tsehai.

Lithwick, Dahlia. 2021. "Our Never-Ending Empathy for Everything Is Backfiring." *Slate*, August 21, 2021. https://slate.com/technology/2021/08/empathy-overload-try-this-instead.html.

MacGillivray, Lindsey. 2009. "I Feel Your Pain: Mirror Neurons and Empathy." *Health Psychology* 6 (1): 2009: 16–20.

McAlister, Elizabeth. 2004. *Race, Nation, and Religion in the Americas*. New York: Oxford University Press.

Meyer, Birgit. 1999. *Translating the Devil: Religion and Modernity among the Ewe in Ghana*. Edinburgh: Edinburgh University Press.

Meyerowitz, Eva. 1952. *Akan Traditions of Origin*. London: Faber and Faber.

Miles, William F. S. 2019. "Who Is a Jew (in Africa)? Definitional and Ethical Considerations in the Study of Sub-Saharan Jewry and Judaism." *Journal of the Middle East and Africa*, 10 (1): 1–15.

Mirecki, Paul, and Marvin Meyer, eds. 1995. *Magic and Ritual in the Ancient World*. Boston: Brill.

Olupona, Jacob, and Rowland Abiodun, eds. 2016. *Ifá Divination, Knowledge, Power, and Performance*. Bloomington: Indiana University Press.

Parfitt, Tudor. 2013. *Black Jews in Africa and the Americas*. Boston: Harvard University Press.

———. 2020. *Hybrid Hate: Conflations of Antisemitism and Anti-Black Racism from the Renaissance to the Third Reich*. New York: Oxford University Press.

Pobee, John S., and Emmanuel H. Mends. 1977. "Social Change and African Traditional Religion." *Sociological Analysis* 38 (1): 1–12.

Ratner, Austin. 2021. "How Tales of Jewish Resistance Inspire a 21st Century Nazi Hunter." *Forward*. August 17, 2021. https://forward.com/culture/474201/how-tales-of-jewish-resistance-inspire-a-21st-century-nazi-hunter/?fbclid=IwAR3BzOzFdhN4wxVh-pGwLpldcK20MRjDXIDWVPBpNd_ysd1TM9-xKOL5NjY.

Robinson, Dylan. 2020. *Hungry Listing: Resonant Theory for Indigenous Sound Studies*. Minneapolis: University of Minnesota Press.

Rosaldo, Renato. 1993. "Introduction: Grief and the Headhunter's Rage." In *Culture and Truth: The Remaking of Social Analysis*. Boston: Beacon Press.

Salamon, Hagar. 2001. "Ethiopian Jewry and New Self-Concepts." In *The Life of Judaism*, edited by Harvey E. Goldberg, 227–58. Berkeley: University of California Press.

———. 2003. "Blackness in Transition: Decoding the Stories of Ethiopian Jews." *Journal of Folklore Research* 40 (1): 3–32.

Schechner, Richard. 1985. "Restoration of Behavior." In *Between Theater and Anthropology*, 35–116. Philadelphia: University of Pennsylvania Press.

Shelemay, Kay Kaufman. 1989. *Music, Ritual, and Falasha History*. East Lansing: Michigan State University Press.

Subedi, Binaya. 2006. "Theorizing a 'Halfie' Researcher's Identity in Transnational Fieldwork." *International Journal of Qualitative Studies in Education* 19 (5): 573–93.

Summit, Jeffrey A. 2003a. *The Lord's Song in a Strange Land: Music and Identity in Contemporary Jewish Worship*. New York: Oxford University Press.

———. 2003b. *Abayudaya: Music from the Jewish People of Uganda*. Recorded, compiled, and annotated. Smithsonian Folkways Recordings, SFW CD 40504.

———. 2008. "Music and the Construction of Identity among the Abayudaya (Jewish people) of Uganda." In *The Garland Handbook of African Music*, edited by Ruth M. Stone, 312–24. 2nd edition. London: Routledge.

———. 2013–2014. "The Participating Observer: Fieldwork in Jewish Settings." *Musica Judaica* 20 (5774): 117–42.

Taruskin, Richard. 1995. "The Pastness of the Present and the Presence of the Past." In *Text and Act: Essays on Music and Performance*, 90–154. New York: Oxford University Press.

Turner, Rory. 2019. "Radical Critical Empathy and Cultural Sustainability." In *Cultural Sustainabilities: Music, Media, Language, Advocacy*, edited by Timothy J. Cooley, 32–42. Bloomington: University of Illinois Press.

Tyler, Stephen A. 1986. "Postmodern Ethnography: From Document of the Occult to Occult Document." In *Writing Culture: The Poetics and Politics of Ethnography*, edited by James Clifford and George E. Marcus, 122–40. Berkeley: University of California Press.

Williams, Sean. 2022. "Poetry Writing as Transgressive Ethnography." *Ethnomusicology* 66 (3): 361–77.

Wong, Deborah 2004. *Speak It Louder: Asian Americans Making Music*. New York: Routledge.

Zilkha, Gabrielle, dir. 2016. *Doing Jewish: A Story from Ghana*. Four Corners Productions.

Notes on Contributors

AMA OFORIWAA ADUONUM is a professor of ethnomusicology, public scholar, and performance artist at Illinois State University. Aduonum's work focuses on the performance traditions of Africa, African America, and middle-passage focused areas. She is interested in understanding how our ways of walking, sound, sensorial/emotional experience, and multimodal listening can be pivotal to conceiving an ethnography. Aduonum is the creator of the performance art pieces *Walking with My Ancestors: Elmina Castle* and the award-winning *Walking with My Ancestors: Cape Coast Castle*. University of Rochester Press published her book, *Walking with Asafo in Ghana: An Ethnographic Account of Kormantse Bentsir Warrior Music*.

CATHERINE M. APPERT is an associate professor in the Department of Music at Cornell University. She holds a PhD in ethnomusicology with a graduate certificate in women's studies from the University of California, Los Angeles. Her research on popular music in Senegal, The Gambia, and US urban centers focuses on questions of globalization, migration, and diaspora; the ethnographic study of musical genre; global racial constructs; and gender and research methods. Her book, *In Hip Hop Time: Music, Memory, and Social Change in Urban Senegal*, was published in 2018 by Oxford University Press.

LESLEY N. BRAUN is a research associate at the Institute for Social Anthropology, University of Basel, Switzerland. She is a recipient of the Swiss National Foundation's Ambizione Grant (2020–24). Her research investigates the gendered dimensions of transnational mobility and how gender and sexuality impact, as well as shape, women's activities in the public sphere. Her book, *Congo's Dancers: Women and Work in Kinshasa*, will be published by the University of Wisconsin Press in Winter 2023.

STEVEN CORNELIUS teaches at University of Massachusetts Boston. Previous academic positions include Boston University, Bowling Green State University, and University of Wisconsin-Madison. From 1996 to 2006 he served as a music critic for the *Blade*, the daily newspaper of Toledo, Ohio. Books include *Music: A Social Experience* (with Mary Natvig), *Music of the Civil War Era*, and *The Music of Santería: Traditional Rhythms of the Batá Drums* (with John Amira). Performances as a percussionist include the Metropolitan Opera, New York City Opera National Company, Opera Orchestra of New York, and Radio City Music Hall. He holds a PhD from

UCLA; an M.M. from Manhattan School of Music; and a B.M.Ed. from the University of Wisconsin-Madison.

DANIELLE DAVIS is a doctoral candidate at Florida State University. Her dissertation research interprets the cultural productions of the Alt-Hip-hop band N.E.R.D., the production duo the Neptunes, and Pharrell Williams' solo career as Afro-Filipino futures within the twenty-first-century American soundscape. She is a violist and the music director of the Florida State University Middle Eastern World Music ensemble. She has additional research interests in public popular music pedagogy and education, Afrofuturism, Black sound studies, African diasporic musics, and musics of the Arab world.

DEBORAH KAPCHAN is a professor of performance studies at New York University. A Guggenheim fellow, she is the author of *Gender on the Market: Moroccan Women and the Revoicing of Tradition* (1996), *Traveling Spirit Masters: Moroccan Music and Trance in the Global Marketplace* (2007), as well as numerous articles on sound, narrative, and poetics. Her translated and edited volume titled *Poetic Justice: An Anthology of Moroccan Contemporary Poetry* (2020) was shortlisted for the National Translation Prize for Poetry by the American Literary Translators Association in 2021. Other works include *Intangible Rights: Cultural Heritage in Transit* (2014) and *Theorizing Sound Writing* (2017).

MICHELLE KISLIUK is an associate professor of music at the University of Virginia, where she teaches graduate and undergraduate students. She has conducted ethnographic research with BaAka forest people in the Central African Republic, focusing on musical life, dance, and the arts and politics of everyday. Additional field research focused on African popular musics and American bluegrass. Conceptual areas of interest include ethnographic poetics, sound/listening studies, improvisation, play, dance and gesture, Jewish identities, performance theory, conceptual and experimental performance/art, environmental activism intersecting with creative/expressive life, the interests of African hunter-foragers, and the politics of indigeneity.

SIDRA LAWRENCE is a percussionist and an associate professor of ethnomusicology at Bowling Green State University. She takes an intersectional approach to the ways that race, gender, and sexuality shape meaning in the music and soundworlds of Africa and the African diasporas. Her forthcoming book explores sonic performativity as a mode of articulating an indigenous feminist politics in Ghana and Burkina Faso. She has publications in *Feminist Studies, Ethnomusicology, African Music, Africa Today, The Senses and Society,* and *Ethnopornography: Sexuality, Colonialism, and Archival Knowledge.* Her research has been supported by the Woodrow Wilson National Fellowship Foundation, the National Endowment for the Humanities, and the West African Research Association.

MARK LOMANNO is an ethnomusicologist and jazz pianist currently serving as director of applied music and assistant professor at Albright College. A former Consortium for Faculty Diversity Fellow, Lomanno is co-founder of the Jazz Studies Collaborative, the current media editor for the journal *Jazz Perspectives*, and a former chair of the Society of Ethnomusicology's Improvisation Section. Their ethnographic, performance, and scholarly work is based in the Afro-Atlantic world. In addition to a forthcoming monograph on intercultural collaborations in global jazz, Lomanno is co-editor of the forthcoming volume *The Improviser's Classroom: Pedagogies for Cocreative Worldmaking*.

TRACY MCMULLEN is a saxophonist, composer, an associate professor of music at Bowdoin College, and an ACLS Frederick Burkhardt Fellow at the Berklee Institute of Jazz and Gender Justice (through 2023). She is currently researching her second book, *Jazz Humanism: Responsibility and Blur in the New Human*, which investigates jazz as a moral practice. As a saxophonist and composer, she has recorded on Cadence, Parma, and Plutonium Records and most recently provided film scores for the 4-disc Bluray/DVD box set *Cinema's First Nasty Women* (available on Kino Lorber).

CAROL MULLER is a Cape Town, South Africa–born professor of music at the University of Pennsylvania. She is currently working on a podcasting project on South African jazz and community music programs, and a third edition, now co-authored with Glenn Holtzman, Bongani Ndodana-Breen and Nduduzo Makhathini, of *Focus: Music of South Africa* (Routledge). She is writing *Music of Contemporary Africa* (Routledge) and is embarking on a new project with aboriginal Australians. Along with Tshepo Masango, she is co-authoring *The Faith of Our Fathers,* about apartheid-era faith and political resistance, focused on the work of our Presbyterian minister fathers who were friends in difficult times.

Index

Note: Figures are indicated by page numbers in *italics*.

ableism, 63–64, 72, 80
Abu-Lughod, Lila, 103, 200, 234n92
acoustemology, 64, 64n16, 77, 79, 80n49
Aduonum, Ama Oforiwaa, 6n10, 114–45, *133–34, 140–41*
Afro hairstyle, 119, 119n10
Afrofuturism, 151
age, 96–97
agency, erotic, 11–12
Ahenkorah, David, 219n60
Aidoo, Ama Ata, 118
Amadie, Jimmy, 75
Another Country (Baldwin), x, 40
Anzaldúa, Gloria, 9
apartheid, 162–64, 172–73
Appert, Catherine M., 107–13
appropriation, 34–35, 37n25, 39, 42, 154, 205
Arbery, Ahmaud, 114
Artaud, Antonin, 195, 198
Arthur, John, 121n13

Ba, Mariama, 127
BaAka, 202n20, 205n23, 206, 219n61
Baldwin, James, x–xi, 23, 40, 42, 43n35
Barad, Karan, 1
Baraka, Amiri, 36
Bataille, George, 179
Beauregard, Julie, 13n29
bebop vocabulary, 32n19

becoming, 159–74
Behar, Ruth, 9, 200
Benjamin, Sathima Bea, 169
Between the World and Me (Coates), 152
Biehl, Amy, 163
Birk, Lara, 71
Bisset Perea, Jessica, 196n5
Black Lives Matter, 114, 139, 142, 151
Black sound, 33, 33n20
Blackness, 25, 28, 32, 39, 115, 151–52
Bofane, Jean, 178–79
Bonilla, Yarimar, 123
Braden, Daniel, 226n72
Braun, Lesley N., 175–91
Brecker, Michael, 29, 29n7, 30–31
Brooks, Daphne, 37, 37n24
Brown, Brené, 196n3
Brown, Danielle, 4
Brown, Jayna, 37
Buddhism, 23 25, 196n3
Bulu, Leon Tsambu, 185n10
Burnim, Mellonee, 151

Cage, John, 31–32, 155
Carrington, Terri Lyne, 44n36
"Case for Reparations, The" (Coates), 41
Castille, Philando, 115
class-based discrimination, 95
Clifford, James, 235
Coates, Ta'Nehisi, 40–41, 152

Collins, Patricia Hill, 151–52, 154
colonialism, 4–8, 12, 116–77, 116n3, 126, 208n31, 221, 229n78
"Color of Supremacy, The" (Leonardo), 153n11
colorism, 119, 121n13
Coltrane, John, 26, 32, 32n19, 33n21, 43n36, 65
Comaroff, Jean, 167n9
combines, football, 29n9
competition jazz, 29–31
Congo, Inc. (Bofane), 178–79
Coplan, David, 166n8
Cornelius, Steven, 47–56
COVID-19, 151–52, 162, 172
Crawley, Ashon, 43n36
critical practice positioning, 196, 196n5
cultural appropriation, 34–35, 37n25, 39, 42, 154, 205
Cusick, Suzanne, 67, 68n27, 91
Cyrus, Miley, 38–39

dancing, mirror, 175–91
Dargie, Dave, 164, 165n5, 172
Daughtry, Martin, 203
Davis, Danielle, 150–57
De Boeck, Filip, 176
decolonization, 8–9, 103, 162
DeJohnette, Jack, 68
Dennis, Kelly, 4n5
desire, 86–104
Devir, Nathan P., 211, 212n42, 213n44, 214n46, 219n60, 221n67, 224n71, 226n72
diaspora, 116–17, 120–21, 126, 130–32, 160
difference, inherent, 6
Dilemma of a Ghost (Aidoo), 118
discrimination
    class-based, 95
    against Jews, 201, 226
    literacy-based, 95
Dlamini, Sazi, 166
Dorsey, Thomas, 138
DuBois, W. E. B., 127
Dwyli, Nofinish, 165–66
Dyani, Johnny, 164, 169

ecstatic abandonment, 179
"effortless mastery," 61n3, 80
emancipation, 3
embodiment, 25, 183, 225–33
"emotional justice," 116, 116n3, 132, 140, 143
"emotional patriarchy," 115, 115n2
empathy, xi–xii, 5, 13, 139, 150–57, 195–96, 199–202, 200n9–200n10, 203–5
Erlmann, Veit, 164
erotic agency, 11–12
erotic subjectivity, 2, 8, 10, 87–89, 92, 180
erotics, 8–12, 16, 62, 68, 76, 159–74
ethics of intersubjectivity, 61, 61n5
ethnographic knowledge, 4–8, 12, 87, 89, 91, 103
ethnography
    fidelity in, 77
    as healing, 61
    and its double, 195–96
    performance, 92
    power dynamics in, 2
    pure, 4n5
    reflexive turn in, 235
    reflexivity and, 197
    vulnerable, 9–12
ethnomusicology, 4–8, 89, 154, 156n17, 159–74
exchange, 99, 103–4
exotification, 28. See also Othering
Express Yourself (Madonna), 38

Fargion, Janet Topp, 164

field research, 162–72
Fisk University, 118n9
flesh, x–n1
Floyd, George, 114, 130
Floyd, Samuel, 33n20
football, 29n9
Forté, Marjani, 125
Foucault, Michel, 190
Franko, Mark, 191

Gabbard, Krin, 35
gender
    categories, 7
    ethnography and, 10n20
    identity, 128, 143
    inequity, 34, 173
    mimicry, 39
    norms, 43
    researcher, 10n20, 87, 155n14
gendered subjectivity, 91
gendered violence, 15, 91
Ghana, 51, 114, 118, 194–236
"going native," x
Goldman, Emma, 142
gyil, 88, 88n3

Hall, Edward T., 121n14
Han, Quan Trai, 166n6
Hancock, Herbie, 24
Hanh, Thich Nhat, 197, 200n10, 203
Harris, Barry, ix
Hawkins, Seton, 171
Hayes, Eileen M., 6n10
Haynes, Bruce, 210n36, 211, 211n40, 213n44, 222, 226n73
Hentoff, Nat, 40
Herzfeld, Michael, 183
hierarchy, racial, 33n21
hipness, white female, 36–40
Hoffman, Alex, 31–32
Holocaust, 201
hooks, bell, 114, 151

Hurston, Zora Neale, 156

Ibrahim, Abdullah, 166–67, 169
Imus, Don, 39
intersectionality, 2, 74n40, 197
intersubjectivity, 9, 61–63, 61n5, 76–77, 102, 194, 196, 224, 234, 236
intimacy, 1–2, 9–12, 17, 56, 61, 64, 66, 79–81, 116–17, 120–21, 130–32, 172, 183
Isay, Dave, 159

Jackson, Michael, 38
Jarrett, Keith, 64, 66–69, 67n21, 68n27
Jazz Life (Hentoff), 40
jazz music, 23–26, 74n40
    competition jazz, 29–31
    masculinity and, 75–76
    "paying dues" and, 40–44
    racial identifications in, 26–36
Jews, 209–21, 210n36–210n37, 212–13, 213n44, 214n46–214n47, 219n60, 222, 224n70–224n71, 225–34, 233n91
Jews for Jesus, 233n91
Jones, Omi Osun, 17–18, 62
justice, emotional, 116, 116n3, 132, 140, 143

Kaepernick, Colin, 139
Kapchan, Deborah, ix–xii
Kelly, Ed, 24
King Tha. *See* Mazwai, Thandiswa
Kirshenblatt-Gimblett, Barbara, 195n2, 210–11
Kisliuk, Ingrid, 201n16
Kisliuk, Michelle, x, 92, 194–236
knowledge, ethnographic, 4–8, 12, 87, 89, 91, 103
knowledge production, 5, 90n4

Kulick, Don, 10–11

Lateef, Yusef, 26, 28–30, 33n21, 43, 43n36
Lawrence, Sidra, x, 86–104
Leonardo, Zeus, 151, 153–54, 153n11
Levi, Janice, 214n47, 224n71
listening, 159–74
literacy-based discrimination, 95
Lomanno, Mark, xi–n10, 57–81
Lomax, Alan, 156
Lorde, Audre, 11, 43, 159–62
Lott, Eric, 37n25
Lubet, Alex, 69n30, 74–75

Madonna, 38–39
Malinowski, Bronislaw, 8, 8n16
Mami Wata, 188–89, 188n11
masculinity, 37, 66n20, 75–76, 95–96, 101
Mazwai, Thandiswa, 159, 161
Mbembe, Achille, 179
McCormack, Ryan, 78n48
McKittrick, Katherine, 155n14
McMillan Cottom, Tressie, 39
McMullen, Tracy, x–xi, 23–44
memory, 127–30
Menakem, Resmaa, 115n1
Merleau-Ponty, Maurice, x–n1
Minh-ha, Trinh, 91
minstrelsy, 154
mirror dancing, 175–91
mirror neurons, 204–5
misogynoir, 154–55
Monson, Ingrid, 33, 33n20, 36, 37n25
Moreno, Eva, 12n29
Muller, Carol, 159–74
Murphy, John, 25–26
Murray, Albert, 33n20
Mwana, Tschala, 182

"near enemies," 196
Ness, Sally Ann, 176

Nettle, Bruno, 151
Nietzsche, Friedrich, 179
Nnaemeka, Obioma, 126
Noland, Carrie, 176
Nussbaum, Martha, x

objectivity, x, 155, 235
Of Other Spaces (Foucault), 190
"On Touching" (Barad), 1
osteogenesis imperfecta, 75
Othering, 8, 153. *See also* exotification
Otherness, 1, 4–5, 7, 25, 180–81, 188n11

pain, 12–13, 71–74, 76–79
pandemic, 151–52, 162, 172
patriarchy, 32, 36, 115, 115n2, 161–63, 196
"paying dues," 40–44
Payton, Nicholas, 26
Perdomo, Enrique "Kike," 58, 69n33
performance
    ableist conceptions of, 64
    Black male, 31
    Black masculinity and, 37
    of desire, 91, 99, 101, 104
    disembodied, 67
    embodied, 62, 70–71, 80
    ethnography, 92
    micro-, of gesture, 183
    pain and, 61, 69, 71, 73–74
    socioaesthetic vision of, 195
    of status, 95–96
    transcendent, 72
    transformative power of, 116
Peterson, Oscar, 69n30
Petrucciani, Michel, 75–76
pianism, 63–70, 73–76
Politics of Passion (Wekker), 12n29
power, x–xi, 2, 5, 8–10, 87, 90–91, 90n4, 92, 94, 102, 104, 112, 116, 204, 233
praxis, 204–5, 219, 225–33

privilege, xii, 5, 39, 41, 61, 71, 98, 101–2, 153n11, 156–57, 181, 203, 205
Pujol, Ernesto, 161

queer subjectivity, 88

Race Talk (Sue), 151n4
racial apartheid, 162–64, 172–73
racial hierarchy, 33n21
racial identifications, in jazz, 26–36
racial imagination, 4n5, 6–7
racial violence, 115–16, 143
racialization, 4, 12, 98, 157
racism, 33n21, 35–36, 38–39, 41–42, 118, 142, 151–54, 156–57, 167, 200n12, 209, 220. See also discrimination
Rebelo, Pedro, 67n23, 68n25
reflexive turn, 235
reflexivity, 197, 235
reparations, 41
researcher gender, 10n20, 87, 155n14
rhythm, 225–33
ritual, 225–33
Robinson, Dylan, 197
Rosaldo, Renato, 197n6

Santería, 47–50, 54–55
Senegal, 127–30
sexual assault, 107–13
sexual harassment, 88–89, 107–13
Shaw-Taylor, Yoku, 121n13
Shembe, Isaiah, 167
Shorter, Wayne, 31
Sieczynski, Rudolf, 201n14
Sigal, Pete, 9
Sister Outsider (Lorde), 43
Smith, Mamie, 37, 37n24
solidarity, 126, 156n17, 157
"Speaking in Tongues" (Anzaldúa), 9
Stoever, Jennifer Lynn, 33n21

subjectivity, 38, 161
  erotic, 2, 8, 10, 87–89, 92, 180
  gendered, 91, 101
  queer, 88
Sudnow, David, 67n21
Sue, Derald Wing, 151, 151n4
Summit, Jeffrey, 217n54, 233n91
symmetry, 32, 32n19
Syms, Martine, 151

Taboo (Kulick), 10, 12n29
Taylor, Breonna, 114
Teachings on Love (Hanh), 197
Theater and Its Double, The (Artaud), 195
"This Morning, This Evening" (Baldwin), 42
Titlestad, Michael F., 69n32
tokenism, 197
Tonda, Joseph, 188
Tortorici, Zeb, 9
transformation, 12–13
trauma, 3, 12–13, 116–17. See also sexual assault; violence
"trauma ghosted," 115n1
Trump, Donald, 170
Tucker, Sophie, 37
Turner, Victor, 121
Tyler, Steven, 195n2

University of North Texas, 29–30
Urban Bush Women (UBW) (dance company), 116–17, 119–27

Vasconcelos, Nana, x
violence, 2, 15, 44n36, 88–89, 91, 98, 110, 115–16, 143, 163, 179, 203
visibility, 93–96, 102, 184–85, 188, 190–91
vulnerability, 197–99, 203–4
vulnerable ethnography, 9–12
Vulnerable Observer, The (Behar), 200

Walking with My Ancestors (Aduonum), 116, 132–41, *133–34, 140–41*
Waterman, Ellen, 11, 62, 67n23, 68n27
Watznauer, Kelsey, 132n32
Ways of the Hand (Sudnow), 67n21
Wekker, Gloria, 11n22, 12n29, 98n2
Werner, Kenny, 67
West, Mae, 37, 37n24
white fragility, 35, 157
white guilt, 153–54
white innocence, 157
white-body supremacy, 115, 115n1, 142
Whitehead, Neil L., 7
whiteness, 5, 31n14, 32n18, 42, 101, 129, 153n11, 154, 156, 180, 185, 211, 222n68
Williams, Sean, 195n2
Williams, Walter L., 118n9
Wilson, Olly, 33n20

Winehouse, Amy, 37
women. *See also* gender
  controlling images of Black, 152
  exchange and, 99
  misogynoir, 154–55
  Othering of Black, 153
  as researchers, Black, 155n14
  through "Western eyes," 88
  white female hipness and, 36–40
Women Writing Culture (Behar), 9
Writing Women's Worlds (Abu-Lughod), 200

Xaba, Ntsikana, 164

Yoruba, 47–50, 54–55

Zilkha, Gabrielle, 224n71, 226n74, 228n76
Zollar, Jawole Willa Jo, 120, 125

www.ingramcontent.com/pod-product-compliance
Lightning Source LLC
Chambersburg PA
CBHW070236240426
43673CB00044B/1817